Artificial Intelligence in Cultural Production

This book offers an in-depth academic discourse on the convergence of AI, digital platforms, and popular culture, in order to understand the ways in which the platform and cultural industries have reshaped and developed AI-driven algorithmic cultural production and consumption.

At a time of fundamental change for the media and cultural industries, driven by the emergence of big data, algorithms, and AI, the book examines how media ecology and popular culture are evolving to serve the needs of both media and cultural industries and consumers. The analysis documents global governments' rapid development of AI-relevant policies and identifies key policy issues; examines the ways in which cultural industries firms utilize AI and algorithms to advance the new forms of cultural production and distribution; investigates change in cultural consumption by analyzing the ways in which AI, algorithms, and digital platforms reshape people's consumption habits; and examines whether governments and corporations have advanced reliable public and corporate policies and ethical codes to secure socio-economic equality.

Offering a unique perspective on this timely and vital issue, this book will be of interest to scholars and students in media studies, communication studies, anthropology, globalization studies, sociology, cultural studies, Asian studies, and science and technology studies (STS).

Dal Yong Jin is a Distinguished SFU Professor in the School of Communication at Simon Fraser University.

Routledge Studies in New Media and Cyberculture

42 **Digital Gambling**
Theorizing Gamble-Play Media
César Albarrán-Torres

43 **Digital interfacing**
Action and perception through technology
Daniel Black

44 **Women and the Digitally-Mediated Revolution in the Middle East**
Applying Digital Methods
Chiara Bernardi

45 **The Discursive Power of Memes in Digital Culture**
Ideology, Semiotics, and Intertextuality
Bradley E. Wiggins

46 **Digital Media, Sharing and Everyday Life**
Jenny Kennedy

47 **Digital Icons**
Memes, Martyrs and Avatars
Yasmin Ibrahim

48 **Artificial Intelligence in Cultural Production**
Critical Perspectives on Digital Platforms
Dal Yong Jin

49 **Loving Fanfiction**
Exploring the Role of Emotion in Online Fandoms
Brit Kelley

50 **Posthuman Capitalism**
Dancing with Data in the Digital Economy
Yasmin Ibrahim

Artificial Intelligence in Cultural Production

Critical Perspectives
on Digital Platforms

Dal Yong Jin

LONDON AND NEW YORK

First published 2021
by Routledge
2 Park Square, Milton Park, Abingdon, Oxon OX14 4RN

and by Routledge
605 Third Avenue, New York, NY 10158

Routledge is an imprint of the Taylor & Francis Group, an informa business

© 2021 Dal Yong Jin

The right of Dal Yong Jin to be identified as author of this work has been asserted by him in accordance with sections 77 and 78 of the Copyright, Designs and Patents Act 1988.

All rights reserved. No part of this book may be reprinted or reproduced or utilised in any form or by any electronic, mechanical, or other means, now known or hereafter invented, including photocopying and recording, or in any information storage or retrieval system, without permission in writing from the publishers.

Trademark notice: Product or corporate names may be trademarks or registered trademarks, and are used only for identification and explanation without intent to infringe.

British Library Cataloguing-in-Publication Data
A catalogue record for this book is available from the British Library

Library of Congress Cataloging-in-Publication Data
A catalog record for this book has been requested

ISBN: 978-0-367-75844-8 (hbk)
ISBN: 978-0-367-75845-5 (pbk)
ISBN: 978-1-003-16425-8 (ebk)

Typeset in Sabon
by Apex CoVantage, LLC

Contents

Preface		vi
1	Artificial intelligence in popular culture	1
2	Convergence of AI, digital platforms, and popular culture	16
3	AI, cultural policy, and the rise of counter-neoliberalism	35
4	Artificial intelligence and cultural production	54
5	Netflix's effects in transforming global cultural norms	75
6	Personalization of culture in the AI era	94
7	AI journalism, social media platforms, and fake news	113
8	New media ethics in the age of AI	133
9	Conclusion	151
	References	158
	Index	180

Preface

My academic interests in digital platforms have continued to advance since the early 2010s. When I published my first monograph *Korea's Online Gaming Empire* (2010), I did not expect that video games could be one of the primary subjects in platforms studies. However, digital games have become some of the most significant areas in platform studies in the early 21st century. With the rapid growth of several cutting-edge digital technologies, including search engines, social media, and smartphones, as well as digital games, people's curiosity in digital platforms has concomitantly grown, and I have also decided to improve my research and teaching interests on digital platforms from various perspectives, including critical political economy. While there are diverse approaches and frameworks, I have especially analyzed the increasing role of digital platforms in the process of globalization, as several digital platforms based in the U.S. play a pivotal role in comparison to local-based digital platforms in countries like Japan, Korea, and China in the global platform spheres. My works on digital platforms have thus discussed the power relationships between the global forces and the local forces.

Under these circumstances, I have been able to publish several articles and monographs on digital platforms, including *Digital Platforms, Imperialism, and Political Culture* in 2015. Many scholars in media studies, sociology, and political science have continued to develop the notion of platform imperialism as one of the major theoretical frameworks in media studies, sociology, and geography, which demands me to further develop my research on similar subjects. Consequently, my second book on digital platforms came out with the title of *Globalization and Media in the Digital Platform Age* in 2019. Unlike other books mainly focusing on the relationships between traditional media and globalization, this book emphasizes the crucial role of digital platforms in the globalization process. Almost at the same time, I started to progress another book project by combining digital platforms with artificial intelligence (AI) in cultural production. In this latest book, I mainly attempted to converge three major areas, including AI, digital platforms, and popular culture, in order to understand the ways in which platform and cultural industries have transformed AI-driven algorithmic cultural production and consumption, as AI and digital platforms together have fundamentally transformed business models and cultural production formats with the emergence of big data and algorithms. As a shifting media ecology drives us to stipulate popular culture from different perspectives in the age of artificial intelligence, I wanted to discuss not only the emergence of AI but also its convergence with digital platforms in cultural production and its implications in a timely manner. Indeed, from social media platforms like YouTube and Facebook to over-the-top (OTT) platforms, including Netflix and Disney+, digital platforms have swiftly adapted AI technology and transformed our cultural activities and daily routines. Due to their close connection with AI, digital platforms have on a large scale reshaped cultural production, from the production of culture to the consumption of culture, which should be fully analyzed and discussed.

I am fortunate to have been able to focus on digital platforms as one of my major research agendas for the past ten years. During this period, many scholars have jumped on the bandwagon, and therefore, discussions on digital platforms have become commonplace in various academic venues. I hope that the current book provides some convincing discussion topics to many scholars, students, and policy makers who are interested in the roles of the convergence of AI and digital platforms. It is certain that digital platforms in conjunction with AI will intensify their roles in the realms of popular culture and journalism. Without understanding the convergence of AI and digital platforms, we cannot fully comprehend the rapidly shifting media ecology surrounding cultural industries. As I have developed my academic interests on digital platforms since the early 2010s, I will continue my academic discourses on digital platforms over the next decade. Throughout continuing research and discussions, I expect to shed light on current debates and discussions on digital platforms to place them in perspectives that have relevance for future digital platform studies. This book's critical discussions of the convergence of AI and digital platforms in cultural production, as well as my two previously published books on digital platforms, will guide me to contribute to advancing digital platform studies in the realms of popular culture and journalism.

Overall, this book is the outcome of my long academic journey, and now I really want to express my sincere gratitude to several editors at Routledge, in particular Suzanne Richardson, who showed their consistent support and patience, while professionally dealing with the streamlined production of these three books on digital platforms. Most of all, my special thanks go to my family: my wife Kyung Won (Eustina) Na and our two daughters Yu Sun Jin and Yu Young Jin. Their endless support has been my blessing at all times.

1 Artificial intelligence in popular culture

Introduction

> David (22) who lives in Vancouver, Canada, always checks cultural content on digital platforms, in particular his Apple iPhone. After watching a movie trailer of *Morgan*—created through artificial intelligence—a 2016 American sci-fi horror film on YouTube in March 2020, he immediately enjoyed the movie on Netflix. Right after, he also watched *Kingdom*—a Korean television series produced in 2019—on Netflix, partially due to social distancing regulation in the COVID-19 era.

Three major components that directly influence David's cultural activities at this particular juncture are artificial intelligence (AI); digital platforms, including Netflix and smartphone; and popular culture. The interaction among these three seemingly not connected areas has been greatly increasing, a relatively new development, as AI has recently jumped into the realm of media and popular culture. Although AI is the latest comer in the cultural sphere, it has suddenly become one of the major forces transforming people's cultural consumption habits, as well as the production of popular culture.

AI has been with us for many years, and the huge wave of AI breaks across several areas, such as robots, self-driving cars, Google Maps, Amazon, healthcare, and online education. In early 2020 when COVID-19, referring to an infectious disease starting in late fall or early winter 2019, was rampant globally, for example, the Canadian federal government signed a contract with BlueDot, a Toronto-based digital health firm to track the spread of the virus, the latest tool in the AI toolbox being deployed against the public health crisis. The federal government announced a CDN$1 billion COVID-19 response fund on March 11, 2020, with $275 million dedicated to research. A little less than $52 million has already been doled out to the 96 researchers and research teams across the country, and three of those projects are using AI (Chamandy, 2020).

Several information technology (IT) firms and universities have also developed not only online education tools but also advanced technological systems that subtract students' participation and concentration on online

2 *Artificial intelligence in popular culture*

education via AI technologies (Choi, J.H., 2020). Due to the rapid spread of the disease, universities in many countries, including the U.S., the U.K., Canada, and Korea, canceled in-class education and introduced online class systems. As the COVID-19 situation continues, and the new normal in the post-coronavirus era is evident, many universities and tech companies have continued to develop various forms of online education tools, mainly supported by AI. In other words, the rush to adopt new digital technologies during COVID-19-driven remote learning led educators at all levels, from elementary school to university, to use more tools powered by advanced AI (Rauf, 2020). As of late January 2021, many universities around the world still practice remote learning, which was started in March 2020, and therefore, AI-supported educational mechanisms have continued to deeply embed in people's daily lives in the near future.

Meanwhile, AI is saturating in the realm of popular culture, in which humans have been traditionally primary actors. Many AIs now "act invisibly in the background of activities conducted on smartphones and computers; in search engine results, social media feeds, video games and targeted advertisements" (Dyer-Witheford et al., 2019, 2). As Elliott (2019, xx) points out, "The digital universe has a direct connection with AI." Furthermore, today's changes in the field of popular culture are far more encompassing in scope than AI alone as digital platforms; both social media platforms like YouTube and over-the-top (OTT) service platforms like Netflix also play a major role in the transformation process in conjunction with popular culture. Consequently, people around the globe live in a new cultural world of technological innovation that AI and digital platforms create and develop.

Since the mid-2010s, AI has been applied to quite diverse applications, including predictive text assistance in smartphones, the identification of objects and faces for photos, the interpretation of video material linked to self-driving cars, the evaluation of performances recorded as data, and many more—"a list which shows that the technology of machine learning is being used in multiple sectors and for a broad range of activities, some sensitive and others more playful" (Bunz, 2019, 264). The swelling use of AI in media and culture in tandem with digital platforms, however, came unplanned with a few exceptions, right after Korea hosted a Go match telecast live where Google DeepMind's AlphaGo defeated Lee Sedol, one of the best Go players in the world, in 2016 (Figure 1.1).[1] The AlphaGo AI program triumphed in its final game against Lee to win the series 4–1, providing a landmark achievement for an AI program (Borowiec, 2016; Choi, W.W., 2016).

As evidenced in the Go match between AlphaGo and Lee Sedol, AI can easily beat humans in Go and chess. Watching AlphaGo's victory over Lee put people, not only in Korea but also around the globe, into shock, as many global GO fans watched those five matches.[2] Everyone was suddenly talking about AI, and many global cultural and platform firms started to invest in this particular new technology. All this is in anticipation of the "Fourth Industrial Revolution," which "proponents say differs from the third digital

Artificial intelligence in popular culture 3

Figure 1.1 Go Match between AlphaGo and Lee Sedol in 2016 (*SBS*, 2016)

revolution in its emphasis on AI technology.[3] Some speculate this could affect the digital economy as much as its shipping, automobile and electronics industries" (Volodzko, 2017). AI has seemed to become a core technology in the media and cultural industries in the age of the Fourth Industrial Revolution (Kim, K.H. et al., 2018).

Starting in the late 2010s when they saw the AlphaGo phenomenon, the global cultural industries, as in other industries, have rapidly transformed their industrial structures and the ways in which they produce cultural content. In both advanced economies, including the U.S., the U.K., Canada, and Japan, known as the Global North, and a few developing countries like China and Korea, namely, the Global South, AI, algorithms, and big data are reshaping all media-related industries, from platform to cultural sectors, as new digital technologies, including AI and digital platforms, are expected to provide opportunities for many ICT (information and communication technology) firms to create jobs and engender prosperity (McKelvey and MacDonald, 2019). These countries have already achieved substantial growth in their ICTs—internet and smartphones—and cultural industries. Mega media and cultural giants in these countries now focus on AI to further develop and produce new forms of popular culture, and therefore, the digital economy.

AI is becoming a ubiquitous part of our cultural lives, and the adoption of AI is indeed noticeable in media and cultural sectors like music, film, game, and webtoon, as well as journalism. As Caramiaux et al. (2019, 6) point out, "Creatives have always been in demand of new tools that they can use to enrich the way they work, making them early adopters of technological innovations. AI is not an exception." AI seems to be suited to the particular

4 *Artificial intelligence in popular culture*

requirements of the contemporary cultural industries that are shifting principal paradigms. In particular, AI is deeply associated with digital platforms, such as Google, Facebook, YouTube, Netflix, and smartphone technologies.

The paradigm shift in the realm of media and culture in tandem with AI has been controversial. Some admit that AI is a big part of the cultural sector, while others claim that it is only lip service. What is interesting, though, is that there has been a clear trend toward the adoption and actualization of AI in media and cultural production. As Gunkel (2012, 20) argues, in communication studies,

> the operative paradigm—the framework that has defined what is considered normal science—situates technology as a tool or instrument of message exchange between human users. This particular understanding has been supported and codified by the dominant forms of communication theory. . . . Because this conceptualization has been accepted as normative, the computer and other forms of information technology have been accommodated to fit the dominant paradigm.

What he emphasized is that the computer has not effectively challenged long-standing assumptions about the role and function of technology in communication. For him, "The computer is not necessarily a new technology to be accommodated to the theories and practices of communication studies," but the current situation has fundamentally changed (Gunkel, 2012, 20).

Now, it is certain that the computer and AI have actualized a paradigm shift in digital media and popular culture. The emphasis has switched to machine learning (ML), meaning a subset of AI, in communication and/or cultural studies. "With huge datasets available and cheaper hardware, machine learning has been gaining ground over conventional search and discovery applications. The future lies in machine learning and it is maturing at a faster pace and finding diverse applications" (Frankel, 2018, 10). As Benchmann (2019, 82) points out, data in ML processing becomes an issue not only in terms of the quality of data input itself but also its suitability for training the algorithms to recognize patterns and clusters. The more data and the more diversified training data people have, the better people's algorithm potentially is at recognizing new data. Here the algorithm can only interpret data and predict patterns from the data that it has already seen from training data.

Many governments around the world have embraced the AI phenomenon. They firmly believe that AI can reshape the industry structure and is able to bring new energies to the digital economy. Governments have developed new supporting measures, both legal and financial, so that governments and corporations can work closely together to enhance the AI-driven digital economy. Governments, digital platform firms, and cultural corporations like broadcasting companies and music firms discuss a whole host of agendas surrounding the remarkable emergence of AI in general, as our contemporary society is "becoming increasingly visible and bullish on its own investments in AI" (Walch, 2019). The media landscape has been transformed so deeply that it is now unrecognizable. For many governments and corporations, how to utilize new digital technologies, in particular AI, for the growth of popular culture, and in general cultural production, becomes a key issue.

Cultural production can be explained from various perspectives, and it means "the making, circulation and reception of cultural forms and to cultural practices and processes in situ"; therefore, cultural production, sometimes, implies "processes whose outcomes or products are specialized and well defined" (Henderson, 2013, 3).[4] In cultural production studies, it has also "addressed industrial contexts and professional routines to understand why films, television programs, and popular music genres are what they are" (3). However, in this book, cultural production refers to "the social processes involved in the generation and circulation of cultural forms, practices, values, and shared understandings" as well as "the work of the culture industry" (Oxford Reference, 2019). Cultural production is also "used as a shorthand term to refer to industrialized or semi-industrialized symbol making and circulation in modern societies" (Hesmondhalgh and Saha, 2013, 181). In other words, cultural production does not narrowly define the actual production of cultural content, but the overall process, including production, distribution, exhibition, and consumption of media content and popular culture and, recently, embedded in AI use.

Due to the significant role of digital platforms and their users who also participate in the process of cultural production and circulation, this book broadly includes the digital platform industry as well as the cultural industries as major parts of cultural production.

Digital platforms and cultural industries have transformed the production and distribution of cultural content, while people shift their consumption habits with the help of AI and digital platforms, differentiating the cultural sphere from the traditional norms that traditional media, including terrestrial broadcasting, have created. In the early 21st century, people, in particular global youth, equipped with new digital technologies enjoy popular culture and news on digital platforms instead of physically going to theaters or buying and possessing cultural materials.

On the one hand, recent data certainly proves the increasing use of AI in the ICT and cultural sectors, which asks us to contemplate the convergence of AI and platform/culture in the production of culture. According to Statistics Canada (2020), several different industries have invested and used AI technology. Among these, the information and cultural industry was the second highest in terms of AI usage at 25.5%, only behind the finance and insurance industry (32.2%), while the average usage of AI was recorded at 10.1% in 2017 (Table 1.1). This data includes only large companies who have more than 250 employees. The ranks are still similar when we include small businesses, although the percentage of AI usage slightly decreases.

6 Artificial intelligence in popular culture

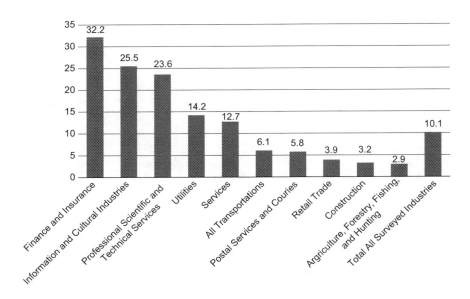

Table 1.1 AI usage by industry in Canada in 2017 (unit %)
Source: Statistics Canada (2020). Table 27-10-0367-01 Use of advanced or emerging technologies by industry and enterprise size.

This certainly implies that IT, including digital platform and mobile sectors, and culture have already deeply integrated with AI technology, and we can expect that new media and cultural sectors will continue to use AI at the highest level in our contemporary capitalist society.

On the other hand, AI has greatly transformed people's consumption patterns in media and popular culture, as people enjoy media and cultural content on digital platforms, including social media platforms and OTT platforms (e.g., Netflix), rather than on traditional media like television channels and at theaters. People watch movies and listen to music recommended by AI and algorithms on Netflix and Spotify. As Frankel (2018, 10) argues, as user interfaces have advanced to

> help TV viewers more easily find content amid an ever-expanding field of choices, the data science used to achieve true personalization in many cases has moved beyond the scope of human capabilities. The blending of voice recognition into the user search and recommendation process only serves to further the need for AI.

The rise of digital platforms, such as Facebook, YouTube, and Netflix is vital "in the transformation of social into data-minable business ventures," which means that people enjoy popular culture through digital platforms backed by machine learning and algorithms that recommend cultural content to individual users (Langolis et al., 2015, 4). As Lobato (2019, 40) also aptly puts it, one major characteristic of digital platforms is "a reliance on algorithmic recommendations." Netflix, for example, has played a major role in "the development and popularization of recommendations" since its inception. Several OTT platforms, including Netflix, Disney+, and Amazon Prime, and music streaming service platforms, such as Spotify and Apple Play, function as contemporary distribution platforms and connect production and consumption.

However, new digital technologies, including AI and algorithms, have raised some serious concerns, as several global mega platform giants like Facebook and Netflix preoccupy and utilize them to make huge profits, resulting in socio-economic disparities between platform owners and platform users (Fuchs, 2014; Jin, 2015; Srnicek, 2016). While providing extraordinary opportunities, contemporary technological innovation driven by AI has brought about unprecedented risks.

As one of the major caveats, several researchers (Barocas et al., 2019; Reisman et al., 2018) argue that the rapid growth and use of AI have brought about potential cultural and social problems—so-called representational harms—to our contemporary society. This particular harm occurs because AI requires the agency of people who adopt AI

> to make assumptions or predictions about cultural or social factors that vary enormously within and between communities and geographic areas. This practice often results in findings only reflecting potential impacts on a dominant culture and omitting or misinterpreting the impacts on marginalized communities and individuals.
>
> (Reisman et al., 2018, 18)

Compared to allocative harms, which are caused when a system withholds an opportunity or resource to certain groups, representational harms occur when agencies and systems reinforce the subordination of some groups along the lines of identity—age, class, ethnicity, gender, and so on (Barocas et al., 2019):

> Representational harms have long-term effects, and resist formal characterization. But as machine learning becomes a bigger part of how we make sense of the world—through technologies such as search, translation, voice assistants, and image labeling—representational harms will leave an imprint on our culture, and influence identity formation and stereotype perpetuation. Thus, these are critical concerns for the fields of natural language processing and computer vision.
>
> (Barocas et al., 2019, 30–31)

Meanwhile, globally, it is not surprising to learn that leading platforms, including Google, Facebook, and Netflix, armed with big data, algorithms, and AI are characterized "by an avid tendency to colonize and converge into

8 *Artificial intelligence in popular culture*

ever-new markets" (Schwarz, 2017, 384). Many governments and corporations seem to advance some mechanisms to secure socio-economic fairness and equality; however, these measures are not practical, nor transparent, in the majority of countries, whether in the Global North or in the Global South.

Major goals of the book

Media scholars, sociologists, cultural anthropologists, and computer scientists have explored the emergence of AI, algorithms, and big data in tandem with media and culture. Several existing books (Langolis et al., 2018; Andrejevic, 2020; Gunkel, 2020) address the roles of AI and big data; however, there is no single book discussing the convergence of AI, digital platforms, and popular culture other than digital games (Yannakakis and Togelius, 2018; Togelius, 2019). For example, in *The Culture of AI*, Elliott (2019) discusses the ways in which intelligent machines, advanced robotics, accelerating automation, and big data[5] impact people's day-to-day lives and contemporary societies. His understanding of the reordering of everyday life highlights the centrality of AI to everything people do—from receiving Amazon recommendations to requesting Uber and from getting information from virtual personal assistants to talking with chatbots. These academic books on AI are valuable sources, as they offer intriguing case studies of and/or theoretical discussions about new media technologies, AI in this case.

Nevertheless, these books have provided insufficient comprehensive studies of the use of AI in media and popular culture. When they did, they tended to focus on a particular cultural genre—namely, gaming—rather than examining this cultural trend involving various cultural genres, such as music, variety shows, TV dramas, and films. Thus, they could not adequately examine how structural factors and audience engagements interplay in the rise of AI. In other words, AI is currently discussed and used everywhere in the media; however, its impact on popular culture is rarely analyzed. In particular, these studies did not focus on the nexus of AI, digital platforms, and popular culture. Some scholars in several fields seem to understand the convergence of these areas but rarely focus on the nexus of these areas, given the short history of the subject matter.

Unlike previous works, this book offers a comprehensive yet critical understanding of AI as a major force in cultural production, which means that it explores cultural production in the age of AI. I explore the impact of AI on culture, focusing on the situation as it relates to cultural creators, the cultural industries, and the public as consumers, in both the Global North and the Global South, "at a time when the large digital platforms are taking over bigger chunks of the value chain" (Kulesz, 2018a, 5). This book not only discusses several major exemplary cultural forms, including music, gaming, and webtoon as the format of the nexus of AI and culture, but also offers a critical understanding of the convergence of AI, digital platforms,

Artificial intelligence in popular culture 9

and popular culture. This book's evidence-based analyses of AI in the media and cultural industries from a political-economy perspective make significant theoretical and empirical contributions to the literature in several academic fields, including media and cultural studies, science and technology studies (STS), and globalization studies. In so doing, it will also put forward new ideas on the ongoing AI phenomenon.

This book, as the first academic discourse on the conjunction of AI, digital platforms, and popular culture, attempts to understand the ways in which the digital platform and cultural industries have reshaped and developed AI-driven algorithmic cultural production, distribution, and consumption. As can be seen throughout the book, with the emergence of big data, algorithms, and AI, cultural industries have fundamentally transformed their business models and cultural production formats in order to maximize the benefits from these cutting-edge technologies, as well as to appeal to audiences who are tech-savvy and delicate consumers. In the age of artificial intelligence, this changing media ecology demands that we examine the cultural production of popular culture from new perspectives through our understanding of the nexus of AI, digital platforms, and popular culture. Furthermore, AI-driven cultural transformation has required us to adequately grasp contemporary society's socio-cultural, economic, and political spheres, which play pivotal roles in the process.

To begin with, this book examines the ways in which media and cultural industries utilize AI and algorithms to advance the new forms of cultural production, including the production of culture, distribution, and exhibition. By selecting a few major media and cultural industries that use AI and big data the most, such as the music, game, and webtoon sectors, as well as AI journalism, it discusses how these new digital technologies influence the transformation of cultural production. This part of the discussion also includes the role of AI and algorithms in both distribution and exhibition. Due to the recent surge of some local cultural content, including Korean popular culture in the global markets, and local cultural firms' endless efforts to develop popular culture in tandem with AI and big data, the discourses embedded in the convergence of AI, digital platforms, and popular culture focus on the particular local sphere both in the Global North and the Global South. However, as these new technologies and cultures are transnational, the analyses are naturally global, which means that it interprets the discourses between the global and the local so that readers can comprehend several major characteristics in the production of culture.

Second, it investigates change in cultural consumption as part of cultural production by analyzing the ways in which AI and digital platforms reshape people's consumption habits, including in relation to COVID-19. As digital platform firms and cultural corporations who develop AI and algorithms supported by big data are mega giants, it maps out how global platform giants transform local platforms, and therefore, consumers. In fact, Nieborg and Poell (2018, 4279) focus on "the inherent accumulative tendency of

10 *Artificial intelligence in popular culture*

capital and corporate ownership and its subsequent effects on the distribution of power and the precarious and exploitative nature of cultural and (immaterial) labor of both producers and end-users." Subsequently, this book maps out whether new business models protect people's preferences and diversity in culture. The analysis in this particular perspective certainly examines the power relationships between platform firms who use AI and big data and the users who do not have AI technology, but consume recommended cultural content. "AI's purpose can loosely be summarized as algorithmically-driven automation that drives the improvement of service from both a business and user perspective"; therefore, it is critical to understand the AI-driven digital platform environment from both production and consumption sides (Easton, 2019).

Third, as an extension of the discussion above, it maps out the transformation of people's consumption habits toward personal culture. As AI-equipped digital platforms have advanced "personal culture," compared to mass culture, it addresses the nature of the personalization of popular culture. In a media context, digital platforms supported by AI and algorithms like Netflix have recommended particular programs to individual users so that these audiences consume popular culture personally and selectively, which characterizes contemporary cultural scenes. Many digital platforms, from social media platforms to OTT platforms, "aim for increased levels of personalization" (Pangrazio, 2018, 12). Personal culture, as one of the most distinctive characteristics of the contemporary cultural sphere, can be referred to not only as popular culture and media-produced and recommended by AI-equipped cultural producers and digital platforms but also as cultural consumption conducted individually on and through digital platforms, including social media platforms. Since AI and algorithms in the realms of popular culture and media have developed personalized recommendation systems, personal culture implies the entire process of cultural production, distribution, and consumption in the age of digital platforms.

Fourth, it documents and discusses governments' own rapid developments of AI-relevant policies in cultural production, as AI interlaces with the nation-state, the contemporary phase of globalization, and geopolitics. In particular, it draws on the active engagement in the process and builds on the legacy of digital platforms and cultural policies. Governments around the globe fiercely invest in AI and big data, as they are drivers for the growth of the digital economy. The governments have developed new policy measures through their legal and financial arms in order not to be left behind. Therefore, this book does not only identify key policy issues relevant to AI in tandem with media and popular culture, but it also attempts to critically interpret major issues occurring in the early 21st century.

Last, but not least, as a continuation of the previous discussion, it examines whether governments and corporations have advanced reliable public and corporate policies and ethical codes to secure socio-economic equality. It is not clear whether AI and big data achieve socio-cultural progress in addition to economic prosperity. As one of the most significant concerns in our contemporary cultural environment is the disparity between the haves and the have-nots, as well as fake news on social media platforms, it discusses whether new ethical codes are able to develop socio-economic justice and equality so that we may contemplate the future of the AI-driven media and cultural sphere. In addition, it examines whether AI embedded in popular culture advances diversity and cultural identity, which are crucial components of democracy in the realm of popular culture.

As a major analytical framework, this book employs critical political economy, as it is important to explore the relationship between technological development and the political economy of contemporary culture. There are high stakes in debates over the use of digital technologies in cultural industries; therefore, it is significant to investigate the relationship between technological development and growth, mainly AI and digital platforms in this book, and the political economy of contemporary media and culture. Unlike other approaches, political economy gives priority to comprehending "social change and historical transformation." This means that people need to understand "the great capitalist revolution, the upheaval that transformed societies" (Mosco, 2009, 26). As political economists are also concerned about power and politics, it takes a historical and normative approach toward the growth of digital technologies, including AI and big data (Mosco, 2009). As Susan Strange (1994, 125) already pointed out, digital technology, including AI, has been "made to serve the interests of the state and to reinforce its power." Therefore, policy mechanisms and AI initiatives must be understood "from a critical perspective that considers development, deployment, and impact from a wide diversity of voices beyond the tech sector" (McKelvey and MacDonald, 2019, 44). Digital platforms like Facebook and Netflix use AI and algorithms to assemble databases about customers and to target campaigns "based on information gathered through their surveillance." Surprisingly, users are "often willing to exchange personal information for specialized services," which consequently allows major digital platforms supported by AI to expand their revenues (Klinenberg and Benzecry, 2005, 9). In particular, in an ever more AI and digital platform–centric world, the media and cultural infrastructure industries and their close relationship with popular culture are now the center of gravity around which our contemporary society and culture revolve (Winseck, 2016).

As such, this book discusses relevant questions from a critical political-economy perspective that emphasizes not only power relationships between politics and the economy but also between cultural creators and consumers. In other words, it is critical to discuss the role of AI in shifting production and consumption patterns in the context of media and culture, because it brings new imperatives for understanding power relations between two major actors—cultural creators and cultural consumers—within as well as outside of traditional state/market disparities (Youngs, 2007). This critical political-economy approach in the age of AI and digital platforms, in

12 *Artificial intelligence in popular culture*

particular, in tandem with the coronavirus pandemic, will shed light on our current debates on the convergence of AI, digital platforms, and popular culture to determine the dominant power of AI and digital platforms in the vicious circle of cultural production in the near future. This approach also allows readers to critically ponder whether AI and digital platforms have developed cultural diversity in terms of the creation and preservation of plural ideas and diverse cultural tastes and, therefore, cultural democracy in the early 21st century.

Organization of the study

The study is organized as follows. After providing the fundamentals of the book in this chapter, the following chapters discuss detailed information, key issues, and future directions. In Chapter 2, I historicize and theorize the convergence of AI, digital platforms, and popular culture. Given their short histories in the realms of media and culture, it is necessary to define the major characteristics of AI and digital platforms, which also becomes a foundation for the convergence of AI and popular culture. In this chapter, I first construct how the histories and concepts of AI and digital platforms were originally developed for the media and cultural research. I especially discuss the ways in which we understand AI in the realms of media and popular culture. Then, I address the role of digital platforms in cultural production. Finally, I develop the ideas of convergence between AI and digital platforms in the cultural sector in order to understand the nexus of AI, digital platforms, and popular culture as one of the most significant trends in the early 21st century. The final part focuses on the theoretical development of our perspectives on the possibility of AI as a digital platform.

Chapter 3 investigates state-led AI policies in tandem with the media and cultural industries. It compares and contrasts AI policies between the Global North and the Global South, which eventually provides the discourses on AI-related policies in the cultural industries. The chapter discusses the reasons why these countries have adopted AI, big data, and algorithms as the drivers of popular culture and, therefore, the digital economy, both nationally and globally. As several leading countries in the Global North have continued to advance neoliberalism, while a few countries in the Global South have focused on developmentalism to support AI-related technologies and businesses, I offer some vantage points to compare relevant policy standards in conjunction with AI. In particular, it examines whether governments in several countries must continue their emphasis on either neoliberal tendencies or developmentalism in the age of AI. Most of all, it discusses the possibility of a human-centered norm in the cultural sector in the AI era.

Chapter 4 examines the nexus of popular culture and AI in production. AI is one of the most versatile technologies that can be utilized in almost the entire process of game development, including production and data analytics. By addressing the complexity and specialty of the convergence of AI and

Artificial intelligence in popular culture 13

popular culture, this chapter attempts to offer new insights on the global cultural industries that vehemently work with AI and big data. It examines the nexus of popular culture, such as films, music, digital gaming, and webtoon and AI in production. While admitting the significance of Korean popular culture, including music (K-pop) and webtoons in the global cultural markets, it especially explores some Korean cultural sectors as among the most important cultural industries to converge AI and popular culture. It maps out how local entertainment houses have partnered with AI companies; therefore, it compares AI-supported cultural production between countries in the Global North and countries in the Global South. Finally, it discusses whether the encounters of AI and popular culture have advanced cultural democratization and creativity or not and whether audiences have enjoyed the benefits of AI-driven cultural production. There are high stakes in this particular dispute over the use of AI in cultural production and cultural industries; thus, it is critical to examine the relationships between AI development and the political economy of contemporary popular culture.

In Chapter 5, I explore the convergence of AI, algorithms, and digital platforms, focusing on Netflix, and in general OTT platforms. Netflix has played a key role in transforming the global entertainment markets. Having mostly conquered the Western markets, including Canada (2010) and the U.K. (2012), Netflix has pivoted east and vehemently sought to rack up its number of subscribers from Asia starting in 2015. Netflix entered Japan in 2015 and has a presence in most Asian countries. Young and increasingly digital populations in Asia present an incredible opportunity to ramp up Netflix's international subscribers, and subscriptions in Asia already surpassed that of the U.S. at the end of 2018 (Gilchrist, 2018). The chapter first discusses the major characteristics of Netflix as one of the most significant OTT platforms, one that controls the vicious chain of the broadcasting and film industries. Second, it examines the ways in which Netflix, utilizing AI and algorithms, influences the content production industry in the global cultural industries, as the content industry has rapidly shifted its methods of production and distribution by learning from the Netflix model. Then, it investigates Netflix's effects in the global OTT industry, including the Korean market. Through these discussions, it eventually articulates whether Netflix actualizes an asymmetrical relationship of interdependence between the West, primarily the U.S., and many developing countries, based on its crucial role in reshaping global platforms.

Chapter 6 examines the crucial role of consumers in the age of artificial intelligence and big data. As is well known, several digital platforms like OTT services, including Netflix and Amazon Prime, and music streaming service platforms, such as Spotify and Apple Play, connect production and consumption. While these digital platforms and cultural industries have transformed their production and distribution, people have also shifted their consumption habits with the help of AI and algorithms. In the early 21st century, global youth equipped with new digital media enjoy popular culture

14 *Artificial intelligence in popular culture*

and news on digital platforms instead of physically going to theaters or buying and possessing cultural materials.

However, these consumers sometimes function as free labor—working as non-wage workers in return for their use of digital platforms—which triggers a severe disparity between platform owners and platform users. Understanding the concept of users as free labor is a crucial step in developing well-balanced approaches in the realm of digital platforms and popular culture. Then, it discusses the personalization of culture directed by AI so that people can understand AI's impacts on people's consumption trends. This chapter, therefore, investigates not only the transformational force of AI in production but also in consumption.

Chapter 7 explores the convergence of journalism and digital technology, focusing on AI, as it has especially transformed the journalism industry. In particular, it raises the question of fake news in tandem with digital platforms, such as Facebook, Twitter, and TikTok, as much of the fake news circulates on social media platforms. In fact, one of the most existential questions of the digital age is about the ways in which social media platforms are caught so unprepared for the rise of fake news, misinformation, disinformation, and digital falsehoods, which eventually work as tools of democratic destruction. This chapter maps out the implications of AI and big data in the realm of journalism, which must be foregrounded in the larger context of the digitization of media—a transition toward algorithms and social media—and, therefore, examines the ways in which AI and big data have transformed journalism as an institution (Lewis, 2019). By raising the question of what AI means for journalism, it aims to discuss how AI and big data have transformed the journalism landscape as we have known it. AI technologies, regardless of how transformative they prove to be in the long term, might be understood as part of a broader story of journalism's reconfiguration in relation to new data and computer-driven systems (Lewis, 2019). In particular, this chapter attempts to analyze digital platforms, such as Facebook and TikTok as some of the most significant news platforms, which often produce and disseminate fake news. By discussing the platformization of journalism, it critically discusses the increasing role of AI in producing a news culture and its effects in journalism.

Chapter 8 discusses new media ethics in the age of AI. Governments and media corporations around the globe seem to advance mechanisms to secure socio-economic fairness. By emphasizing social security, transparency, and accountability, these standards underscore whether AI-driven industrial policies present any biases or produce reliable results and ethical frameworks for society. However, due to AI's fast and recent growth, these measures are not practical or transparent. Thus, this chapter addresses whether governments and corporations have advanced reliable ethical codes to secure socio-economic equality. It answers these questions from a critical political-economy perspective which emphasizes not only power relationships between politics and the economy but also socio-economic justice and fairness. Chapter 9 summarizes the major characteristics of the convergence of AI, digital platforms, and popular culture and discusses several implications in conjunction with COVID-19 to provide some foreseeable topics to be addressed in the near future.

Notes

1 Go is a game of two different players or teams who take turns putting black or white stones on a 19 × 19 grid. Players win by taking control of the most territory on the board. Meanwhile, AlphaGo is a computer program to play the Go game. AlphaGo's algorithm uses a combination of ML and tree search techniques. AlphaGo has built up its expertise by studying recorded games and teasing out patterns of play (*BBC News*, 2016).
2 In December 2019, when Lee Sedol finally retired, he expressed that he would no longer play professionally, partially because AI is impossible to overcome. During his interview with the media, he said, "with the debut of AI in Go games, I have realized that I am not at the top even if I become the No. 1 through frantic efforts. Even if I become the No. 1, there is an entity that cannot be defeated" (Webb, 2019).
3 Simply put, the Fourth Industrial Revolution refers to how technologies like AI, autonomous vehicles, and the internet of things (IoT) merge with humans' physical lives. These technological changes are drastically altering how individuals, companies, and governments operate, ultimately leading to a societal transformation (Schulze, 2019). This Fourth Industrial Revolution is fundamentally different from previous revolutions, as it is characterized by a range of new technologies, including AI, that are fusing the physical, digital, and biological worlds, impacting all disciplines, economies, and industries (Schwab, 2016, 12).
4 Although it is not perfect, Bourdieu (1983) already argued that to understand a work of art, people must look not only at the piece of art itself but also at the conditions of its production and reception, because these socio-cultural environments characterize the field of cultural production and, therefore, people can determine the way in which the production of culture, back then, mainly literature and pure art, relates to the wider fields of power and class relations.
5 The term 'big data' appeared in the late 1990s, and big data mainly refers to "data sets whose size or type is beyond the ability of traditional relational databases to capture, manage and process the data with low latency. Big data has some common characteristics: high volume, high velocity or high variety. AI, mobile, social and the IoT are driving data complexity through new forms and sources of data. For example, big data comes from sensors, devices, video/audio, networks, log files, transactional applications, web, and social media—much of it generated in real time and at a very large scale" (IBM, 2020).

2 Convergence of AI, digital platforms, and popular culture

Introduction

AI has been a major consideration in contemporary digital capitalism and culture. Although AI is considered a new digital technology, AI already seems to be ever present in our modern era. While "we are still many years away from having robots at our beck and call, AI has already had a profound impact in more subtle ways" in several areas such as weather forecasts; Google's search predictions; and voice recognition, such as Apple's Siri. What these new technologies have in common are "machine learning algorithms that enable them to react and respond in real time" (Shani, 2015). The role of AI has also continued to increase in the media and cultural sectors on a large scale, and AI technology has especially been utilized with digital platforms, such as search engines, social media, and smartphones, as well as over-the-top (OTT) service platforms like Netflix, which has been consequently reshaping the media and cultural industries, since the early 21st century. Due to AI's increasing role in cultural production, from the production of popular culture and media information to the consumption of this media and cultural content, it is crucial to understand AI-related technologies and digital platforms, as well as relevant socio-cultural mechanisms, including policy measures, together and to examine their convoluted relationships.

It was not long ago when people talked about the influence of digital technologies in cultural production. Only about 20 years ago, people were interested in what happened to cultural products when they were crafted and distributed through digital channels. Historically, the most influential digital technologies like the internet "reduced the price of entry into a cultural field, creating openings for actors and organizations who were previously unable to get their work into the public" (Klinenberg and Benzecry, 2005, 8). For example, artists could easily change and repackage digitally recorded music and video, sampling tunes or assembling images into new work, occasionally with high commercial or aesthetic value. News companies could repurpose content across platforms, adapting a single digital file to suit a newspaper article, internet publication, or teleprompter script. This was a significant

AI, digital platforms, and popular culture 17

transformation since it changed the meaning of cultural products and, in turn, the status of professional journalistic labor (Klinenberg and Benzecry, 2005, 8). With AI, algorithms, and big data, people's interest in and use of these cutting-edge digital technologies have soared. This has not been limited to cultural producers but includes users as consumers.

Therefore, it is necessary to define the major characteristics of AI and digital platforms, which also becomes a foundation for the convergence of AI and popular culture. In this chapter, I first construct how the histories and concepts of AI and digital platforms have evolved in media and cultural research. I especially examine the ways in which we understand AI in the realms of media and popular culture, not only in the production of popular culture and media content but also in the distribution and consumption. Then, I address the role of digital platforms supported by AI in cultural production, focusing on their role as mediators, and therefore, I attempt to discuss the crucial connection of these two fundamental digital technologies. Eventually, this chapter develops the ideas of convergence between AI and digital platforms in the cultural sector in order to understand the nexus of AI, digital platforms, and popular culture as one of the most significant trends in the early 21st century. The final part discusses the theoretical development of our perspectives on the possibility of AI as a digital platform.

What is artificial intelligence in popular culture?

Artificial intelligence is not a new concept, and the origin of AI goes as far back as Greek antiquity. Nevertheless, it was less than 100 years ago that the technological revolution took off and AI went from fiction to plausible reality (Shani, 2015). Due to its complexity, there are various definitions of AI, which means that no single definition encompassing what this new digital technology means was made. In fact, the notion of AI still evolves, and therefore, I do not seek to lay down a general, all-purpose definition of AI that can be applied in any context in this book. Instead, this book attempts to arrive at a definition that is suited to the cultural sector that uses AI, big data, and algorithms to produce, distribute, and consume cultural content. While historicizing the concept of AI, it provides the best relevant notion of AI in the media and cultural sectors—in particular, in conjunction with cultural production. AI, machine learning (ML), and deep learning (DL) are each a subset of the previous field. AI is the overarching category for ML, and ML is the overarching category for DL. AI can be "applied to fields as wide as computer audio or visual recognition, self-driving vehicles, robots that can respond autonomously to their environments, recommendations of films via Netflix, and financial analysis" (New European Media, 2018, 5) (See Table 2.1).

In our modern era, the definition of AI was originally developed by John McCarthy, an American computer scientist, pioneer, and inventor, who was

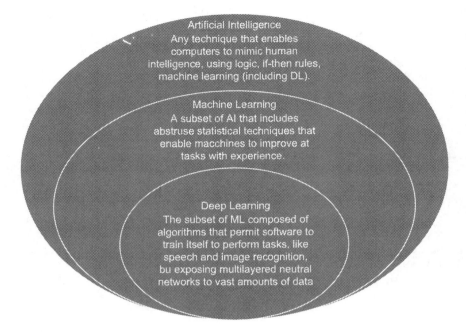

Table 2.1 Relationships of AI, ML, and DL
Source: Moore (2019, 8).

known as the father of AI after playing a seminal role in defining the field devoted to the development of intelligent machines. He coined the term "AI" during the 1956 Dartmouth Conference, the first AI conference (Gunkel, 2020). As is well documented (Childs, 2011) in the *Independent* of the U.K., "The objective was to explore ways to make a machine that could reason like a human, was capable of abstract thought, problem-solving and self-improvement." He believed that "every aspect of learning or any other feature of intelligence can in principle be so precisely described that a machine can be made to simulate it" (Childs, 2011). Since then, many computer scientists, science and technology study (STS) scholars, and sociologists have developed the concept of AI.

Through the 1960s and 1970s, the excitement further grew as computers became more accessible. Nevertheless,

> it became apparent that AI was not living up to the hype. This led to what has been called the AI winter, a period through the late 1980s and 1990s when investment in AI research and commercial efforts slowed significantly. In recent years, excitement about AI has increased due to some high-profile successes.
>
> (Moore, 2019, 6)

AI, digital platforms, and popular culture   19

AI has been mainly the preserve of computer science, information science, mathematics, linguistics, psychology, and neuroscience. However, it took several more decades for people to acknowledge the true power of AI. As the Go match between AlphaGo and Lee Sedol explained in Chapter 1 proves, AI has finally become one of the most popular and influential terms that people remember in recent years.

While there are several major differences, one of the major variances of AI from other digital technologies is its capacity to replace human beings. The word "artificial" "has come to denote that machines can be made to replicate or simulate human intelligence, and hence the affinity between artificial intelligence and digital technologies (including advanced robotics and accelerating automation)" (Elliott, 2019, 2). Of course, this notion itself is controversial because AI cannot replace humans entirely, but partially. In the media sector, for example, journalists are concerned about the increasing role of robot journalism because they believe that robots may replace human journalists in writing and editing processes. However, as is fully discussed in Chapter 7, it is premature to confirm this kind of new trend or phenomenon, as humans are still major actors in media journalism with the help of robots.

More specifically, in the 2010s, AI was defined, in general, as the "simulation of human intelligence through computers, mainly referring to machine learning. Put simply, machine learning is a form of data" (Asia Pacific Foundation of Canada, 2019, 6). This general definition seems to identify three major areas—AI, machine learning, and big data—involved in AI interchangeably. From a slightly different tone, AI is also defined "as a set of algorithms that is able to cope with unforeseen circumstances" (Berendsen, n.d.).[1] Here, AI is compared with algorithms in that AI involves analyzing big data and looking for patterns.

On the one hand, an algorithm is a set of instructions—a preset, rigid, coded recipe that gets executed when it encounters a trigger. On the other hand, AI—which is an extremely broad term covering a myriad of AI specializations and subsets—is a group of algorithms that

> modify its algorithms and create new algorithms in response to learned inputs and data as opposed to relying merely on the inputs it was designed to recognize as triggers. This ability to change, adapt and grow based on new data, is labeled as intelligence.
>
> (Ismail, 2018)

AI systems especially learn from experience and over time get a better understanding of what people, in particular, managers, operators, and designers need for their operations. When these algorithms are automated, it is called AI (Lengnick-Hall et al., 2018). As Broussard (2018, 94) also points out, "An algorithm is a series of steps or procedures the computer is instructed to follow."[2]

Gonfalonieri (2019) also claims that an algorithm is a "process or set of rules to be followed in calculations or other problem-solving operations,

20 AI, digital platforms, and popular culture

especially by a computer." Here "the goal of an algorithm is to solve a specific problem," defined by someone as a sequence of steps. An algorithm is a shortcut that helps people give instructions to computers. An algorithm simply "tells a computer what to do next with an 'and,' 'or,' or 'not' statement." However, traditional algorithms have an issue. Indeed, people have to tell to create a step-by-step process to reach their objective. Rather than following explicitly programmed instructions, some computer algorithms are designed to allow computers to learn on their own. Putting these definitions together, UNESCO (2020) states,

> AI involves using computers to classify, analyze, and draw predictions from data sets, using a set of rules called algorithms. AI algorithms are trained using large datasets so that they can identify patterns, make predictions, recommend actions, and figure out what to do in unfamiliar situations, learning from new data and thus improving over time. The ability of an AI system to improve automatically through experience is known as ML.
>
> (4)

Another major element that characterizes AI is whether AI can learn automatically, and it is considered that machine learning is a set of algorithms that arguably enable the software to update and "learn" from previous outcomes without the need for programmer intervention, although the process is not entirely automatic. It is fed with structured data in order to complete a task without being programmed how to do so. Machine learning is made up of a series of algorithms. Basically, AI is designed to learn in the same way as a child. Thanks to a data set, an AI can find patterns and build assumptions based on those findings (Gonfalonieri, 2019). In this light, Niranjan Krishnan, head of data science at Tiger Analytics said (Ismail, 2018),

> AI is like a gear system with three interlocking wheels: data processing, machine learning and business action. It operates in an automated mode without any human intervention. Data is created, transformed and moved without data engineers. Business actions or decisions are implemented without any operators or agents.

He continued to state that the system learns endlessly from the accumulating data and business activities and outcomes are getting better with time.
  More narrowly, AI could refer to

> a branch of computer science focused on simulating human intelligence, one that recently has been especially engaged in the subfield of machine learning: the training of a machine to learn from data, recognize patterns, and make subsequent judgments, with little to no human intervention.
>
> (Lewis, 2019, 673)

In a similar vein, Elliott (2019, 4) defines AI as "encompassing any computational system that can sense its relevant context and react intelligently to data." AI and machine learning often seem to be used interchangeably. However, they are not quite the same thing, but the perception that they are can sometimes lead to some confusion. "Both terms crop up very frequently when the topic is big data, analytics, and the broader waves of technological change which are sweeping through our world" (Marr, 2016). Simply speaking, "AI is the broader concept of machines being able to carry out tasks in a way that we would consider smart," while "machine learning is a current application of AI based around the idea that we should really just be able to give machines access to data and let them learn for themselves" (Marr, 2016).

In the realms of media and culture, focusing on its relationship to communication, "communicative AI refers to AI technologies—such as conversational agents, social robots, and automated-writing software—that are designed to function as communicators, often in ways that confound traditional conceptions of communication theory and practice" (Guzman and Lewis, 2019; cited in Lewis, 2019, 673). As Andrejevic (2020) especially points out,

> as automatically generated information comes to play a central role in the rationalization of production, distribution, and consumption, artificial intelligence robotizes mental labor: it promises to augment or displace the human role in communication, information processing, and decision-making.
>
> (3–4)

What he emphasizes is that "AI resuscitates the promise of automation in the mental sphere: to be faster, more efficient, and more powerful than humans" (Andrejevic, 2020, 4).

Again, this does not mean that AI entirely replaces human beings. Rather, the focus should be the interaction between technologies and people, both creators and consumers, as they are the developers as well as the users of AI and algorithms, which create new forms of cultural content and consumption patterns. It must be clear from the outset that we use AI to make the work more innovative and workers' role more rewarding, instead of simply cutting costs by replacing human workers (Britt, 2019). While admitting that various explanations exist, this book defines AI as the simulation of human intelligence through computers supported by and connected with big data and algorithms to not only "intermediate" human-machine interactions but also "mediate" production and consumption of media and culture through the convergence of intelligent technology and human creativity.

What is significant is that AI symbolizes innovation in the early 21st century, and many countries around the globe have emphasized the increasing

22   AI, digital platforms, and popular culture

role of AI and invested in this particular area. As Robin Mansell (2017, 4286) points out,

> Investment in the development and use of novel digital applications, including intelligent or social machines and robots, supported by algorithms and machine learning, is expected by many industry leaders to raise income levels and foster movement along a singular pathway through a fourth industrial revolution.

As Shah (2013, cited in Shorey and Howard, 2016) also argues, "What should be done with AI and big data, and what other kinds of relevant knowledges could it help produce" are among the major agendas for the government, industries, and cultural creators. What they commonly pursue is the enhancement of digital economy, driven by the use of AI and big data, as several digital platforms like Google and Facebook already prove.

Specialists such as digital platform workers, game designers, music composers, and webtoon creators have already utilized AI and big data to dramatically enhance the experience of enjoying and playing, "resulting in increased popularity and soaring profits" (Klinenberg and Benzecry, 2005, 9). Since AI has rapidly taken on a major role in the digital platform and cultural industries, which are very significant sectors for the national economy and society, both governments and corporations have enthusiastically invested in AI and big data. As usual, several Western countries lead the AI sector, followed by a few Asian countries. China and Korea are latecomers in the realm of AI; however, they have already advanced their AI-related platform and cultural industries to the level of potentially leading contenders globally (Walch, 2019). The use of various digital technologies, such as high-speed internet and smartphones, proves that these two major actors show sometimes cooperative and at other times conflicting relationships in the development of an AI-saturated industry structure.

On the one hand, governments have acknowledged the significance of AI and vehemently developed relevant policies, in both financial and regulatory standards. As a policy matter,

> AI operates at the intersection of big data and automation. On one side, machine learning—an algorithm that improves through experience, and the kind of AI most talked about in many countries—requires massive amounts of training data to optimize its algorithms, a privacy issue. Once trained, AI requires proper implementation, and should be used only when experts deem it acceptable.
>
> (McKelvey and MacDonald, 2019, 44)

On the other hand, major platform and cultural firms have invested heavily in developing synergistic relationships between several media holdings, "integrating their production processes into convergence systems that yield content for different outlets, cross-promoting programs in different media,

AI, digital platforms, and popular culture 23

and establishing lines of vertical and horizontal integration in production and distribution" (Klinenberg, 2000, cited in Klinenberg and Benzecry, 2005, 10). In other words, like other digital technologies, such as smartphones, games, and the internet, AI and big data have facilitated the growth of large media conglomerates. In *The Guardian*, Paul Nemitz, a senior European Commission official (Chadwick, 2018) argues, "We need a new culture of technology and business development for the age of AI which we call 'rule of law, democracy, and human rights by designs.'"

The reality is highly controversial because the business practices supported by the government have not guaranteed diversity, democracy, and equality, unlike their expectations and promises, and instead they raise new levels of concern due to concentration of ownership and skills. AI and big data have even seemed to intensify asymmetrical power relationships between mega platforms like Facebook and Google, big venture capitals, and media giants, and small- and mid-sized cultural firms as well as cultural producers and cultural consumers. This book, therefore, offers several critical discussions on the use of AI in popular culture, which transforms entire cultural industries.

Digital platforms as mediators in the global cultural sphere

The increasing use of AI is visible in digital platforms. Digital platforms equipped with AI and big data have continued to grow and are becoming among the most significant players in the global cultural industries. A platform refers to "the online services of content intermediaries, both in their self-characterizations and in the broader public discourse of users, the press and commentaries" (Gillespie, 2010, 349). In other words, Gillespie seems to consider that platforms are and can be neutral. For example, he (2018, 41) argues that "social media platforms are 'intermediaries,' in the sense that they mediate between users who speak and users who might want to hear them, or speak back," although social media platforms create several negative impacts like fake news and surveillance. Evens and Donders (2018, 4) also argue that "apart from the underlying software and algorithmic configuration, we put emphasis on the intermediary (and gatekeeping) position platforms have when connecting programming to consumers." Digital platforms, therefore, could be defined as large-scale online systems premised on user interaction and user-generated content—including Facebook, Twitter, YouTube, OTT services, and smartphones (Jin, 2015; Lobato, 2019).

Digital platforms have different dimensions according to their primary areas and purposes. For example, OTT service platforms (e.g., Netflix) are different from social network site platforms (e.g., Facebook) and user-generated content platforms (e.g., YouTube). It is indeed controversial to categorize OTTs, including Netflix and Amazon Prime, as digital platforms. In this regard, Lobato (2019) points out:

> Netflix is not a platform in the same way as social media services like Facebook or Twitter are. Netflix is not open, social, or collaborative.

24 AI, *digital platforms, and popular culture*

> One cannot upload content to Netflix or design software applications to run within it. In this sense, it is fundamentally different from video sites containing both user-uploaded and professionally managed content (YouTube, Youku, etc.). . . . Netflix is closed, library-like, professional; a portal rather than a platform; a walled garden rather than an open marketplace.
>
> (31–32)

However, due to several of their unique characteristics—data-driven, commercially oriented, and mediated—it is possible to define OTT services as digital platforms, at least as quasi digital platforms.[3]

More specifically, Netflix is an on-demand video-streaming platform in that it connects content providers and final consumers. Although people or companies could not run their software programs on Netflix, this particular OTT service mediates content producers and consumers, and by providing their watching habits to Netflix, the customers fulfill their sociality on Netflix. Kulesz (2018b, 80), for example, emphasizes, "a platform facilitates interaction between users—buyers and sellers, creators and consumers, etc.—in a highly efficient way, and in this regard adds great dynamism to the cultural fabric," instead of focusing on technological aspects. Netflix has continued to transform its own major characteristics, from a distribution channel to a production company to now a digital platform. Therefore, it is not dicey to discuss Netflix through digital platform approaches.

Due to the rapid growth and massive influence of digital platforms, academic discourses on digital platforms are widespread with three major focal elements. To begin with, as in the case of AI, the digital platform must be understood comprehensively, instead of narrowly focusing on technological aspects. Several scholars (Jin, 2015; Srnicek, 2016; van Dijck et al., 2018; Nieborg and Poell, 2018; Flew, 2018b; Mansell, 2021) argue that digital platforms encompass various unique characteristics. For many, a platform is a programmable architecture designed to organize interactions between platform users. Therefore, many people consider platforms simply as technological tools that allow the users to do things online: "sharing content, making connections, ranking cultural artifacts, and producing digital content" (Gehl, 2011, 1228). However, "these online activities hide a system whose logic and logistics are about more than facilitating: they actually shape the way we live and how society is organized" (van Dijck et al., 2018, 9).

Among these, van Dijck et al. (2018, 9) especially point out that "a platform is fueled by data, automated and organized through algorithms and interfaces, formalized through ownership relations driven by business models, and governed through user agreements." Prior to this, Jin also (2015) argues, digital platforms could not be fairly understood without contemplating three major areas: technological sphere, corporate sphere, and political sphere. While developing the notion of the platformization of cultural production, Nieborg and Poell (2018) emphasize the significance of the analysis

AI, digital platforms, and popular culture   25

of overall ecology relevant to digital platforms. They argue (2018, 4276) that platformization can be defined as

> the penetration of economic, governmental, and infrastructural extensions of digital platforms into the web and app ecosystems, fundamentally affecting the operations of the cultural industries. So far, this process has been examined from three perspectives: business studies, political economy, and software studies.

As such, the digital platform shapes the communications, interactions, and consumption that it facilitates—through interface design, moderation policies, and terms of service (van Dijck, 2013). The platforms' commercial interest in gathering user data implies that people cannot study a single layer but must acknowledge the complicated relationship between the technical affordances and the underlying commercial interests (Jørgensen, 2019).

Second, digital platforms must be treated as mediators, not as intermediaries. As discussed, Gillespie (2010) and Evens and Donders (2018) define platforms as content intermediaries. This certainly explains the partial nature of digital platforms; however, it does not focus on digital platforms' true nature as one of the most powerful communication systems. In contrast to this, van Dijck (2013, 29) points out that a platform is a mediator rather than an intermediary, because it shapes the performance of social acts instead of merely facilitating them. Bratton (2015) especially considers the platform as "the third institutional form alongside nation-states and markets, mainly due to platforms' increasing power in our contemporary society." Compared with traditional media conglomerates, digital platforms are guided by business models that foreground connectivity between users and producers over the creation of products, not only by cultural creators but also general users, and therefore, they tactically mediate these two major components for their financial gains (Cunningham and Craig, 2019).

As such, digital platforms work not only as simple conveyors and/or distributors of value neutral technologies but also play a key role in manipulating and controlling the entire vicious circle of the entertainment industry for their own business successes. The ways in which digital platforms mediate access to cultural content through the use of AI algorithms ask us to question if and how these platforms are not only distributing but also reproducing media information and popular culture. What I am arguing here is that digital platforms supported by AI should be considered as powerful entities able to control the entire process of cultural production due to their role as mediators.

Third, digital platforms are global, and the process of globalization in the realm of platforms has been the fastest thus far. Several digital platforms, from search engines like Google to social media such as YouTube and Facebook, have clearly attempted to target global users, not only national users. By penetrating the global markets, these platforms have continued to gain

26 AI, digital platforms, and popular culture

huge profits from foreign countries, while dominating the flows of information and culture. Equipped with AI supported by big data gathered from global users, several major platforms, which were mostly developed in the U.S., dominate the global markets, as more than 90% of search engine users mainly rely on Google (StatCounter, 2019). Facebook and Netflix have also garnered more revenues in the global markets than the U.S. market due to the increasing number of international users since many years ago.

In fact, ever since it began streaming in the U.S. in 2007, Netflix has become one of the largest and most significant global OTT service platforms. Netflix, as an interesting example of a digital platform as well as television source due to its unique characteristics—"a computational, software-based system that can produce a television-like experience" (Lobato, 2019, 35)— has greatly reshaped both the global audio-visual industries and people's habits in consuming cultural content. Since digital platforms have heavily relied on data that they garner from their users, a handful of mega platform giants, including Facebook, Google, and Netflix, have certainly controlled the global markets, which is also one of the major reasons why they are major actors in the age of AI, which also depends on the quantity and quality of data.

Digital platforms, including social media platforms, OTT platforms, and smartphones have greatly influenced people's daily activities and cultural lives. Digital platforms as some of the most significant mediators rather than intermediaries should be understood from various perspectives, including technological, commercial, and global standards. In particular, it is critical to understand the significance of the nexus of AI and digital platforms—the two most important digital technologies in the early 21st century—in the vicious circle of cultural production.

Convergence of AI, digital platforms, and popular culture

AI and digital platforms go hand in hand, as digital platforms are the major users of AI in the realms of media and popular culture. Several traditional media and cultural areas like music, film, and newspaper have gradually utilized AI for cultural production. However, the use of AI in the digital platform sector has been larger and much faster than in these traditional media, which means that the convergence of AI and digital platforms, not only technologically but also commercially, has become very common and powerful. Media convergence is mainly about the integration of old media and new media as well as digital technologies and popular culture as Jenkins (2006) explains. However, popular culture now can be produced and circulated by AI and digital platforms, sometimes together, at other times separately, and the boundary of old media and new media is not clear; therefore, we may say that the convergence of AI and digital platforms can be made possible as part of the broader notion of media convergence or as a new form of media convergence.

AI, digital platforms, and popular culture   27

Taking Netflix as an example, convergence has been one of the most important practices for Netflix, as it has grown based on the convergence of new media and popular culture since the late 1990s when broadband, the internet, and smartphones consecutively helped the integration of popular culture and these new digital technologies. Broadband services became accessible in tandem with other digital technologies. The rise of cable channels expanded the number of "available programming choices and promoted the idea that content should be tailored to niche audiences. The proliferation of smartphones and wireless connections shifted expectations about accessibility and convenience, popularizing presumptions that culture circulates best on an on-demand basis" (McDonald and Smith-Rowsey, 2018, 2).

Netflix later utilized algorithms converged with AI to create one of the most powerful recommendation systems in the media and cultural industries, while YouTube, Facebook, and Twitter have used AI to develop their business models to attract customers. Netflix and Facebook represent two different business models (see Chapter 6). As one of the most noticeable cases in the field of popular culture, Netflix develops AI-based algorithmic recommendations as a new business model that other OTT service platforms follow. As Plummer (2017) points out, "Netflix uses machine learning and algorithms to help break users' preconceived notions and find shows like movies and television dramas" that they might not have originally selected.

Netflix's recommendation engine—a set of algorithms that connect people to content they want—is "the most well-known element of the Netflix AI system" (Frank et al., 2018). In fact, Netflix itself improves over time. As people use it more, it learns about people's tastes and serves up the best content available in a highly personalized way. The core of the Netflix system is a remarkable piece of software design and engineering, which is nearly invisible (Frank et al., 2018). Machine-learning algorithms are excellent at predicting whether a person engages with a video clip or not. As Tercek (2019) points out, Netflix is at the forefront of applied AI in every stage of video delivery. However, AI also helps to govern the quality of service to the subscribers. Netflix uses AI to monitor bandwidth in the network and optimize a particular household's video and audio streams based on available bandwidth and network congestion.

> Netflix even uses AI to monitor whether subscribers share their passwords. AI can also aid monetization of video by improving the environment for advertising. Today several firms compete to offer systems powered by AI for brand safety, efficient targeting and more completed views.
>
> (Tercek, 2019)

With the rapid growth in the number of its global subscribers, Netflix has changed its algorithms that recommend what users should watch next since 2016. Instead of suggesting recommendations based on regional models,

28 AI, *digital platforms, and popular culture*

Netflix started to recommend movies a customer may enjoy and looks to other users with similar tastes around the world regardless of where they live (Brownell, 2016). For Netflix, algorithmic recommendations are used to auto-curate selections of content geared around individual users' data profiles. Every video selection that appears on TV or mobile gadgets is the result of intricate calculations based on user-submitted data, collaborative filtering, and manual coding of content for all conceivable metadata points (Lobato, 2019). As a Western-based OTT platform, Netflix has increased its capital gains through algorithmic recommendations. Netflix is working as a mediator: the platform strategically groups people based on their common interests in order to maximize its profits. Netflix offers space for consuming entertainment products (Srnicek, 2016), not as a simple intermediary, but as a crucial mediator.

The major problem here is that people as the subscribers of Netflix lose cultural diversity and, therefore, cultural democracy. Since the personalization engine algorithms utilized by Netflix don't display different ideas and tastes, subscribers mostly see similar cultural content. In other words, the recommendation system "carries the risk of the extinction of diversity" (Filibeli, 2019, 99). As digital platform users, when people use Netflix, Facebook, and Twitter, they get easily biased cultural content and information based on their preferences, but intensified by these platforms' recommendation systems. People who have far-right ideology may never see cultural content, including news, on leftwing politics or vice versa (Filibeli, 2019). When they start to enjoy some particular genres of movies, they have no opportunities or less opportunities than other subscribers in enjoying movies portraying different genres and themes. As diversity has been one of the most significant characteristics in cultural democracy, this business norm certainly hurts not only cultural pluralism but also cultural democracy. Furthermore, what Netflix implements is the intensification of established hierarchies of cultural authority and power (Hadley and Belfiore, 2018) that must be challenged. Netflix equipped with AI and algorithms has strengthened the digital platform's power in people's cultural activities and, therefore, continues to harm cultural democracy.

Arguably, Netflix is one of the most significant examples of a digital platform, as it not only circulates cultural content but also produces cultural products, and therefore, Netflix backed by cutting-edge AI and algorithms controls the entire cultural chain, from production to distribution. Characterized by unequal technological and cultural flows, the state of platform development implies a technological and relevant socio-economic domination of U.S.-based or U.S.-origin firms that have tremendously influenced the majority of people and countries. Unlike other fields like culture and hardware, in which the method for sustaining unequal power relations among countries is mainly the exportation of goods and related services, the means of dominating foreign countries in digital platforms are commercial values that are embedded in platforms, which are significant for the expansion of power and capital accumulation (Jin, 2015).

Meanwhile, Facebook as one of the largest social media platforms has used deep learning as deep learning algorithms become more sophisticated, and they can increasingly be applied to more data that people share, from simple text to pictures to videos (Marr, 2016). Deep learning is used to gain value and help Facebook achieve its goals of providing greater convenience to users. "Facebook utilizes deep neural networks—the foundation stones of deep learning—to decide which advertisements to show to which users. This has always been the cornerstone of its business," but by tasking machines themselves to find out as much as they can about the users, and to cluster the users together in the most insightful ways when serving the users ads, "it hopes to maintain a competitive edge against other high-tech competitors" such as YouTube and Twitter who fight for supremacy of the social media market (Marr, 2016).

Facebook as a digital platform has increased its influence in the social media market and now uses AI to attract users. As *The Intercept* (Biddle, 2018) reported, Facebook's new advertising service expands the ways in which it sells corporations' access to Facebook's users and their lives.

> Instead of merely offering advertisers the ability to target people based on demographics and consumer preferences, Facebook instead offers the ability to target them based on how they *will* behave, what they *will* buy, and what they *will* think. These capabilities are the fruits of a self-improving, artificial intelligence-powered prediction engine, first unveiled by Facebook in 2016 and dubbed "FBLearner Flow."
>
> (Biddle, 2018)

Of course, as will be fully discussed in Chapter 7, the same social media company utilizes AI to control fake news. Facebook has increased its use of AI, both for good and bad, and therefore, the convergence of AI and Facebook has been practically real.

As such, AI-equipped Netflix and Facebook have substantially influenced local cultural industry firms, cultural creators, and customers, while greatly appropriating the global media and cultural markets. This means that the convergence of AI and Facebook and, in general, social media and Netflix and other OTT platforms plays a crucial role for digital platforms to intensify the disparity between AI-equipped platform owners and platform users who provide data to platforms in the early 21st century.

AI moves toward a digital platform

Many governments and corporations around the globe have rapidly pursued the Fourth Industrial Revolution in the early 21st century, and AI,

30 *AI, digital platforms, and popular culture*

algorithms, digital platforms, and big data are key technological tools that they have had to focus on for this. Although they do not emphasize the media and cultural industries as some of the major industries, AI has gradually become a new digital technology that cultural creators and cultural industries companies adopt to enhance the quality of media and cultural content (see Kim, K.H. et al., 2018). For these actors, the common belief is that machine learning is more powerful than it actually is. As the magazine *Forbes* (2017) aptly observed,

> Machine learning is good at things machine learning is good at and, of course, it's bad at everything else. If you listen to some people though, you'd believe you could throw a neural net at any problem and get a solid solution.

Most of all, the increasing role of AI in the cultural industries has related to the growth of digital platforms as a new player of the cultural sector. Several digital platforms, such as social media platforms, OTT service platforms, and smartphones are rapidly becoming primary actors in the production, distribution, and consumption of media content and popular culture. In the realms of media and culture, digital platforms like Facebook and Netflix mainly function as the distribution tools of media and cultural content; however, these digital platforms equipped with AI, algorithms, and big data have produced media and cultural content themselves, while people enjoy popular culture produced and distributed on these platforms. Facebook and Netflix are no longer distribution channels, but as platforms produce their own cultural content and media information and actively mediate other cultural providers and consumers. Netflix is a good example of the increasing convergence of AI, digital platforms, and popular culture, and therefore, it is necessary to discuss the ways in which AI has deeply influenced cultural production.

What is interesting is that AI itself will in turn become a digital platform. As discussed, AI has transformed the media and cultural spheres. That is just the beginning. Stanford University's AI Index 2019 annual report has found that the speed of AI is even outpacing Moore's Law—how processor speeds double every 18 months to two years—meaning application developers can expect a doubling in application performance for the same hardware cost. The Stanford report released in December 2019 especially found that AI computational power is accelerating faster than traditional processor development. According to the report, prior to 2012, AI results closely tracked Moore's Law, with compute power doubling every two years. Post 2012, however, compute power has been doubling every three to four months (Saran, 2019). The speed is important for the cultural sector as well. As AI becomes a normal standard and technology, the media and cultural landscape will be transformed deeply. In this regard, Tercek (2019) argues that "AI as platform" will happen eventually because of competition, which

AI, digital platforms, and popular culture 31

means that one way or another, it seems inevitable that AI as an on-demand service like Netflix will be widely available soon.

> Usually, when we think about the future of media, we do not consider AI. . . . The folks in the media and advertising business are intensely pre-occupied with streaming video platforms, including on-demand services like Netflix and (considerably less so) with live streaming systems like Twitch. In their defense, this myopic focus makes sense because stream-ing video has permanently altered consumer behavior, but at this point it is also kind of an obvious trend: there are more than 200 OTT stream-ing videos services available in the United States today, and thousands outside the US. What comes next after OTT? In my speech, I aimed to push past the obvious trends like streaming video to explore something that is still emerging and evolving. To me, right now, that is AI for media.
>
> (Tercek, 2019)

In reality, we may need to wait longer to witness the growing role of AI as a digital platform itself in the cultural sector, including in both produc-tion and consumption, as it is a long way from buzzwords to reality. As discussed, the implementation of AI in cultural production is certain, and people are surely experiencing the increasing role of AI in media and cul-ture, although the process is rather slow. This implies that the transformation of the cultural sector in tandem with AI is real, but gradual, as opposed to expectations.

The role of AI will furthermore grow to become one of the most signifi-cant components, even as a digital platform itself, in our cultural lives. This is why we have to consider AI not only as a new digital technology, but also as a platformitized entity, which means that we critically analyze AI as one of most profitable and dominant mediators in the global context. AI is the only digital technology to learn itself to control the entire value chain in the media and cultural industries. It is only a matter of time before AI is platformitized too beyond its role as a cutting-edge digital technology. As Shani (2015) points out in *Wired,* "While the discussion occasionally turns to potential doomsday scenarios, there is a consensus that when used for good, AI could radically change the course of human history. And that is especially true when it comes to big data." In other words, "The very premise of AI technology is its ability to continually learn from the data it collects. The more data there is to collect and analyze through carefully crafted algo-rithms, the better the machine becomes at making predictions."

Regardless of the increasing role of AI in the traditional media sectors, including broadcasting, film, and music, AI has closely connected to digital platforms in contemporary capitalism. In other words, AI can be identified

> as an instrument of capital, with all this entails in terms of both the exploitation in and ejection from waged work of human labor, and the

32 AI, *digital platforms, and popular culture*

concentration of wealth and social power in the hands of the corporate owners of high technology

(Dyer-Witheford et al., 2019, 3)

AI has been

the product not just of a technological logic, but simultaneously of a social logic, the logic of producing surplus-value. Capitalism is the fusion of these technological and social logics and AI is the most recent manifestation of its chimerical merging of computation with commodification.

(Dyer-Witheford et al., 2019, 3)

Understanding AI in the cultural sector is not isolated from socio-cultural and economic conditions surrounding the growth of AI, which means that we have to analyze AI within the broader context of our society. We need to analyze AI and digital platforms, and therefore, the convergence of AI and digital platforms in popular culture comprehensively and critically, from technological perspectives to commercial spheres and to socio-cultural aspects.

Conclusion

This chapter has constructed the histories and theories of AI and digital platforms toward the convergence of AI and digital platforms. It addressed how people understand AI in the realms of media and popular culture, while discussing the increasing role of digital platforms in cultural production. Through this process, it developed ideas of convergence between AI and digital platforms in the cultural sector in order to understand the nexus of AI, digital platforms, and popular culture. The convergence of AI and popular culture is currently in its early stage. However, there are several platforms and media firms that utilize AI for the production of popular culture, and therefore, it may not take long to witness massive production supported by AI. The use of AI in cultural production is faster than expected, at least for a handful of powerhouses in the Global North, such as the U.S., the U.K., Canada, and Japan, and in the Global South like Korea and China, as will be discussed in the next chapters.

What is significant at this stage is that AI actualizes its possibility in cultural production and prepares for the new era. For example, the potential power of AI in the media and cultural sectors will be further increased by the opportunity to combine it with other emerging technologies, especially virtual reality and augmented reality (PricewaterhouseCoopers, 2018). Revenues from VR apps, gaming, and video, which were US$3.9billion in 2017, are expected to soar more than fivefold by 2022. In the VR space, the installed base of headsets is projected to grow substantially, helped by

Facebook launching its US$199 untethered Oculus Rift in the second quarter of 2018 for gaming, education, and enterprise use. The price point is significant: the Rift originally sold for US$599 and required a computer costing several hundred dollars to power the related VR experiences and games. Blending AI and VR/AR can have a transformational impact on the ability to derive actionable data on consumers' behavior. The VR analytics company Retinad has developed heat-map technology that tracks where a person in a virtual environment looks and for how long. In the future, apps equipped with AI could harness that data to create experiences geared to specific individuals (PricewaterhouseCoopers, 2018, 19–20).

AI and digital platforms have substantially worked together in the realms of media and culture in the early 21st century. In particular, with people practicing social distancing due to the onset of COVID-19 and experiencing lockdowns worldwide mainly in 2020 and 2021, the use of digital platforms has been soaring. While AI functions as a technological tool to control the process of cultural production, digital platforms are one of the strongest mediators, which not only simply connect production and consumption, but also actively govern the vicious circle of the cultural industries. Cultural production, again, encompassing the entire process of cultural activities, such as production, distribution, and consumption, has been rapidly connected to AI and digital platforms, and the convergence of AI, digital platforms, and popular culture will be a new dominant norm in the near future, which is the primary reason why we have to pay attention to this new trend. AI itself has also platformitized to become one of the most powerful mediators in the realms of media and culture, which will affect cultural production.

Notes

1 In the early 21st century, "algorithms have expanded and woven their logic into the very fabric of all social processes, interactions and experiences that increasingly hinge on computation to unfold; they now populate our everyday life, from the sorting of information in search engines and news feeds, to the prediction of personal preferences and desires for online retailers, to the encryption of personal information in credit cards, and the calculation of the shortest paths in our navigational devices" (Roberge and Seyfert, 2015, 2).

2 There are mainly two types of algorithms: 'rule-based algorithms' and 'machine-learning algorithms'. The former refers to "a set of instructions designed by a human and are direct and unambiguous" in order to achieve a given goal, whereas the latter refers to a type of algorithm that is able to define its own rules based on a well-designed training process (Fry, 2018, 10). In the case of rule-based algorithms, a human as the programmer needs to know in advance all the necessary steps to achieve a given task, which is another way of saying that "rule-based algorithms will only work for the problems for which humans know how to write instructions." Machine-learning algorithms, by contrast, will themselves generate a set of rules based on a training process. The problem is that the result of that training "often won't make a lot of sense to a human observer" (Fry, 2018, 11; see also Bueno, 2020, 74).

34 *AI, digital platforms, and popular culture*

3 Several recent works have defined Netflix as a platform. For example, Gerald Sim (2018, 186) called Netflix "an online video platform." Two of the most recent books published in Korea (You, G.S, 2019; Kim, K.D. and C-Rocket Research Lab, 2019) also designated OTT services, including Netflix and Amazon Prime, as well as YouTube, as digital platforms with no particular discourses. Since they published in the latter part of 2018 and 2019, media scholars and practitioners automatically take for granted Netflix as one of the major digital platforms.

3 AI, cultural policy, and the rise of counter-neoliberalism

Introduction

Governments and cultural industries firms around the globe are riding an AI phenomenon. Starting in the late 2010s, several countries, both in the Global North and the Global South, have reshaped their industrial structures by emphasizing the increasing role of AI, big data, and algorithms. In a handful of advanced economies in the Global North, including the U.S., the U.K., Germany, and Canada, AI and big data are transforming all industries, including platform and cultural industries. Several countries like China and Korea in the Global South have also vehemently invested in AI and big data, as they are new drivers for the digital economy, although the majority of countries in the Global South cannot develop AI-related technologies comparable to a few Western countries due to the lack of money and manpower. It is certain that AI can streamline industry structure and bring new energies to the national economies, and therefore, many countries have to adapt to nascent technological shifts like AI (McKelvey and MacDonald, 2019). Again, because of the possibility of economic prosperity, these countries have also developed various supporting measures, both legal and financial, so that governments and corporations can closely work together to enhance the AI-driven digital economy.

Given its short history, AI policies in many countries are relatively new, and these countries mentioned above do not have well-advanced policy measures yet. In particular, these countries rarely develop AI policy pertinent to the cultural industries with a few exceptions. The trend itself is shifting, of course, due to the significance of AI in media and culture, as well as other industries. As Kulesz (2018a, 2) points out, "AI can help to empower numerous creators, make the cultural industries more efficient and increase the number of artworks, which is in the interest of the public." Accordingly, governments, digital platform firms, and cultural corporations discuss a whole host of agendas surrounding the remarkable emergence of AI in general. From governments to cultural industries to cultural creators (e.g., film directors and music composers), how to utilize AI and algorithms for the digital economy and cultural production is one of their key concerns.

36 *AI, cultural policy, counter-neoliberalism*

Governance in media and platform companies has been gradually emphasized in this shifting trend over the past several years; however, the current form of government policies does not emphasize cultural diversity, as many governments provide disproportionately favorable policy measures to AI and platform owners instead of the users.

This chapter aims to document the ways in which several countries, both in the Global North and the Global South, have shaped and developed AI-related media and cultural politics. It analyzes the governments' own rapid development of AI policies in tandem with neoliberalism, which emphasizes small government while guaranteeing the maximum liberty of the private sector or developmentalism—"a state-driven political doctrine coined by the state to combat harsh domestic economic conditions" (Lee and Kim, 2010, 315)—entailing government intervention to promote economic development for large conglomerates. It discusses AI policy in a few leading countries and in developing countries in order to critically compare and contrast relevant policy standards—in particular, in the media and cultural sectors. It draws on the active engagement of governments in the process and builds on the legacy of digital platforms and cultural industries firms in the neoliberal era, which is not what the proponents of neoliberalism expect to see. Finally, it addresses the possibility of a human-centered policy norm in the cultural sector in the age of AI.

AI policies and the increasing tendency of counter-neoliberalism

AI development and use are some of the major indicators for the growth of AI and relevant policies around the world. To begin with, according to the Government AI Readiness Index 2019 produced by Oxford Insights (2019), U.K. (2), Germany (3), U.S. (4), Canada (6), and Japan (10) lead the global AI society, while China ranked at 20 and Korea ranked at 26. Although there are some exceptional cases—for example, Singapore was ranked in the top position—this index certainly proves the great divide between a few Western societies and non-Western societies showing an insurmountable gap. Another survey published by Tortois in December 2019 indicates a similar trend. As Table 3.1 explains, only three countries, China, Singapore, and South Korea, are ranked in the top ten list of The Global AI Index.

There are a few different perspectives, of course. According to the 2018 China AI Development Report, by the end of 2017, the international AI talent pool had 204,575 people, densely distributed in North America, Western Europe, Northern Europe, East Asia, and South Asia. At the country level, AI talent is concentrated in a few countries, with the top ten countries representing 61.8% of the global total. The U.S. takes the lead with as many as 28,536 AI talents, representing 13.9% of the global total; followed by China in the second place with 18,232, representing 8.9%; India in third place with 17384; Germany in fourth place with 9,441; and the U.K. in fifth place

Table 3.1 The Global AI Index

Country	Talent	Infrastructure	Operating environment	Research	Development	Government strategy	Commercial	Total rank
U.S.	1	1	6	1	2	13	1	1
China	18	3	3	2	1	1	2	2
U.K.	5	8	1	3	11	7	4	3
Canada	4	23	5	8	10	4	5	4
Germany	9	12	7	4	12	5	9	5
France	8	30	2	12	9	8	7	6
Singapore	2	4	39	16	15	30	6	7
South Korea	28	5	30	22	3	31	25	8
Japan	26	16	17	6	7	12	8	9
Ireland	6	2	28	28	6	40	20	10

Source: Tortois (2019).

38 *AI, cultural policy, counter-neoliberalism*

with 7,998 (China Institute for Science and Technology Policy at Tsinghua University, 2018). With some variations like China, these data explain that there is an AI divide between a few Western countries and many developing countries. As a global economic divide has intensified the gap of people's lives between these two areas, the AI divide has shown a symptom to worsen the already existing gap between the Global North and the Global South, both technologically and economically.

The growth of AI in these countries mentioned above, either in the Global North or in the Global South, has closely related to national information and communication technology (ICT) policies, which means that several countries around the world have vehemently developed AI policies in the early 21st century. Although each country's focuses are dissimilar, they commonly admit the importance of policy measures to advance AI-supported economy and culture while avoiding potential risks rooted in the growth of AI use. They develop regulatory schemes in order for AI to drive the transformation of our contemporary society, both economically and culturally. In regard to the increasing role of governments in AI, people have seen unprecedented investment in AI governance and ethics in recent years. As Gunkel stated in his university's newspaper (Parisi, 2019), the 2020s will see an amplification of this effort as stakeholders in many parts of the planet as North America, Europe, and China compete to dominate the AI policy and governance market. AI-related technology might be global in scope and controlled by borderless multinationals. But AI policy and governance is still a matter of nation-states. Merkie (2018, 2) also points out the significance of relevant AI policy, not only focusing on the digital revolution, including AI revolution, but social and cultural change as well, as the world we are currently understanding is much more than technical. Digitization, here developed by AI, must be "accompanied by enlightened state cultural policies, if opportunities for access and participation, individual and collective creativity with respect to diversity are to be fully used." What these scholars generally emphasize is the leading role of nation-states in the AI era, unlike neoliberal proponents who argue that governments must take hands-off policy measures.

As is well documented, governments in the Global North and the Global South have deregulated and liberalized their domestic markets and industries to guarantee the maximum profits for corporations, including cultural firms. As McChesney (2008) clearly points out, neoliberal norms imply that governments should remain large so as to better serve corporate interests, while minimizing their hand-on activities that might undermine the free rule of business. Proponents of neoliberalism claim that the market itself is alive and that governments must leave everything in the invisible hands of market forces (Friedman, 1982).

Contrary to neoliberal economic policy, governments around the globe, both countries in the Global North and the Global South, have expanded their involvement in the field of AI. Several leading and emerging economies have had to advance AI policy, mainly because of AI prosperity, meaning AI certainly improves business productivity, government effectiveness, and the nation's future. Public policy is a key driver for achieving AI prosperity because it sets the rules and conditions for success (Deloitte, 2019, 4). From the U.S. to China, governments have increased their financial investments and legal supports for the growth of AI-related areas.

Governments around the globe believe that AI is one of the most significant cutting-edge technologies that should be supported by the governments rather than leaving it in the hands of the private sector only. As Joseph Stiglitz (2019) argues, "Contrary to what many in the financial sector would like to think, the problem was not too much state involvement in the economy, but too little," and therefore, these governments have turned their gazes to directly nurturing AI-related fields, although they are not giving up on their neoliberal tendencies. This does not mean that the private sector has lost its crucial role to the public sector in advancing AI. Many IT corporations and venture capitals have continued to develop AI and relevant technologies, and many governments have closely worked with them to advance AI.

There is another major reason for the continuous involvement of the government. For many nation-states, people who may be negatively affected by AI should be protected. Public policy measures, therefore, need to focus on not only economic prosperity but also fairness and justice. Since governments are the major players in this regard, it is necessary for nation-states to formulate supportive, but still normative and ethical policy mechanisms, as also discussed in Chapter 8. Media and culture are unique in both production and consumption, as they are directly related to humans' daily cultural activities, which asks nation-states to play a leading role in nurturing AI-driven media and cultural content through their articulated cultural policies. The necessity of AI-involved media and cultural content triggers the revival of nation-states, which intensifies counter-neoliberal tendencies in the 2020s.

State-led AI policies in the Global North

There are several exemplary cases showing the increasing involvement of nation-states in the field of AI. To begin with, as one of the leading countries in the development of AI, the Canadian government has actively shaped diverse AI policies, as briefly discussed with the case of COVID-19 in Chapter 1. In Canadian policy, nurturing AI is crucial for the government, as AI greatly operates at the intersection of automation and big data. On one side, ML that improves through experience requires massive amounts of training data to optimize its algorithms. "Once trained, AI requires proper implementation, and should be used only when experts deem it acceptable"; thus, the Canadian government's recent movements with AI are part of "a global rush to codify rules and regulations on AI. Several relevant standards have been proposed to govern AI and its underlying data" (McKelvey and MacDonald,

40 *AI, cultural policy, counter-neoliberalism*

2019, 44). Many of these mechanisms are concerned with ensuring transparent practices and establishing accountable methods of "securing the role of facts in public debate" (Marres, 2018, 424).

More specifically, in March 2017, Canada became the first country in the world to announce a national strategy for AI, with a CD$125 million investment over the next five years by the federal government (UNESCO, 2018). A few factors inspired the Canadian government to act. Canada had the talent advantage, but it needed to act quickly to maintain that lead. International demand for talent, especially from the U.S., was putting Canada's prior investments in AI research and talent development at risk. There was concern in both the Canadian government and in the private sector that this brain drain would compromise Canada's capacity to become an early adopter of this new technology (UNESCO, 2018).

Canada's top-notch research expertise in the field of AI has led to significant recent investment. But far fewer resources have been dedicated to the governance, ethics, or social responsibilities of AI, leaving many different local initiatives to try to fill the gap as well. People cannot deny that AI already affects their everyday lives, and people's activities are the major sources for the growth of digital platforms. With each "like" and comment on Facebook, people as the users are already contributing individual data to improve AI applications. Better processors, advances in algorithms, as well as big data, often gathered from people's online interactions, have driven key advances in deep learning. Advances in these fields have been heralded as a net benefit to humans. However, treating AI as inherently good overlooks the significant development needed for ethical, safe, and inclusive applications. Poor data or rushed deployment can lead to AI systems that are not worth celebrating (McKelvey and Gupta, 2018).

Consequently, the Canadian government experimented with a highly open consultation process during the development of its AI self-regulation. The public, but mostly experts, could join its Artificial Intelligence Policy Workspace, where other civil servants shared news and reports (Karlin, 2018). The paper, titled "Responsible AI in the Government of Canada," summarized the benefits and risks of AI to the federal government (McKelvey and MacDonald, 2019, 45). The Canadian government tool provides a risk assessment based on 1) impact on individuals and entities, 2) impact on government institutions, 3) data management, 4) procedural fairness, and 5) complexity. These criteria drew on the report's final section on "Policy, Ethical, and Legal Considerations of AI," where it discussed bias and fairness in data, transparency, and accountability, as well as acceptable use. This tool is just now being used across the federal government due to the 2019 Directive on Automated Decision-Making. Applications to date seem low risk, but it also seems clear that though we might know how the government considers AI, we are not privy to who engages with it—and whether high-risk situations such as immigration should be considered a no-go zone (McKelvey and MacDonald, 2019, 45–46). While the Canadian government started to develop new policy mechanisms, it has not shown any crucial policy measures to deal with some issues embedded in the growth of AI.

The U.S. has also rapidly developed its AI policy, deploying a hands-on policy, not one based on neoliberal trends, which is interesting. It is especially critical to understand American AI-related policy, as the country is arguably the home of cutting-edge digital technologies, including AI and platforms, as well as neoliberalism. The U.S. government has been active in developing policies and implementing strategies that accelerate AI innovation since President Trump issued an executive order launching the American AI Initiative on February 11, 2019 (Office of Science and Technology Policy of the U.S., 2019). The executive order explained that the federal government plays an important role not only in facilitating AI R&D (research and development) but also in promoting trust; training people for a changing workforce; and protecting national interests, security, and values. As the Future of Life Institute (2019) points out, the American AI Initiative is guided by five principles: 1) driving technological breakthroughs, 2) driving the development of appropriate technical standards, 3) training workers with the skills to develop and apply AI technologies, 4) protecting American values including civil liberties and privacy and fostering public trust and confidence in AI technologies, and 5) protecting US technological advantage in AI, while promoting an international environment that supports innovation.

On March 19, 2019, the U.S. federal government launched AI.gov to make it easier to access all the governmental AI initiatives currently underway (White House, 2019). There is no doubt that the U.S. has initiated and developed neoliberal policy in most areas, including economy. In the realm of digital platforms, both social media platforms and OTT platforms, private corporations and venture capitals have been the major actors. However, the U.S. government has no choice but to take a leading role for the growth of AI due to AI's significant role for the national digital economy. This initiative, though, does not include media and culture as major areas that the U.S. government has to support with priority. As Table 3.1 shows, under favorable government initiatives, the U.S. has continued to become the leading country in several AI areas, including talent, infrastructure, research, and commercial.

Several European countries have also developed strong and practical legal and ethical guidelines. As one of the leading countries in the field of AI, Germany has emphasized legal stability and security to users since the early years of AI initiatives. For Germany, "advancing the development of AI is important from societal and ethical perspectives" since legal standards and ethical principles were considered as important elements during development and rollout of AI systems. The German government has developed "verifiable requirements concerning transparency, information efficiency, formal privacy guarantees and the integrity of AI" that could become features of AI

42 AI, cultural policy, counter-neoliberalism

development (Harhoff et al., 2018, 24). In August 2019, a government panel also stated that "businesses are free to develop tools for AI but also must weigh a variety of factors and ethical restrictions." The German government established the Data Ethics Commission in July 2018 to develop ethical guidelines and recommendations for protecting "the individual, preserving social cohesion, and safeguarding and promoting prosperity in the information age" (Radu, 2019), and the Data Ethics Commission proposed 75 recommendations to regulate automated decision-making by AI and algorithms in October 2019. Although many aspects of the commission's report remain blurry, the recommendations encouraged the German government to provide more funding to current oversight bodies and to support self-regulation initiatives (Data Ethics Commission, 2019).

Meanwhile, Japan has advanced its own policy to advance AI technology in the name of Society 5.0 since early 2019. Japan's new blueprint for a supersmart society, Society 5.0, is a more far-reaching concept than the Fourth Industrial Revolution, for it envisions completely transforming the Japanese way of life by blurring the frontier between cyberspace and physical space. Society 5.0, also called "the 'super-smart society,' envisions a sustainable, inclusive socio-economic system, powered by digital technologies such as big data analytics, AI, the Internet of Things and robotics" (UNESCO, 2019). In Society 5.0, many products or services will be optimally delivered to people and tailored to their needs.

> In Society 5.0, autonomous vehicles and drones will bring goods and services to people in depopulated areas. Customers will be able to choose the size, color and fabric of their clothing online directly from the garment factory before having it delivered by drone.
>
> (UNESCO, 2019)

As such, AI policies in many countries are relatively new, and these countries have developed several different policy mechanisms. Although these countries in the Global North have heavily depended on neoliberal policy for national economy, they provide necessary funds and supporting measures for the growth of AI. On the contrary to neoliberal tendencies, emphasizing small government, these governments have to initiate some mechanisms to advance AI and relevant technologies in their infancy. Due to AI's nascent development, however, these countries have not yet developed AI policy for the cultural industries, other than a few exceptional cases. State policies on the cultural industries thus far have been mainly concerned with fostering and supporting the production of cultural content, such as television dramas, documentaries, feature films, and other forms of audiovisual content like music by domestic producers (Jin, 2018). With increasing involvement of AI, cultural policy in many countries needs to be changed, as AI becomes a new key player in cultural production.

State-led AI policies in the Global South

Several countries in the Global South have attempted to build new digital economies based on AI, and their primary mechanism has been developmentalism instead of neoliberalism. As several Asian countries, including Korea, China, and Singapore, have developed their national economy through strong developmentalism, they have greatly advanced AI policy for the enhancement of national economy—in particular, digital economy. Developmentalism in these countries has been "a state-driven political doctrine coined by the state to combat harsh domestic economic conditions" (Lee and Kim, 2010, 315). However, the situation in the Global South is not much different in that they have not paid much attention to media and cultural areas in their major AI policy measures.

As one of the leading investors in AI around the globe, China has developed several AI master plans. In July 2017, the State Council of China (2017) released the New Generation Artificial Intelligence Development Plan (AIDP), which outlines China's strategy to build a domestic AI industry worth nearly US$150 billion in the next few years and to become the leading AI power by 2030.[1] This officially marked the development of the AI sector as a national priority, and it was included in President Xi Jinping's grand vision for China. This policy initiative also emphasized that the Chinese government will provide necessary support to digital platforms but did not mention the cultural industry itself. The plan clearly indicates that China will construct innovative platforms of AI and strengthen support for the application, research, and development of AI. According to State Council of China (2017), AI open source hardware and software infrastructure platform focuses on building a unified computing framework platform supporting knowledge reasoning, probability statistics, depth learning, and other AI paradigms and forms a promotion of AI software, hardware, and intelligent clouds between the ecological chain. The group intelligent service platform focuses on the construction of knowledge resource management based on the large-scale cooperation of the internet and forms the platform and the service environment for the innovation of the industry and university.

China's government incentives and growing leadership in the digital economy has led to a data advantage. Chinese platform giants like Tencent, Alibaba, and Baidu have "an unparalleled view into the minutiae of everyday economic activities across hundreds of millions of consumers," data that feeds into deep learning systems that power AI-related applications (Sundararajan, 2019). There is no doubt that China will become one of the world's premier AI innovation hubs; however, the country is still busy developing new master plans for other major industries, and not yet for the media and cultural sectors.

Meanwhile, Korea has developed its unique AI policies in the digital platform and cultural sectors. Unlike other countries, Korea has developed AI policy somewhat relevant to the cultural industries, which distinguishes it

44 *AI, cultural policy, counter-neoliberalism*

from other countries, although its AI policy mainly focuses on digital platforms. As the Korean government was the major actor during the developmental era between the 1970s and the 1990s, it once again has played a key role in the development of the AI-driven industrial revolution starting in the late 2010s and the early 2020s. In fact, Korea has advanced one of the strongest state-led developmental models, which pursued a top-down and export-led economy (Lee and Kim, 2010; Kwon and Kim, 2014; Ryoo and Jin, 2020). In Korea, developmentalism entails government intervention to promote economic development in tandem with large conglomerates. Although the Korean government has advanced neoliberal economic policies, emphasizing the increasing role of the private sector while reducing its own functions (McChesney, 2008), the Korean government cannot give up its developmental paradigm and continues to develop necessary industrial policies to support AI-related technologies and businesses.

There are several small-scale AI policy developments in various ministries, and one of the most recent policy measures is the National Strategy for Artificial Intelligence (The Korean Government, 2019a) announced in December 2019. Under the strategy, Korea plans to leverage its prowess in memory chips to build the world's most competitive AI chip industry, with new semiconductors having 25 times the processing speed and just one-thousandth the power consumption of existing integrated circuits. The Korean government states that the plans will help create an industrial, social, and governmental ecosystem that can stimulate and sustain growth in next-generation technology and potentially add upward of 455 trillion won (US\$389 billion) to the economy by 2030. During a press conference, Science and ICT Minister Choi Ki-young said, "The latest AI strategy is centered on making full use of our country's existing strengths so as to effectively compete with rivals and respond swiftly to technological changes" (The Korean Government, 2019a). This national strategy, however, does not show any big difference from that of the previous government nor emphasize the convergence of culture, digital platforms, and AI.

Nevertheless, the Korean government has developed three major AI-related initiatives—in particular, in relation to digital platforms and cultural sectors. As was briefly explained in the introductory chapter, the entire Korean society was shocked when AlphaGo developed by DeepMind defeated Lee Sedol in GO games, forcing the country to acknowledge the significance of AI for their future. Right after the event, the Korean Ministry of Science, ICT and Future Planning (MSIP, now Ministry of Science and ICT) created an Artificial Intelligence Information Industry Development Strategy in 2016 (Government of the Republic of Korea Interdepartmental Exercise, 2016). The policy report titled "Mid- to Long-Term Master Plan in Preparation for the Intelligent Information Society: Managing the Fourth Industrial Revolution" focuses on the role of AI alongside other converging technologies such as cloud computing, big data analysis, and mobile technologies in reshaping Korea's industrial systems.

AI, cultural policy, counter-neoliberalism 45

The report provides a framework for collaboration between technology, industry, and civil society with a 30-year time frame, which is promising, but not practical. This seemingly overwhelming plan reflects the Korean government's basic approach to AI, and the plan is rearticulated in more detail through the Presidential Committee on the Fourth Industrial Revolution (PCFIR), which was established by President Moon Jae-in (2017–present) in November 2018. Operating under the motto "led by the private sector, supported by the government," the PCFIR features a roster of private sector leaders and academics alongside five ministers from relevant departments and the science advisor to the president, totaling 25 members (Asia Pacific Foundation of Canada, 2019, 24). As the first major AI-related policy, it certainly shows a unique Korean-style top-down initiative.

The Mid- to Long-Term Master Plan in Preparation for the Intelligent Information Society mainly discusses a range of implications of AI related to the workforce and economy as well as lifestyles and living environments. The strategy defined in the report highlights some key issues, fostering an intelligent information society on the basis of public-private partnership, with businesses and citizens playing leading roles and the government and research community providing support. As usual, the same strategy emphasizes industrial competitiveness and social security (Government of the Republic of Korea Interdepartmental Exercise, 2016). It was supposed to lead to the definition of specific policy aims and tasks related to technological development, the promotion of industry, and proactive steps to reform education. Based on these fundamental and basic strategic plans, various ministries in the Korean government (2019b) have developed diverse initiatives. In 2019, several ministries, including the MSIP as a leading ministry, developed a five-year plan titled "Data, AI Economy Promotion Plan." This policy measure emphasizes that the success of the Fourth Industrial Revolution in the Korean context relies on marketable high-quality data, cutting-edge AI technology, and ecological convergence of big data and AI.

Against this backdrop, the Korean government aims to develop the data market, from 14 billion Korean won in 2018 to 30 billion won in 2023, while the number of workers in the fields of AI and data is anticipated to be 10,000 by 2023 to position Korea as the country in which people handle AI and data safely. The government specifically plans to establish 100 big data centers and ten big data platforms by 2023, while developing a hub to provide relevant services, such as data, algorithms, and computer power to corporations. As of January 2019, several ICT and telecommunications firms, including Samsung, LG, SKT, KT, and Kakao lead the development of AI in Korea, although the scales of their operations and reach are not comparable to several global ICT and platform firms like Amazon, Google, and Facebook (The Korean government, 2019b).

The continuous intervention by the Korean government in the AI era certainly implies that the Korean government remains as the major player, not only an organizer of governance but also a coordinator of socio-economic

46 AI, cultural policy, counter-neoliberalism

actions (Lee, H.K., 2019, 146–147); "culture became decoupled from statist ideological propaganda; however, it has still been taken as a determining factor and strategy for the survival, prosperity and success of the nation state." In this light, "culture is uninterruptedly perceived as intrinsically instrumental. The hands-on cultural governance was replaced by a liberalized approach of governing at distance; yet, the actual distance between the state and the populace is not very far." In particular, digital technologies, which need an ample amount of research and development (R&D) investment, are drivers for the national economy, and the government cannot leave it alone. As evidenced in the cultural industries, the Korean government has continued to support cultural production through legal and financial resources, and now it actualizes its developmental approach in the neoliberalism era.

Meanwhile, Singapore has taken a developmentalism model. Singapore released its National Artificial Intelligence Strategy in November 2019, and it is taking a whole-of-nation approach to the development, use, and governance of AI. This approach is enabled by a strong bureaucracy and positive track record of national coordination. The newly created National AI office, which is part of Singapore's Smart Nation Office, is responsible for managing the National AI Strategy. Singapore adopts an application-focused approach by leveraging its smaller size and ability to coordinate through its strong, top-down bureaucracy. Singapore's government has successfully implemented its socio-economic development agenda through centralized action—known as a developmental state, although this model has been criticized for inhibiting innovation (Kim and Loke, 2019).

These countries aforementioned in the Global South have certainly relied on developmentalism in different ways for the national economy, and they, once again, have advanced top-down AI initiatives. In the realm of AI, they do not want to be left behind, which is one of the major reasons for their AI drive. However, these countries other than a few exceptional cases have not focused on the nexus of AI and culture. What is significant is that media and culture, including digital platforms, are some of the most important and largest industries that AI can develop on a large scale. Therefore, several governments in the Global North and the Global South have gradually focused on the use of AI in the realms of media and culture in the early 21st century.

Counter-neoliberal AI policies in the media and cultural spheres

Several governments in the Global North and the Global South are deeply involved in the growth of AI and relevant areas, again, mainly due to AI's role in their digital economies. As discussed in the previous sections, however, these governments have not initiated the growth of media and cultural industries in tandem with AI. For them, media and cultural industries are not good enough to be prioritized. Nevertheless, a very few countries have certainly emphasized the leading role of AI in the media and cultural sectors.

Among these, the Korean government has acknowledged the significance of the convergence of AI and popular culture and developed several AI

AI, cultural policy, counter-neoliberalism 47

policies in the fields of digital platform and culture. From popular music to film to webtoon, cultural industries corporations have continued to develop their business strategies to encompass AI-related technologies for both production and consumption. Korea has rapidly increased its digital Hallyu (Korean Wave) with the growth of smartphones, digital gaming, and webtoon (Goldsmith et al., 2011; Jin, 2016), and the convergence of culture and AI is a natural direction. As Caramiaux et al. (2019, 6) point out, "The scope of applications involving AI is growing in the media and creative industries," and Korea is at the forefront.

The Korean cultural industries and the government have developed collaborative relationships in cultural production based on AI, which is not surprising, given the developmental policy stance pursued by the Korean government. In 2018, the Ministry of Culture, Sports, and Tourism (2019a) emphasized the significance of research and development in the realm of culture technology and, in particular, focused on the intensification of its investment in the creation of intelligent content or surreal content by combining AI, VR (virtual reality), and AR (augmented reality), which are core technologies of the Fourth Industrial Revolution. The total amount of R&D in this category was 56.1 million won, up from 34.3 million won in a previous year.

When the Ministry of Culture, Sports, and Tourism (2019b) announced its plan titled "The Third Culture Technology R&D Basic Plan" in January 2019, it included several key agendas: cultural planning and creation, production of intelligent content, participatory cultural sharing, resolving cultural divide in experience, and emphasis on intellectual property. Cultural planning and creation is identified as the major area that the government supports by developing necessary skills in conjunction with AI. This is especially important as much of the cultural industry heavily relies on narration and storytelling in the areas of broadcasting, film, games, and webtoon. "Story remains the backbone of an experience," and "digital storytelling is at the heart of the new digital media in today's creative industries and the ability to tell stories in various formats for multiple platforms is becoming increasingly important" (Caramiaux et al., 2019, 17). What is significant in this context is AI plays an increasing role in digital society.

The Korean government (2019b) also plans to secure rich stories as sources for popular culture by developing databases rooted in cultural heritages and legend supported by data mining and AI. It also aims to develop a cultural curation system that provides two-way information and communication supported by IoT (internet of things) and AI. What is certain, though, is that these developments do not show any feasible plans that cultural industries firms and cultural creators can benefit from, as government plans and corporate practices do not offer any practical and tangible methods of support.

Due to the imminent necessity, the Korean Creative Content Agency hosted the Next Content Conference with the theme of the impact of new technology, including AI, in October 2017; however, several participants pointed out the lack of plans to enhance people's well-being and cultural

48   AI, cultural policy, counter-neoliberalism

diversity, unlike the government's expectation. Lev Manovich, as one of the keynote speakers, indeed pointed out, with the rise of K-pop from late 2000s, Korea's entertainment industry has been successful, and global social media platforms have paid attention. Korean films seem extremely successful. He believes industrialized culture has to die and urges talented Korean minds to devise ways in which culture can thrive without being forced into an industry (Doo, 2017).

What Manovich called for is the end of culture as an industry. Although he emphasizes the significance of AI in the ICT and cultural industries, he clearly argued that culture could not be treated as general commodities. Prior to this, Manovich (2012, 470) already questioned the justice issue for big data. He argues that big data as part of AI creates a new class hierarchy in which its "people and organizations are divided into three categories: those who create data (both consciously and by leaving digital footprints), those who have the means to collect it, and those who have the expertise to analyze it." As Christians (2019, 8–9) aptly puts it, "This elite stratification in the era of big data represents a new social domain that may reinforce digital inequality. It raises ethical questions such as privacy intrusion and business manipulation without informed consent from consumers." At the same conference, Zheng Quanzhan, head of Tencent Research Institute, interestingly said, "AI is also making ripples in the Chinese content industry. In China, AI writes articles and even poems, and paints paintings. But in the end, AI is equipped with the algorithms and data that humans program into it" (Doo, 2017).

As such, both theoreticians and practitioners commonly emphasize the significant role of creativity and humans. Popular culture is "an irreplaceable means of expression of the human genius, its infinite innate inventiveness and creativity, its power of self-determination and its manifest human rights" (Merkie, 2018, 1). As discussed in Chapter 2, several definitions of AI describe systems that replace aspects of the human brain. Unlike other industries, popular culture used to operate within a definition of humanity that was not reduced to rationality. Culture stimulates "active engagement and creativity in citizens and hence diversity in production" (Merkie, 2018, 2). As O'Regan and Goldsmith (2006, 70) also claim, "Long-established government commitments to the direct and indirect support of cultural production have come under pressure as governments seek to come to terms with changing market conditions and new priorities for the allocation of state revenues." In the cultural industries, well-prepared cultural policy would be a key element for the growth of AI-led cultural production.

A few governments and cultural industries do not focus on these matters, as their major priority is, as usual, an economic imperative. They did not seem to learn from previous negative experiences that economy-focused cultural production in tandem with cultural policy had brought about during the development era, such as asymmetrical growth, socio-cultural inequality, and the lack of diversity. Cultural politics in the AI era must focus on not only supporting measures but also policies to secure cultural democracy and diversity.

AI as in other sectors like big data has come to be dominated by just a few firms—in particular, digital platforms in the cultural sector. As Stiglitz (2019) points out, these mega giants have used

> their market power to enrich themselves at the expense of everyone else. . . . With the help of new technologies, they can, and do, engage in mass discrimination, such that prices are set not by the market (finding the single price that equates demand and supply), but by algorithmic determinations of the maximum each customer is willing to pay.

In the era of AI, people may be negatively influenced by AI, and it is crucial that governments protect humans and offer them other opportunities. Media and culture are particularly exceptional, as they heavily rely on people's creativity and diversity, which demands necessary support from the government. AI has already made inroads into the media and cultural industries, and governments must develop relevant policy measures to protect creativity, diversity, and cultural equality. Of course, governments still need to consider economic benefits as well. While it is not easy to achieve both of these different goals, if the government and cultural creators together develop human-centered norms, they will be able to reduce any unnecessary socio-cultural risks. Neoliberal norms have not cared about humans, simply financial profits for corporations, but AI asks us to develop counter-neoliberal tendencies where humans in conjunction with new digital technologies are honored and protected. This implies that AI as the most recent cutting-edge digital technology has interestingly driven governments to take a developmental model, while emphasizing fairness, justice, and human creativity.

Necessity of human-centered norms in the AI era

There is no doubt that AI has gradually become a primary player in the media and cultural sectors, and its role in cultural production will be furthermore increasing in the near future, as can be seen in Chapter 4 as well. With big data and algorithms, AI will continue to transform media and culture so that audiences will be experiencing new forms of culture—from cultural content to business models—that are unprecedented. The degree of involvement of AI in media and culture cannot be predictable due to its complexity and speed; however, in a nutshell, it is certain that AI will become a major component in the media and cultural industries. Again, this does not mean that AI replaces human creators and workers, as media and culture have been mostly human activities unlike other industries, including auto, chemistry, and smart city projects. AI has to collaborate with humans instead of replacing them in most cases, and therefore, government AI policy in many countries must emphasize the close and cooperative relationship

50   AI, cultural policy, counter-neoliberalism

between AI and popular culture. Popular culture lends itself to "surprising co-operation with AI-based systems to allow for the protection and promotion of the diverse cultural heritage" in many parts of the globe. "The majority of current AI applications are in predictable arenas, dominated by consumer electronics. AI could offer great help in the domain of preserving and advancing the issues of massively heterogeneous and rich human heritage" (Merkie, 2018, 2–3).

Popular culture is more complicated than expected, because it is directly related to people's feelings. In other words, media and popular culture are different from other industries mainly because the media and cultural sectors are two major areas in which creativity and people's feelings play a key role in the entire process of cultural production. As the *Harvard Business Review* (Kosslyn, 2019) points out, two non-routine kinds of work seem to be difficult to automate—emotion and context. On the one hand, emotion plays a significant role in human communication. It is involved in virtually all forms of nonverbal communication and in empathy. Furthermore, popular culture also plays a key role in

> helping us decide what needs to be attended to right now as opposed to later in the evening. Emotion is not only complex and nuanced, it also interacts with many of our decision processes. The functioning of emotion has proven challenging to understand scientifically (although there has been progress), and is difficult to build into an automated system.
>
> (Kosslyn, 2019)

On the other hand, human beings are able to take context into account when making decisions or having interactions with others. Context is interesting because it is open ended. Whenever a new story appears, it shifts the context in which people operate. Changes in context is able to introduce new elements and reconfigure the organization of elements in fundamental ways. This is a problem for ML, which operates on data sets that were created previously, in a different context. Thus, taking context into account is a challenge for automation. People's ability to manage and utilize emotion and to consider the effects of context are key components of critical thinking, creative problem solving, adaptive learning, and decent judgment. However, it has proven very difficult for ML to compete with such human knowledge and skills (Kosslyn, 2019).

Unlike other industries, media and culture are fundamentally rooted in the lived human condition, which cannot easily be replaced by AI. The reality is that digital transformation, driven by several major digital technologies, including the internet and smartphones, has begun, but we are still in the very early stages of AI-powered digital transformation. It is coming, but it will not overtake humans and organizations. In other words, AI is not about machines ruling over humans, but machines and humans working together. AI will supply humans with insight and perspective but will

AI, *cultural policy, counter-neoliberalism* 51

not supply judgment and creativity. They are still what people do. When people combine human creativity and passion together with technology, this creates an excitement that can ultimately solve humanity's challenges and change the world. To balance out ML means that people themselves have to become learning machines. People cannot let themselves become disconnected; people need to find their own way to stay intellectually active. There needs to be an active role in keeping people's minds curious and the need for self-improvement (Deyo, 2017). AI algorithms "do not have the power of the human mind in distinguishing right from wrong," which means that "humans can judge the morality of our actions, even when we decide to act against ethical norms. But for algorithms, data is the ultimate determining factor" (Dickson, 2018).

What we have to speculate about is, therefore, the creative and constructive relationship building between humans and AI. Again, media and culture are distinctive because they reflect people's emotions, feelings, and creativity. AI cannot simply overtake humans to become a replacer. Instead, AI, as one of the major actors, actively mediates the entire process of cultural production between humans and technology and between cultural creators and consumers. Replacing humans and mediating the process are not the same thing. As Jeanne Ross, principal research scientist at the MIT Center for Information Systems Research, states (2017), media and cultural industries corporations that seek to implement AI need to be aware of the fundamental flaw in AI implementation. According to Ross (2017), corporations that view AI "purely as a cost-cutting opportunity are likely to insert them in all the wrong places and all the wrong ways." This is because many corporations mistakenly view AI as a replacement for human workers, which cannot be done, nor is it possible in the realms of media and culture.

Humans have been the major actors in cultural production, from production to distribution to consumption, over the past several decades although there are several different digital technologies, including the internet and smartphones. Many engineers and scientists focus on the question of whether AI can ever achieve "human-like" behavior in computational systems while witnessing the rapid advance of AI. In the realms of media and culture, the question is whether AI will replace humans in the long run. However, both questions are not adequate in understanding the role of AI in media and popular culture.

Unlike other major industries, media and culture cannot thrive without humans and their creativity. Culture does not mean anything that is unilateral, but instead consists of interactions between humans, between humans and technology, and therefore, between humans and culture. Without human components, mostly people's creativity, emotions, feelings, and opinions, it is not possible to achieve the true meaning of popular culture. Instead of simply taking the increasing role of AI in media and culture for granted, it is critical to develop and understand the creation of human-centered AI ecosystems. As Gunkel (2020, 276) argues, "Robots and AI that are designed to

52 AI, *cultural policy, counter-neoliberalism*

follow rules and operate within the boundaries of some kind of programmed restraint might turn out to be something other than what is typically recognized as a responsible agent." Consequently,

> this lack of emotion would render them non-moral agents—i.e., agents that follow rules without being by moral concerns—and they would even lack the capacity to discern what is of value. They would be morally blind. If these robots [and AI] were given full independence—absence of external control by humans, which is another condition for full moral agency—they would pose danger to humans and other entities.
> (Coeckelbergh, 2010, 236)

What is significant here is that humans must work with AI to include morality and humanistic emotions and feelings so that humans and AI can work together to reflect both technological functionality and humanistic values in popular culture. As Stiglitz (2019) argues, "Artificial intelligence and robotization are being hailed as the engines of future growth. But under the prevailing policy and regulatory framework, many people will lose their jobs, with little help from government to find new ones." AI and digital platforms have continued to play a role as mediators, fulfilling their mission in contemporary capitalism; however, only humans are able to mediate AI and digital platforms in the realms of media and popular culture with the help of public policy. The major consideration of AI policy in the realms of popular culture around the globe has been to advance the norms that governments and digital platforms must advance this particular characteristic of popular culture.

Conclusion

This chapter has analyzed significant advancements around AI governance in the platform and cultural industries and raised questions about pragmatic support from governments as well as the relationship between the public and private sectors. The exemplary countries advancing AI governance in this chapter develop or adopt new technologies quickly and widely. Within a few years, contemporary society has especially moved toward AI and big data–driven industrial systems in order not to be left behind.

From the Global North to the Global South, several leading and emerging countries in the field of AI not only advance new digital technologies but also establish new policy measures relevant to AI, in contrast to neoliberal trends. Several countries around the globe have created relevant policy mechanisms and invested in AI-related industries. AI is not something governments can disregard easily due to its huge impacts on the digital economy and the fulfillment of the Fourth Industrial Revolution, which focuses on AI, big data, and algorithms. Governments alongside private corporations have had to advance AI through their financial and legal mechanisms, which symbolizes a counter-neoliberal norm in the early 21st century.

Of course, only a few nation-states have developed their cultural policies to support AI-related cultural production. Their interests in media and popular culture have not been significant or practical with a few exceptions. What they do not understand is that media and popular culture are not the secondary sectors in the national economy—in particular, in the digital economy. The cultural industries themselves have become some of the largest segments in the national economy, and AI implementation has been soaring as part of the digital economy, which demands governmental support through various measures. Media and popular culture need to secure financial and legal support from governments, as the growth of AI itself and its involvement in cultural production cannot be fulfilled without proper cultural policies. Digital platforms and cultural industries firms also need to develop their corporate policies to advance AI-driven cultural production, from production to distribution. Governments have acknowledged this necessity and invested in AI-led cultural production; however, the degree of government involvement in the realm of culture has been slow and not practical yet in most nation-states.

What governments and corporations have to advance is the establishment of policy mechanisms, both public and corporate, to build useful relationships between AI and popular culture. Cultural policy in the AI era must focus on the cooperative and close relationship between humans and AI in cultural production, which advances digital culture and economy in the early 21st century. Governments also need to develop cultural policies, including legal and ethical dimensions to advance fairness and justice, while resolving asymmetrical power relations between AI-haves and AI-have-nots. Governments, corporations, and even consumers have to advance some practical measures and commitments, which could "result in a more diverse, vibrant and prosperous creative ecosystem" (Kulesz, 2018b, 83). This is crucial because AI policy in the cultural sector should acknowledge that mainly digital platforms and mega media giants who have already garnered massive profits can benefit further from supportive policy mechanisms. Counter-neoliberal norms, meaning the increasing role of nation-states, cannot be used to support only mega giants, but also small- and mid-sized venture capitals and the majority of customers.

Note

1 Although there had been AI policy initiatives in China previously, the victory for AlphaGo over Lee Sedol (see Chapter 1) contributed to an increase in focus, as indicated by the 2017 'New Generation Artificial Intelligence Development Plan' (Roberts et al., 2020).

4 Artificial intelligence and cultural production

Introduction

In the 2020s, people are living in a world where digital technologies are influencing cultural production as well as people's daily activities. What is different from a decade or so is that the major tools of the transformation in cultural production are now based on AI that is connected to digital platforms, including over-the-top (OTT) services like Netflix, Disney+, and Amazon Prime, as well as traditional cultural industries. In the late 2010s and the early 2020s, the adoption of AI in popular culture is not only real but also surreal. Since AI supported by big data and algorithms has played a pivotal role in the production and distribution of cultural content, cultural industries corporations and cultural creators rapidly pay attention to AI's possibility to produce popular culture. From movie trailers to webtoons (web comics), the use of AI in cultural production has continued to grow. AI is one of the most versatile digital technologies that can be used in the entire process of cultural development, production, and data analytics.

Since the mid-2010s, due to AI's critical role—whether already proven in digital games or potentially growing in other areas—in the production of cultural content, several academic works have paid attention to the convergence of AI and popular culture. In other words, as a reflection of the increasing convergence of AI and popular culture, several scholars already developed analyses on cultural production, focusing on various subjects, including photography (Manovich, 2018), digital gaming (Yannakakis and Togelius, 2018; Togelius, 2019), and automated systems and labor (Andrejevic, 2020). Although their emphases are not the same, they commonly focus on the possibility of the use of AI in cultural production, as well as the actualization of this process. For them, the social impacts of AI in terms of its current development and future institutional forms in the cultural sector have emerged as crucial issues for cultural creators and cultural industries corporations.

As these academic works prove, AI has already become part of cultural production in a few major cultural sectors, from films to digital games to music. AI is also expected to become one of the most reliable digital technologies

AI and cultural production 55

that cultural creators must work with. As defined in Chapter 1, cultural production in this book does not narrowly refer to the actual production of cultural products, but the overall process, including the production, distribution, and consumption of popular culture embedded in AI use. Due to the complexity of the process, the following chapters divide the process into the production of popular culture (Chapter 4), distribution (Chapter 5), and consumption (Chapter 6) so that people can understand the vicious circle of the entire process, where each part is nevertheless closely connected.

By addressing the complexity and specialty of the convergence of AI and popular culture, this chapter attempts to offer new insights on the global cultural industries that vehemently work with AI and big data. It examines the nexus of popular culture, such as films, music, digital gaming, and webtoon with AI in production. It maps out how global cultural industries firms have partnered with AI companies; therefore, it compares AI-supported cultural production between the Global North and the Global South to determine the reasons why they pursue AI-supported cultural content. Finally, it discusses whether the encounters of AI and popular culture have advanced cultural democratization and creativity or not. As such, there are high stakes in this particular dispute over the use of AI in cultural production and cultural industries; thus, it is critical to examine the relationships between AI development and the political economy of contemporary popular culture.

AI and the production of popular culture

AI and popular culture encountering one another is not new. From film to music to Korean webtoons, cultural creators and corporations have rapidly adopted AI to produce their new cultural content. When PricewaterhouseCoopers (PwC, 2018, 19) analyzed more than 150 emerging technologies to pinpoint the most essential ones, it argued that every organization, in both entertainment and media and beyond, must consider formulating its tech strategy, and it claims that AI will dominate. It therefore predicts that "AI will have a pervasive impact on all types of companies involved in entertainment and media and will become the industry's new battleground." The Electronics and Telecommunications Research Institute (ETRI) of Korea also published a report titled "2020 AI Seven Trend: Beyond Perception" in December 2019, and one of the major trends that ETRI predicts is the use of AI in cultural creation, in novel, painting, and film, which means that AI becomes an indispensable component in the realm of culture. The impacts of AI in cultural creations will be many and highly diverse. For example, Netflix's recommendation algorithm is one prominent example of how AI builds consumer engagement and satisfaction. What PwC and ETRI focus on is, however, production. They forecast that over the next few years, more and more digital platforms, telecommunications companies, and broadcasters will work together to launch voice-controlled

56 AI and cultural production

AI assistant interfaces for their pay-TV and smart home products and services (PricewaterhouseCoopers, 2018). What is interesting is that "the true pioneer in AI and automation has been culture, rather than science" (Kulesz, 2018a, 3), which means that media and cultural industries have no choice but to utilize AI in the production of culture.

To historicize the nexus of AI and culture, the term "robot" in the sense of a humanoid device appeared for the first time in the satirical stage play *R.U.R.* (1921), by Czech playwright Karel Čapek. (R.U.R. stands for "Rosumovi Umělí Roboti", literally Rossum's Artificial Robots.) The drama is set in a factory located on an island that is manufacturing synthetic humanoids. This is the text where the word "robot" was coined ("robota" is Czech for forced labor or drudgery) (Roberts, 2006). "The set-up is almost too evidently that of a hypostatized mind/body or masters/workers binary. The robots have been manufactured to free humanity from the drudgery of labor, but have therefore become an oppressed underclass themselves" (Roberts, 2006, 243–244).

As such, it was also almost 100 years ago when "an AI first appeared on the silver screen, and the technology's prevalence has only grown since then" (Tomlinson, 2018). AI was not formed as its own official discipline until the mid-1950s; however, AI first appeared in the movie *Metropolis* in 1927 about a dystopian near-future society in which technology helped the gulf between the rich and the poor to grow, which has inspired other movies in this genre. Several movies in the early 21st century, including *I, Robot* (2004), *WALL-E* (2008), *Morgan* (2016), *Star Wars: The Last Jedi* (2017), and *Blade Runner 2049* (2017) certainly portrayed AI as well. The interaction between AI and popular culture has continued to grow, as humans have been dreaming about the possibilities of AI for far longer.

The convergence of AI and culture in the production of culture has been common in the late 2010s and the early 2020s. When *Culture Machine* (2019)—an international open-access journal of culture and theory starting in 1999—issued a call for papers with the theme of "Machine Intelligences in Context: Beyond the Technological Sublime" in December 2019, the editors of the special issue, Peter Jakobsson, Anne Kaun, and Fredrik Stiernstedt clearly understood that "the supposed blessings that AI may bestow upon datafied societies" are now well-known to the cultural creators and to the general public. As they explained, "Representatives from the tech sector and the world of politics claim that the Fourth Industrial Revolution will be powered by AI and that AI will eventually become ubiquitous within politics, industry, culture and in everyday life."

There are several significant cultural products showing the increasing role of AI in the production of popular culture. Creativity may be the ultimate moonshot for AI, and AI has already helped write pop ballads, mimicked the styles of great painters, and informed creative decisions in filmmaking (IBM, n.d.). Our contemporary cultural sector has been advancing into a new age of AI, and the adoption of AI in the production of culture is expected to soar. This does not mean that all cultural creators, including filmmakers and musicians, adopted AI technology in their cultural work, as only a selected number of cultural industries companies and cultural creators are able to utilize AI due to several limitations, such as money, technique, and know-how. The use of AI in the production of popular culture also varies within different cultural forms, from music to film.

Most of all, digital technologies, including AI, have transformed the cultural scene profoundly. New forms of creation, production, distribution, and access have revolutionized entire cultural industries, such as music and film, in a process that has affected both the Global North and South (UNESCO, 2016). As AI is directly connected to the growth of computers, it is especially natural for digital game companies to utilize AI to create and play games, which means that AI and digital games have had a long history together (Yannakakis and Togelius, 2018). Employing more AI practitioners than any other, the digital game industry is enjoying a screaming success. AI's role in this success of digital games is critical; "its use is essential to producing the needed intelligent behavior on the part of the virtual characters who populate the games" (Franklin, 2014, 24). One of the exemplary cases is *Pokémon GO*, which quickly became a global phenomenon when the game was released in July 2016. Ever since, many people on the planet have enjoyed this new augmented reality (AR) mobile game where players capture pocket monsters using a GPS map on their smartphone and their phone's built-in camera. *Pokémon GO* allows players to scour the real world for characters, including the yellow monster Pikachu, the franchise's mascot (Mochizuki, 2016). While *Pokémon GO* itself was not much supported by AI, Niantic—the maker of *Pokémon GO*, now owned by Google—is reportedly using input from players along with some software-side AI to begin creating AR maps of the real world;

> The basic procedure for the capture is as follows; players use *Pokémon GO's* AR mode to catch Pokemon against a backdrop of the real world around them, and their smartphones' cameras capture that world. Niantic's software interprets what the user's smartphone camera is seeing in order to parse real-world objects and landmarks, then maps out their geometry and dimensions in relation to the space around them. It's possible that previous data on known landmarks could be used to enhance this processing. In any case, once an area has been sufficiently well-captured by multiple players and examined multiple times by Niantic's AI, there is enough data on that space and the things in it to tell what's fixed to the landscape, what comes and goes, and who the living creatures are, allowing Niantic to develop an AR experience around those factors [regardless of privacy issues].
>
> (Fuller, 2018)

This example shows that the growing use of AI has been visible in the media and cultural industries. As briefly discussed in Chapter 1, AI "seems to be

58 AI and cultural production

suited to the specific requirements of the creative industries that is currently profoundly changing prevailing paradigms" (Caramiaux et al., 2019, 6). In several fields of popular culture, cultural creators, such as producers, directors, and designers have used AI to drastically enhance the experience of playing and watching, "resulting in increased popularity and soaring profits" (Klinenberg and Benzecry, 2005, 9).

After analyzing the convergence of AI and photography, Manovich (2018, 12–14) especially points out, AI plays a pivotal role in culture, increasingly influencing our cultural choices, behaviors, and imaginations. For example,

> It is used to recommend photos, videos, music, and other media. AI is also used to suggest people we should follow on social networks, to automatically beautify selfies and edit user photos to fit the norms of good photography, and to generate and control characters in computer games.

Cultural use of AI goes beyond photography, as this new kind of trend includes music recommendations in Spotify, iTunes, and other music services that automatically edit a user's raw video to create short films in a range of styles and the creation of new fashion items and styles as Amazon already plans and actualizes (Shah, 2017). AI provides people options to automate their aesthetic choices (via recommendation engines). It assists in certain areas of production. In the near future, "it will play a larger part in professional cultural production. Its use of helping to design fashion items, logos, music, TV commercials, and works in other areas of culture is already growing" (Manovich, 2018, 159). It is logical to think that

> any area of cultural production which either follows explicit rules or has systematic patterns can be in principle automated. Thus, many commercial cultural areas such as TV dramas, romance novels, professional photography, music video, news stories, website and graphic design, and residential architecture are suitable for automation. For example, we can teach computers to write TV drama scripts, do food photography, or compose news stories in many genres (so far, AI systems are only used to automatically compose sports and business stories).
>
> (Manovich, 2018, 173)

The encounters of AI with popular culture are increasing. In the future, it will not be dicey to claim that almost all cultural products, from literature to audio-visual culture, can be created or at least touched by AI.

AI, as with several previous digital technologies, creates both opportunities and threats for major media corporations and consumers. As usual, only a handful of digital platforms are able to develop and control the AI-driven cultural market and increase their presence in the cultural industries. Again,

AI and cultural production 59

they have heavily invested in developing synergistic relationships between their various media holdings, integrating their production processes into convergence systems that yield content for different outlets, cross-promoting programs in different media, and establishing lines of vertical and horizontal integration in the cultural industries (Klinenberg, 2000; cited in Klinenberg and Benzecry, 2005, 8–9). The adoption of AI in cultural production is more complicated than expected. Both the Global North and the Global South have advanced cultural production, regardless of some tangible gaps due to their level of knowledge, know-how, techniques, capital, and manpower. Here I discuss the production of cultural content in several major cultural areas, both in the Global North and Global South, to demonstrate the role of AI in cultural industries around the globe.

Encounters of AI and popular culture: the Global North

In the early 21st century, cultural industries, such as gaming, music, film, and webtoon, are taking advantage of AI. AI has recently been "trying its hand at various human creative endeavors, from cooking to art, and from poetry to board games" (*The Guardian*, 2016). Other than digital gaming that started its massive adoption of AI earlier than other cultural genres, cultural creators in film, broadcasting, music, and webtoon have mainly begun to use AI to create their cultural content since the mid-2010s.

Among these, the film industry is showing unique growth in the encounters of AI and popular culture, as filmmakers started to create films and film trailers through AI full scale in 2016. After representing AI in several films discussed previously, filmmakers finally used AI in production. When the film studio 20th Century Fox created a movie trailer of *Morgan*, a 2016 British American science fiction horror film directed by Luke Scott, it was recorded as the first ever AI to produce a film trailer. The film studio used the AI supercomputer system called IBM Watson to make the trailer. As Heathman (2018) outlined in *Wired*, in order to create the movie trailer, IBM researchers fed Watson more than 100 horror film trailers cut into separate moments and scenes. It performed several visual, sound, and composition analyses on each scene to get an idea of how to create the dynamics of a trailer. Then Watson processed 90 minutes of *Morgan* to find the right moments to include in the trailer. Once it finished processing *Morgan*, it isolated ten scenes—a total of six minutes of video. A human editor was still needed to patch the scenes together to tell a coherent story; however, the AI shortened the process down to 24 hours, compared to taking around 10–30 days to complete a trailer.

The film studio 20th Century Fox also used AI to predict people's patterns, as specific patterns help predict the future. In other words, the studio used AI to predict what films people will want to see. According to its own paper published in 2018 (Hsieh et al., 2018), several researchers from the

60 *AI and cultural production*

company analyzed the content of movie trailers using machine learning. Hsieh et al. claim that

> temporal sequencing of objects in a movie trailer (e.g., a long shot of an object vs intermittent short shots) can convey information about the type of movie, plot of the movie, role of the main characters, and the filmmaker's cinematographic choices. When combined with historical customer data, sequencing analysis can be used to improve predictions of customer behavior. E.g., a customer buys tickets to a new movie and maybe the customer has seen movies in the past that contained similar sequences. To explore object sequencing in movie trailers, we propose a video convolutional network to capture actions and scenes that are predictive of customers' preferences. The model learns the specific nature of sequences for different types of objects (e.g., cars vs faces), and the role of sequences in predicting customer future behavior.
>
> (2018, 1)

More specifically, "machine vision systems examine trailer footage frame by frame, labeling objects and events, and then compare this to data generated for other trailers. The idea is that movies with similar sets of labels will attract similar sets of people" (Vincent, 2018). For example, *Logan* (2017) is a superhero movie, but it has darker themes and a plot that attracts a slightly different audience. The film studio employed AI to potentially capture those differences. To create their experimental movie attendance prediction and recommendation system, called Merlin, the film studio partnered with Google to use the company's servers and open source AI framework TensorFlow (Vincent, 2018). "Machine learning is, at heart, the art of finding patterns in data. That is why businesses love it. Patterns help predict the future, and predicting the future is a great way to make money" (Vincent, 2018). AI's role in the movies *Morgan* (2016) and *Logan* (2017) and numerous other creative endeavors proves "how far AI has come. Using techniques such as deep learning has enabled tremendous progress, but AI remains relegated to an assistant role—for now" (IBM, n.d.). Such automation has become common in the production of culture.

Another exemplary case in the film sector created in 2016 is the script and movie (*Sunspring*) that was the product of director Oscar Sharp and New York University AI researcher Ross Goodwin. A so-called recurrent neural network, named Benjamin, was fed the scripts of dozens of science fiction movies including such classics as *Highlander Endgame, Ghostbusters, Interstellar,* and *The Fifth Element*. From there it was asked to create a screenplay, including actor directions, using a set of prompts required by the Sci-Fi-London film festival's 48-hour challenge. The resulting screenplay and pop song were then given to the cast to interpret and make into a film. "The actors were randomly assigned to the parts and set to it. The result is a weirdly entertaining, strangely moving dark sci-fi story of love and despair" (*The Guardian*, 2016). Although it is not perfect, these attempts to create movie trailers, scripts, and movies themselves are certainly proofs of the use of AI in the cultural sector.

Music composition programs were also among the first cases of this development (Turner, 2019). Music has been one of the powerful arts that is "as core to the human experience as communicating"; however, in recent years, AI "has increasingly been making headway into some of the more creative pursuits" in music (Walch and World, 2019). In the music industry, there are a range of use cases for AI, including "creating backing tracks for video, helping an artist come up with melodies or lyrics, and automatically creating mood music" (Dredge, 2019).

More specifically, in 1997, a computer program called Mubert in California had written Mozart's *42nd Symphony*, and Mubert "continuously produces a unique music stream created by an algorithm based on the laws of musical theory, mathematics and creative experience" (GVA Capital, 2017). In the popular music sector, as of September 2018, several corporations were developing software that might help people write better songs, even hit songs (Donoughue, 2018). As Marr (2018) clearly points out, music-generating algorithms are now inspiring new songs: "Given enough input— millions of conversations, newspaper headlines and speeches—insights are gleaned that can help create a theme for lyrics." In other words, there are machines such as "Watson BEAT that can come up with different musical elements to inspire composers. AI helps musicians understand what their audiences want and to help determine more accurately what songs might ultimately be hits" (Marr, 2018).

There is indeed an emerging body of activity around popular music production with AI.

> They do this by feeding heaps and heaps of data into a computer program to teach it about music, to the point where, eventually, it can whack out a tune on its own. A team at Google created AI Duet, software that will jam with you. Scientists at Sony's CSL Research Lab went one step better, producing a whole song—in the vein of The Beatles—using AI, though with a little help from their friends (a human composer).
>
> (Donoughue, 2018)

In Australia, one particular corporation named Popgun uses AI to develop software that it hopes will make music composition easy. "It uses a form of deep learning called unsupervised learning, where the AI learns the various features of songs—how a scale or a harmony works, for example—just by studying enough of them." As is well discussed, people consider music to be a very human activity. Unlike in Go—the board game where expert human players were defeated by AI and—"a high-water mark in the world

62 AI and cultural production

of machine learning—in music, there is no clear winner or loser. There are some notes that sound bad in a progression, but lots that sound fine" (Donoughue, 2018).

The rise of music created by AI software has furthermore continued. Sony's AI lab has created software called FlowComposer that is capable of producing a song whose style matches whatever songs people have fed into it. In this case,

> researchers fed it Beatles songs—and indeed, the result sounds a little Beatles-ish. Note that FlowComposer produced only a lead sheet (that is, a piece of music showing the melody and chord symbols); a human then arranged it for instruments, wrote lyrics, recorded it, and mixed it. There are some fresh and intriguing chord sequences in this song, but also some noodling, aimless ones that don't really land.
>
> (Pogue, 2018)

As Ken Lythgoe, head of business development at creative AI technology company MXX, which was founded in 2015 by AI specialist and composer Joe Lyske and Philip Walsh (Davis, 2019) says, "In a world of personalization and on-demand services, music is one of very few remaining static artefacts." MXX has created what it says is the world's first AI tech that allows individual users to instantly edit music to fit their own video footage, complete with rises and fades. Lythgoe says,

> There are two types of AI—the AI that is here to replace us and AI that is here to empower us—we are definitely in the empowerment camp. We are not about computers replacing musicians or editors; we are firm believers in the creative process.
>
> (Davis, 2019)

What they want to develop is a new world where "music can be adapted to perfectly fit certain experiences—such as gym workouts and runs, gaming, user-generated content and virtual or augmented-reality experiences" (Davis, 2019). The convergence of AI and music like in other cultural spheres has been a growth area, and it is certain that the convergence of these two formerly separated areas is likely to last.

Meanwhile, the broadcasting sector has not been left behind. Although network broadcasters are not at the front line in AI-supported cultural production, several global broadcasters began to work to advance AI-supported programs. AI has become more mainstream across the entire entertainment ecosystem. From the front stage (e.g., recommendation engines) through the creative process, scripting, shooting, post-production, and all the way to the backstage (e.g., meta-tagging and distribution), AI is enabling industry newcomers to leverage new business opportunities (Natajaran and Baue, 2019). For example, the BBC project, "Talking with Machines," is an audio drama that allows listeners to join in and have a two-way conversation via their smart speaker. Listeners get to be a part of the story as it prompts them to answer questions and insert their own lines into the story.

(Marr, 2018)

Of course, as mainly discussed in Chapter 5, in the broadcasting sector, Netflix fully uses big data analytics to predict what its customers will enjoy watching. Netflix is increasingly a content creator, not just a distributor, and uses data to drive what content it will invest in creating. Due to the confidence it has in the data findings, Netflix is willing to buck convention and commission multiple seasons of new television shows rather than just pilot episodes (Marr, 2018).

As such, the convergence of AI and popular culture has been widely actualized in the cultural industries, more than we expect. Several cultural forms, including film, music, broadcasting, and digital gaming in several Western countries, are beneficiaries of the interaction between AI and popular culture. From film companies like 20th Century Fox to digital platforms, media giants in these Western countries have vehemently invested in AI-related technologies, either developing these technologies or acquiring firms who already owned these technologies and produced cultural content. AI-supported cultural production is not yet a major force at the end of the 2010s and the early 2020s; however, cultural firms and digital platforms have agreed that the adaptation of AI for the creation of popular culture will be the future of these firms, and therefore, they aggressively attempt to produce cultural content based on further reliance on AI.

Encounters of AI and popular culture in the Global South

As cultural creators in a few Western countries have rapidly paid attention to AI as a new digital tool to produce cultural content, cultural creators in non-Western countries also attempt to adopt AI technologies in their cultural production. Of course, due to the lack of technologies, capital, and manpower, only a handful of non-Western countries are able to utilize AI in tandem with cultural production. Accordingly, AI-supported cultural production in the Global South is not advanced with a few exceptions.

Due to the significance of Korean popular culture, including music (K-pop) and webtoons in the global cultural markets in the early 21st century, I especially explore some Korean cultural sectors as among the most important cultural industries in the Global South to converge AI and popular culture for comparison purposes. Korea has been at the front line in the utilization of the intersection of AI and popular culture. This is understandable because the country has developed both digital technologies, such as broadband, digital games, and smartphones, and popular culture such as the Korean Wave phenomenon—the rapid growth of local cultural industries and the

64 AI and cultural production

expansion of their exports of cultural content in global cultural markets—exemplifies. The convergence of digital technologies and popular culture in Korea has been indeed noticeable, and therefore, the use of AI in cultural production is an already designated path for the local cultural industries. Cultural creators and companies in Korea have emphasized the growth of AI and big data in their production, distribution, and circulation and have vehemently pursued new opportunities in tandem with AI.

A handful of socio-cultural dimensions work in the background of the use of AI in cultural production. In particular, the Korean government—still pursuing its developmental approach, focusing on top-down and direct initiative in the digital economy—has greatly invested in the AI sector.[1] Several cultural sectors have attempted to develop cultural content in conjunction with AI technology.

Most of all, in the music sector, several major music entertainment houses have rapidly advanced their adaptation of AI in order to expand their global reach. As is well documented, K-pop has become one of the most significant global phenomena, representing the contemporary Korean Wave (Lie, 2015; Jin, 2016; Yoon and Jin, 2017; Kim, 2018). SM Entertainment (SME), the largest entertainment agency in Korea, for example, partnered with SK Telecom to work to introduce AI technology into K-pop (Murphy, 2019). Soo Man Lee, the founder and CEO of SME, already explained his plan to combine AI and cultural content in 2017. During one event held in July of the same year, he stated, "From now on, SM plans on expanding its business in Asia, and beyond to provide new contents that combine AI technology and celebrity in the future." In June 2017, SME and ObEN, a full-stack AI company that creates virtual identities, signed an agreement to establish a joint venture, AI Stars Limited (AI Stars). Based in Hong Kong,

> AI Stars became the world's first agency that combines celebrity intellectual property (IP) and AI technology to create entertainment experiences and products. . . . ObEN's AI technology constructs a person's virtual voice, image and personality to create a full-stack virtual celebrity that looks, sounds and behaves like its human counterpart.
>
> (Kwon, 2017)

What SME aims for is to be able to create virtual AI artists via AI Stars and to make new songs and dances through collaborations among AIs. SME also partnered with SK Telecom, Korea's biggest mobile carrier to use SK Telecom's AI technology in separating singers' vocals from music records in January 2019 (Yeo, 2019b).

Another major K-pop entertainment house, YG Entertainment, also started to work with Naver to build a new global music service platform by pooling Naver's technologies, including AI, resources, and global influence in 2017. Under the partnership, Naver and YG's affiliate YG Plus works on expanding their music database to include more diverse genres as well as

K-pop tracks. Naver eventually plans to embark on procedures to build a so-called meta database for the music it owns. In other words, it compiles a standardized database that can describe a particular music track, including the title, artist, and genre. Such standardized labels are critical to building stable and optimized music recommendation features for application to a new music service platform (Shon, 2017).

As expected, the Korean game industry has also rapidly invested in AI. Korea is the second-largest powerhouse in online gaming and one of the most advanced in mobile gaming. As Yannakakis and Togelius (2018, 151–152) point out, AI has expanded its role in game production. In other words, several in-game components and assets, including levels, maps, game rules, textures, stories, items, music, weapons, vehicles, and characters have been supported by AI in the production stage. One obvious reason to generate content by AI is that it could remove the need to have a human designer creating that content, as humans are expensive and slow.

In the field of digital games, several game companies have developed games supported by AI. For example, NCSoft, one of the largest game companies in Korea, has already started to introduce AI into game design and production since 2011 when it created an AI task force, renamed the AI lab in 2012, and then the AI center in 2016. NCSoft has about 100 AI experts, and its two major hubs are the Artificial Intelligence Center, including Game AI Lab, Speech Lab, and Vision Task Force, and Natural Language Processing Center, encompassing Language AI Lab and Knowledge Lab (Oh, D.H., 2018). As Lee Jae-joon, who heads the AI center at NCSoft, said during a media conference held in July 2019, "When creating game characters in the past, game developers had to input each facial expression fitting for lines and situations one by one"; however, "AI helps reduce this kind of repetitive work significantly" (Jun, J.H., 2019b). Other gaming firms like Nexon and Netmarble have also expanded investment in AI to gain a competitive advantage, as people utilize AI in almost the entire process of game development, production, and data analytics.

The latest cultural sector utilizing AI is the webtoon industry. Webtoon—a neologism of web and cartoon, which has been created in Korea in the digital platform era—is one of the nascent cultural genres that fully adapts digital technology and smart media. As people enjoy webtoons on their mobile gadgets—in particular, on smartphones—webtoons rapidly adapt new technologies, including AI. Many leading webtoonists have certainly advanced their use of AI in order to develop both digital storytelling and images. For example, Ha Il-Kwon's *Came Across* (*majuchyeotda*), which was released on Naver in 2017, used not only AI, but also augmented reality (AR) and face recognition technology (Jun et al., 2019). *Came Across* is a webtoon that combines AI, AR, 360-degree panorama, and face recognition technology into the narrative. The analysis applied Chatman's analysis of narrative structure. Each episode was done on how the narrative develops as the technical characteristics incorporated to the new webtoon combines

66 AI and cultural production

with the narrative. The technology of AI and AR broke the barriers between the actual world and the imagined world in this particular webtoon (Jun et al., 2019). In the second episode, for example, AI technology changes the customer's face into the main character of the webtoon. When the customer takes a picture of himself/herself with his/her own smartphone, AI identifies the customer's face and changes it into the webtoon's style. Consequently, the customer enjoys the webtoon as if he/she is a main character (Song, B.G., 2018).

As these several cases certainly exemplify, the encounters between AI and popular culture have been growing in both the Global North and the Global South. The cultural industries in several leading countries in the Global North and a few emerging countries in the Global South have utilized the increasing collaborations between cultural firms, including digital platforms or telecommunications companies, who are equipped with AI and popular culture. While this new trend offers great opportunities to cultural creators and digital platforms, this movement is troublesome, because only a few mega giants in a handful of advanced economies are able to create cultural content supported by AI so that they control the majority of the global cultural markets. The following section discusses the critical perspectives of the convergence of AI and culture.

Political economy of the convergence of AI and popular culture

Cultural industries corporations and digital platforms in both the Global North and the Global South have passionately pursued AI-driven cultural developments. For them, it is critical to utilize AI, big data, and algorithms to create new cultural products that attract new generations who are equipped with new digital culture rooted in AI. Consequently, the increasing role of AI in the media and cultural industries is becoming clear. Although still in its early stage, Roxborough (2019) argues that OTT services equipped with AI and algorithms have already moved into the mainstream in the media and cultural markets and are set to become the main destinations for video viewing around the world. Traditional media, including broadcasters and film companies, need to evolve new services to reflect the viewing preferences of contemporary consumers. It is essential for them to use AI to circulate cultural content, and they also need to develop cultural content supported by AI. In the future, more cultural products will be produced through AI-related technologies, and cultural creators and corporations are afraid of being left behind, if they are not aggressively leading the trend. As Manovich (2018) points out, again, AI recommendation engines suggest what people watch, read, and listen to. Digital devices and services automatically adjust to the aesthetics of captured media. Furthermore, during the COVID-19 era, the traditional norm in cultural products has been transformed, as many content producers work from home, which demands the increasing role of AI. In March 2020, Netflix's VP of networks Dave Temkin indeed claimed, "Right now, it's not unique to us, most content production is shut down around the globe." Therefore, our team "is working on ways to restart aspects of content production like post processing, visual effects and animation—things traditionally not done from home because it requires a significant amount of compute power and bandwidth to move raw encodes around" (Condon, 2020). What he emphasized was the ways in which digital platforms like Netflix get that operating out of people's homes, and it is certainly pinpointing the massive use of AI-related technologies in the production process.

However, cultural production supported by AI has raised some concerns mainly due to several political-economy issues relevant to cultural production. To begin with, AI-supported cultural production blurs the protections from copyright law, as the producers are not only humans but also computers. In the pre-AI era, the work of cultural creators had been protected by strong copyright laws, regardless of rampant piracy in many countries in the Global South; however, as AI has increasingly become a major player, current copyright safeguards lose their primary roles in protecting cultural creators. As Yamamoto (2018, 1) points out, when computers emerged, the copyright issue was discussed, but it was obvious that "computers were not creators of cultural content but just tools with which creators could save labors, time, and money." AI is more complicated than the computers, as AI technology itself backed by big data enables

> computers to judge and decide what people tend to like, feel beautiful, or find funny. . . . The computers then are able to draw pictures, make music, or make stories that satisfy human being's demand by combining expression elements according to people's tendencies. AI works may contain intelligence equivalent to that in the works created by human beings.

Therefore, it is contested whether works made by AI could be protected by copyright (Yamamoto, 2018, 1).

Regarding this, Guadamuz (2017) points out that people are "in the throes of a technological revolution" that requires us to reconsider the interaction between computers and the creative process. For him,

> that revolution is underpinned by the rapid development of machine learning software that produces autonomous systems that are capable of learning without being specifically programmed by a human. A computer program developed for machine learning purposes has a built-in algorithm that allows it to learn from data input, and to evolve and make future decisions.

68 *AI and cultural production*

Therefore, "when applied to art, music and literary works, machine learning algorithms are learning from input provided by programmers." They learn from data to generate a new piece of work,

> making independent decisions throughout the process to determine what the new work looks like. An important feature for this type of AI is that while programmers can set parameters, the work is generated by the computer program itself in a process akin to the thought processes of humans.
>
> (Guadamuz, 2017)

AI-supported cultural production could have very significant implications for copyright law, and how to understand and deal with this are some of the major issues at this particular juncture. Many nation-states, including Japan and Germany, currently protect works created by human intelligence and do not protect works created by machines. Humans still do actual production based on their expertise, regardless of the increasing role of AI in cultural production; therefore, these governments are not prepared for the upcoming years. However, the convergence of human beings and AI arguably needs to be emphasized, and governments have to develop new copyrights so that AI developers, digital platforms, and cultural creators are equally protected by new legal mechanisms.

Second, the proliferation of AI-driven cultural production in addition to distribution has facilitated the growth of large digital platforms, such as Google, Facebook, and Netflix. The period in which AI developed has been marked "by concentration and consolidation of ownership, not openness," as in the cases of other digital technologies (Klinenberg and Benzecry, 2005, 10). Both Western and non-Western digital platforms, including OTT services, have acquired funding from venture capitals, focusing on AI-related technologies, or consolidated to become mega giants. As mainly discussed in Chapter 5, this trend has resulted in the lack of diversity of voice, which hurts our society's cultural democracy. Therefore, it is critical to develop relevant policies for AI that guarantee diversity of cultural expressions. At the same time, it is also vital to "establish incentives for global platforms operating at the national level to contribute useful cultural data for decision making and draw up a national policy on data" (Kulesz, 2018b, 83). The concentration of media and culture in the hands of a few mega giants has not been new; however, in the AI age, the degree has become even steeper and faster than before, as platform giants and a few mega media moguls have enough capital, manpower, and know-how.

In this light, what the U.K. government decided gives us a good lesson. The U.K. government plans to create a technology regulator in 2020 to police platform giants such as Facebook and Google. The regulator, in particular nation-states, will be given powers to implement several new rules,

AI *and cultural production*   69

including an enforceable code of conduct for mega platform giants and greater data accessibility for platform users. The new move comes as several governments "unveil measures to protect citizens from privacy breaches and anti-competitive practices thrown up by the digital economy" in response to widespread calls for a curb on big tech's power. Several governments, including the U.K. and Germany, are concerned that platform moguls like Google and Facebook are so large and have such all-embracing access to data that competitors or mid-sized platforms can no longer compete equally in the market (Murgia and Beioley, 2019).

The Department for Digital, Culture, Media and Sport of the U.K. said that digital services "must work for everyone, so that the incredible benefits of digital technologies are properly harnessed, consumers are protected and innovation thrives across the economy" (Murgia and Beioley, 2019). This implies that the technological disparities intensified by AI between the Global North and the Global South represent a noticeable challenge when it comes to fulfilling a balanced production and circulation of cultural content.

Third, while humans still play a pivotal role in the production of popular culture, it is desirable to ponder the lack of creativity and, again, diversity. As Guadamuz (2017) points out with the latest types of AI, "The computer program is no longer a tool; it actually makes many of the decisions involved in the creative process without human intervention." AI might provide a tool to produce cultural content supported by big data and algorithms; however, the question is that its involvement in cultural production certainly implies a potential lack of diversity and creativity. As several cases in films and music have already proven, AI-driven cultural production emphasized what audiences liked and would like, instead of developing new forms of cultural content. AI, therefore, continues to create similar movies and music that people in the past enjoyed.

The encounters between AI and popular culture are mainly a contemporary phenomenon in that several cultural forms, such as films, music, webtoons, and digital games have rapidly expanded their use of AI in cultural production. In the study of the convergence of AI and popular culture, we must comprehend "what motivated the creation and adaption of AI for cultural production, what affordances the new products offer, and what ways consumers and producers make meaning through them" (Klinenberg and Benzecry, 2005, 16).

> The questions of how people use [AI] for cultural work and what role these practices play in daily life are increasingly important to the study of creativity in action. So too are questions about the balance of power and control in cultural fields, which are dominated by a small number of commercial [platforms] whose reach extends nearly as far as the network itself. The emerging conflict between states, [platforms], and creative actors who aim to harness the power of [AI] in different ways

70 AI and cultural production

promises to be one of the most important policy disputes of the 21st century.

(Klinenberg and Benzecry, 2005, 17)

Last, but not least, the rise of global platforms can be intensified because of the monopolistic possession of available data. As is well known, the life-blood of the cultural system that AI is also rapidly becoming part of is data, and therefore, big data would be one of the key components of the digital economy and digital culture. One of major reasons for the success of large platforms is that they utilize data/metadata—representing a new type of cultural commodity—which can be reused. "In every country, the key to getting the most out of AI is having a 'data-friendly ecosystem' with unified standards and cross-platform sharing." AI depends on data that can be ana-lyzed in real time and brought to bear on concrete problems. Nations that promote open data sources and data sharing are the ones most likely to see AI advances. Having data that are "accessible for exploration" is a prereq-uisite for successful AI development (Barton et al., 2017; West, 2018, 23).

For example, by appropriating big data garnered from the users, they opti-mize recommendation algorithms for the users or sell them to advertisers. OTT platforms like Netflix and mega global media giants "are not simply online intermediaries; they are data companies and, as such, make every possible effort to safeguard and fully exploit their primary input" (Kulesz, 2018b, 81). Almost all forms of user interaction, including liking, friending, following, posting, retweeting, and commenting on digital platforms can be captured as data to turn into valuable commodities. Digital platforms turn these data into commodities, and this datafication process "endows plat-forms with the potential to develop techniques for predictive and real-time analytics, which are vital for delivering targeted advertising and services in a wide variety of economic sectors," including the cultural sector (van Dijck et al., 2018, 33). Given the dominant position of global OTT platforms, local OTT platforms and cultural industries corporations have relatively less usable data than global mega giants, which puts them in jeopardy.

In the AI sector, those who make the most of AI as a technology are expectedly the big tech giants. The clearest examples of profitable, fruit-ful use of AI are Google, Amazon, Facebook, and Netflix (Faggella, 2019). These companies, as mega platform giants, have already had access to more data than any other company in the history of the world. Based on that they have built "a culture of connectivity and data," and they have garnered huge profits. Equipped with AI, based on big data, and supported by algorithms, these digital platforms have produced, distributed, and expedited the global consumption of popular culture. For example,

Netflix's recommendation engines are much more complex than most people assume they are, and are indeed, again, predicated on artificial intelligence on a digital platform in a virtual world where everything is

AI and cultural production 71

potentially trackable. This allows Netflix to collect data that is extremely difficult to collect in the physical world.

(Faggella, 2019)

When people use Netflix, their clicks, watches, pauses, and reviews are tracked by Netflix.

When popular culture encounters AI, several beneficial aspects happen; however, the convergence of these two seemingly separate areas does not guarantee the balanced growth of new digital culture and the digital economy, both nationally and globally. Regardless of its great mechanisms, AI, as with previous digital technologies, has become a major component of digital platforms and mega media corporations as they control big data and capital. In particular, the gap between the Global North and the Global South in this particular form of media convergence has deepened, as global platform giants control local cultural production based on their distribution power and networks. A handful of non-Western countries may advance their own AI and relevant digital technologies so that cultural creators can use them; however, the level of technology is not yet comparable to the AI developed in Western countries. When global OTT platforms and media giants control the flow of cultural content and big data, this divide will widen, not shrink. AI particularly depends on data, which is the driver behind machine learning. However, new and smaller digital platforms and media corporations in the Global South do not have access to as much data to develop powerful AI systems, with a few exceptions in China and Korea, which worsens the disparity between the Global North and the Global South.

The increasing role of AI may hurt democracy in culture and has brought about an AI divide. Several OTT platforms, as AI software developers and holders, will take over the entertainment industries, while traditional media firms centered on less-skilled digital technologies continuously lose their market shares, both nationally and globally. The customers also have no choice but to choose what OTT platforms recommend. Big data and algorithms that are major parts of AI are mostly owned by a few Western-based platforms and mega media giants, and this systemic difference in the global context intensifies the global digital divide, which asks us to develop practical and reasonable standards to share data or distribute the benefits reasonably.

Conclusion

This chapter has addressed the increasing role of AI in the production of popular culture. By discussing several cases in both the Global North and the Global South, it examined the encounters of AI and popular culture in cultural production. As the contemporary phase of AI is dramatically transforming the global order, shifting societies away from a world largely organized around employee-based industrial manufacture to new and future

72 *AI and cultural production*

industries (Elliott, 2019, 157), AI has deeply reshaped the production of popular culture. AI is a recurring theme in popular culture, whether it is through older forms of art such as literature or through contemporary art such as films (Moustachir, 2016).

While many people still do not believe the reality of AI involvement in the production of popular culture, changes made by the adoption of AI in the cultural industries are everywhere, including films, music, games, and television programs. Several digital platforms in tandem with AI have developed their own cultural content. With the escalation of OTT streaming services and the continued influx of capital invested into cultural content, traditional media firms like network broadcasters have advanced their production supported by AI. Several traditional media have also consolidated and formed alliances with AI firms to remain competitive (Foster, 2019).

The necessity of AI in cultural production in the early 21st century leads to a rapid transformation of cultural production. As Kulesz (2018a, 4) points out, "The widespread incorporation of digital tools, and in particular the emergence of large digital platforms, have profoundly transformed the structure of the cultural value chain." People witness a dramatic shift away from a pipeline-like system, in which each link—production, distribution, consumption—processes a good or service and passes it on to the next, toward a network or platform-type model, in which a set of nodes interact in real time. In such an arrangement, an innovation like AI tends to exert a simultaneous influence across the entire chain, rather than just affecting a single link (Kulesz, 2018a). Arguably, AI has powerful social consequences, and the cultural value chain has been experiencing a dramatic shift. As AI develops, deepens, and accelerates, more and more people will be affected, which is unavoidable.

It is expected that AI will take a major role in the production of media and popular culture in the future. For cultural creators and corporations, it is no longer an option of whether to adopt AI technology in their creative work. As AI-driven cultural distribution in the cases of Netflix and Spotify already proves, AI-supported cultural production will be revolutionary and then routine in the media and cultural industries. Machine learning in the realm of popular culture can be utilized to create new forms of interaction between people, creators, and platforms.

However, the rapid use of AI in cultural production does not mean that AI totally changes the production process on a full scale and eliminates humans from production lines. It may take some more time to witness the production of cultural content, which will be entirely relying on AI, because humans will continue to play a key role in cultural production. Therefore, it is important to explore the ways in which people deal with these changes that AI has brought (Elliott, 2019). In other words, what we have to ponder is the relationship between AI and humans in cultural production. As Elliott (2019, 26) points out, "The flow of human action and the production of cultural practices takes place today in the context of complex, powerful

AI *and cultural production* 73

technological and social systems that stretch across time and space," which demand that we develop collaboration between humans and machines in cultural production.

There are a number of major challenges that remain as well. On the one hand, the cultural value chain is rapidly being transformed, and many countries do not have a secure strategy in place to deal with AI-driven shifts. In the Global South, the task is even worse and more complex. Due to the lack of necessary data for traditional media and platform companies in the Global South, AI use in the production of popular culture cannot be fully achieved. As UNESCO (2016) aptly puts it, cultural industries, especially small- and medium-sized enterprises, both nationally and globally, often lack the necessary digital tools and skills, including AI, big data, and manpower. Moreover, migration from analog to digital is often very expensive. The predominance of the platforms in the cultural sector is so strong that it possibly results in an additional danger, which is the inability to produce reliable national statistics on the economy of digital culture. Since exchanges of information between the user and the platform are conducted electronically and are generally encrypted, states do not always have the means to establish which and how goods and services have been consumed or produced by users in the Global South (UNESCO, 2016, 17). On the other hand, the rise and dominance of mega digital platforms in the creative ecosystem may "leave local creative actors defenceless" (Kulesz, 2018b, 83).

Overall, the advance of AI in the production of popular culture cannot be avoided, and there is no doubt that there will be further growth of AI in cultural production. However, it is also true that AI use in cultural production has brought about several significant socio-cultural matters, which asks governments and cultural corporations, including digital platform firms, to advance balanced approaches toward AI-driven cultural production.

Note

1 For example, in spring 2019, the Korea Advanced Institute of Science and Technology (KAIST), Korea University, and Sungkyunkwan University were selected as the institutes to run government-funded graduate schools specializing in AI. The ministry of science and ICT stated that the government planned to inject 9 billion won ($8 million) for the next five years to support these three universities in teaching and developing AI technology. In the long term, the government will invest a combined 19 billion won for the next ten years after conducting performance evaluations. The plan was designed to nurture highly qualified professionals in the AI field, noting that major countries around the world including the U.S. and China have made similar moves (Jun, J.H., 2019a). This clearly demonstrates that the Korean government plans to advance the AI field. On the flip side of the same token, however, it also implies that Korea experiences a lack of talent and corporations; therefore, they must educate people who might want to study and work in the AI sector. This environment also asks local platform and media firms as well as other industries to find their partners in foreign countries, because they cannot fill the positions domestically.

74 AI *and cultural production*

Against this backdrop, Korean telecom and platform giants have aggressively advanced opportunities to work with AI firms and individuals, even from foreign countries. Due to the lack of national talents, again, they have looked abroad to access top AI talents in several Western countries. Naver, as the largest internet portal and platform in Korea, purchased XRCE from France to gain access to 80 top European AI experts. Korea's conglomerates have also been active in Canada. Samsung opened its second North American AI center in Toronto in May 2018, following the launch of its AI lab in Montreal in partnership with the Universite de Montreal's MILA (one of the three AI clusters) in September 2017. LG also established a partnership with the University of Toronto—home to the Vector Institute, another AI cluster—to set up an AI research lab (Asia Pacific Foundation of Canada, 2019). Meanwhile, two other major telecom and platform companies, SK Telecom (2017) and Kakao (2018), established their own AI research labs, indicating massive investments in the fields of AI, big data, and algorithm in Korean society (Asia Pacific Foundation of Canada, 2019). These locally based conglomerates in the fields of smartphones, telecommunications, and digital platforms, focusing on mobility and sociality, have continued to advance their business strategies to have AI in their hands. As they have new technology components and/or digital platforms, they must have AI.

5 Netflix's effects in transforming global cultural norms

Introduction

In the 21st century, the emergence of internet-based over-the-top (OTT) service platforms, known as video-on-demand (VOD) services like Netflix, Amazon Prime, Disney+, and Apple TV+ have tremendously influenced people's cultural activities. Equipped with AI, big data, and algorithms, OTT service platforms have reshaped global cultural markets, as they have changed the norms of the cultural industries. From content distribution to production, to the media industry itself, OTT platforms have substantially transformed the ecology of global entertainment markets, as cultural production and consumption are increasingly happening with the help of AI and algorithms. Cultural consumption in the U.S. and elsewhere has shown a tremendous increase, and it has seen a significant jump from traditional media to digital media. The rise of digital media platforms is challenging the supremacy of television and movie theaters as major entertainment centers.

Admitting that several important OTT platforms exist, Netflix has played a pivotal role in transforming the global entertainment markets, as it "has had a transformative effect in the relationship between consumers and content providers" (McDonald and Smith-Rowsey, 2018, 1). Over the past decade, Netflix has grown as one of the major OTT platforms utilizing big data, algorithms, and AI in order to create the best possible recommendation system, which consequently provides huge profits for platform corporations, while hurting the traditional broadcasting and film industries. Netflix has especially continued to expand its market share in the global cultural markets. Having mostly conquered the Western markets, including Canada and the U.K., Netflix has pivoted east and vigorously sought to rack up the number of its subscribers in Asia starting in 2015. Young and increasingly digital populations in Asia present an incredible opportunity to ramp up Netflix's international subscriber base, and subscriptions in Asia already surpassed the 58 million in the U.S. at the end of 2018 (Gilchrist, 2018). From production to distribution to the OTT industry itself, Asia has experienced a phenomenal shift of the platform and cultural markets mainly because of Netflix's effects. Netflix is commonly received as one of the major hubs of

76 *Netflix transforming global cultural norms*

reflexive distribution (Braun, 2015); however, Netflix has also functioned as a major player in production and exhibition, which is a new business model for many followers in both the Global North and the Global South.

This chapter investigates Netflix's effects as one of the most influential OTT platforms in the global cultural industries, focusing on the crucial nexus of AI, digital platforms, and popular culture. It first discusses the major characteristics of Netflix as the most significant AI-supported OTT service platform, which controls the vicious chain of the cultural industries, from distribution to production. Second, it examines the ways in which Netflix influences the content production industry, focusing on AI and algorithm-driven distribution processes. Then it investigates Netflix's effects in the local OTT industry to understand why OTTs have incorporated AI. Through these discussions, it eventually articulates whether Netflix has expanded an asymmetrical power relationship between the Global North, primarily the U.S., and many developing countries in the Global South. The analysis of the power relationship between them will shed light on the current debates on the increasing role of Netflix utilizing AI, big data, and algorithms on a large scale in the global context.

Emergence of Netflix as a global digital platform

Netflix was founded in the U.S. in 1997 as a video rental service firm and began streaming in 2007. Netflix has been one of the most successful OTT services and has played a key role as a very influential digital platform. Netflix is also one of the most exemplary platforms supported by AI, as "AI represents any technology that can be used to drive automated, complex decision making without requiring low level human input at the individual decision level" (Easton, 2019). This means that in broadcasting "this could manifest as anything from voice assistants and recommendation engines processing TV requests, through to more operational applications of AI such as automated webchat services," which Netflix mostly presents (Easton, 2019).

The presence of AI is becoming more and more ubiquitous, and several mega platforms like Netflix, Facebook, and Spotify deploy AI-related solutions that interact with consumers (Yu, 2019). Netflix has indeed utilized AI and algorithms to develop its powerful recommendation system, which means that its impact in the global cultural markets is not restricted to the distribution sector, but the nexus of AI and culture. Netflix especially uses machine learning and algorithms to present personalized content suggestions to customers (Easton, 2019). Netflix supported by AI and algorithms dominates the entire cultural industries, from production to distribution sectors. Although it started as a distribution outlet, Netflix has produced its own original content to lessen reliance on outside studios while reducing content costs (Kumar et al., 2018). In other words, Netflix utilizes machine learning not only to identify potential projects its customers may like, but also

Netflix transforming global cultural norms 77

to develop worthwhile technical and business decisions, such as planning budgets, finding locations, building sets, and scheduling guest actors, which enable the creative act of connecting with subscribers. In order to actualize this, Netflix analyzes various data sets to predict the cost of several attributes of the production process from pre-production to post-production, including content, location, and scheduling (Kumar et al., 2018). It certainly enhances the possibility for Netflix to recommend the best suitable content to the customers.

Netflix has also transformed itself from a tiny video rental company to the largest OTT platform. As discussed in Chapter 2, Netflix borrows several different aspects from social network sites and user-generated content platforms; however, Netflix also offers several characteristics similar to digital platforms. As van Dijck et al. (2018, 9) point out, again, "A platform is fueled by data, automated and organized through algorithms and interfaces, formalized through ownership relations driven by business models, and governed through user agreements," which puts Netflix in the category of digital platforms. In this regard, Jin (2015) also argues that digital platforms could not be fairly understood without contemplating three major areas: technological sphere, corporate sphere, and political sphere. What they commonly emphasize is that we need to understand Netflix by not only its technological aspects but also its commercial and cultural aspects. Netflix is the largest OTT service utilizing big data, algorithms, and AI to make commercial profit, both nationally and globally, and it is not only functioning as an intermediary, but also as a mediator to control the vicious chain of cultural spheres, starting in the field of distribution, but now also including production and exhibition.

Netflix's business strategy to grab the customer's attention has changed from "its original business model as exhibitor of film content" to "the business of being producer of serialized drama" (Jenner, 2016, 261). Instead of offering an opportunity to catch up with missed television programs and films, Netflix

> offers the first—and for long periods of time only—chance to watch its original dramas, and by turning the familiar chain of first, second and third market distribution on its head, Netflix offers a distinctively different form of media distribution.
>
> (Jenner, 2016, 261)

Netflix like other OTTs, including Amazon Prime and Disney+, as digital platforms, has greatly transformed cultural content and cultural industries. Netflix has continued to advance its unique business models and reshaped global cultural markets. By adding and utilizing several major components, such as AI, algorithms, and big data, Netflix has turned itself into one of the major media giants that change the norms of the cultural sector.

78 *Netflix transforming global cultural norms*

More specifically, Netflix has penetrated other countries since its successful launch in Canada in 2007. When Netflix started its service in Canada, many Canadians hoped that Netflix could offer unlimited movie and television episodes over an internet connection for $7.99 a month, which might allow them to ditch their expensive cable channels. However, Netflix chief executive Reed Hastings said, "That won't be the case," as Netflix is not "an effective competitor" to traditional television. During a press conference held in Toronto before the launch of Netflix in Canada, Hastings stated, "We are like a bicycle compared to their car. We're a supplement" (Nowak, 2010). About ten years later, Hastings' statement proves wrong, as Netflix is not only a strong competitor, but also a replacement, instead of a supplement. The growing trend of people canceling their cable or satellite TV service—known-as cord-cutting—has continued.[1] Originally, Netflix might have seemed as a simple intermediary; however, it has turned into one of the strongest mediators as a digital platform, competing against traditional media. Netflix has consequently challenged the traditional media and their business models in global markets.

Netflix has continued to diversify its market. It first penetrated several Western markets, including the U.K., Ireland, Sweden, Denmark, and the Netherlands, while appearing in Latin America during the early 2010s. Netflix finally moved into the Asian market, including Japan and Korea, in the mid-2010s. Netflix entered Japan in 2015 and has a presence in most Asian countries (Low, 2017). Netflix is not yet available in China. It is also not available in Crimea, North Korea, or Syria due to U.S. government restrictions on American companies.

According to Netflix (2019a), its subscribers with a streaming-only plan could watch TV shows and movies instantly in over 190 countries in 2019, although the content that is available to stream may vary by location. Netflix kept getting bigger, although it was not growing quite as fast as it had been in the U.S., partially because of other competitors including Disney+ (Adalian, 2019). For Netflix, going global is its biggest asset, and increasing international subscribers is among its biggest challenges in the midst of fierce challenges from latecomers, including Amazon Prime, Disney+, and local OTTs.

With its global penetration, Netflix has rapidly increased its revenues, from $6.7 billion in 2015 to $20.1 billion in 2019, as the number of global subscribers has increased from 70 million in 2015 to 167 million in 2019. The number of international subscribers surpassed U.S. subscribers in 2017 (Netflix, 2017, 2018, 2019b, 2020) (Table 5.1). In December 2019, Netflix (2019d) released historical streaming revenue, membership, and average revenue per paying streaming membership by region for the first time. In an 8-K filing with the U.S. SEC (Securities and Exchange Commission), as expected, Netflix reported that in the Asia-Pacific region, revenue over the past two years grew 153% to $382 million at the end of the third quarter of 2019.

Netflix transforming global cultural norms 79

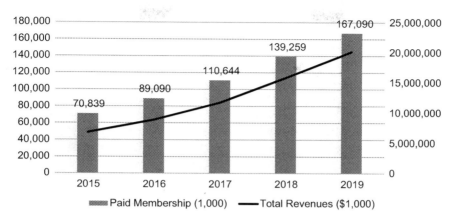

Table 5.1 Netflix membership and revenues (unit: 1,000)
Source: Netflix (2017, 2018, 2019b, 2020).

Streaming subscribers grew by 148% over that time period, to 14.49 million paying customers in Q3 2019. Compared to this, the European region, including the Middle East and Africa (EMEA), showed that subscription revenue increased 132% over the last two years to $1,428 million for the third quarter of 2019. The number of subscribers in EMEA stood at 47.4 million as of the end of the third quarter, up 105% versus two years prior (Spangler, 2019). Asia has been the smallest market, but the growth rate of both revenue and the number of subscribers has been the highest around the globe.

In Asia, Korea is leading the growth, as the number of active streaming subscribers has soared. The service started in Korea in January 2016, and the number of subscribers increased by 5.23 times, from 630,000 in June 2018 to 3.3 million in September 2020, showing one of the fastest growths around the world (Li and Yang, 2020). As of October 2019, by age, people in their 20s are the largest segment at 38%, followed by those in their 30s (31%), 40s (15%), and over 50+ (17%) (Lee, M.K., 2019; *DongA Ilbo*, 2019). More importantly, the number of users of Netflix's mobile app has rapidly increased, from only 80,000 in 2016 to 320,000 in 2017 and to 900,000 in September 2018 (Cho, Y.B., 2019). As is well known (Kim, 2011; Jin, 2017a), Korea is one of the most advanced smartphone-saturated markets, and Netflix also utilizes new media and ICTs in order to increase the number of its users in Korea. For Netflix, digital generations who are used to working and playing with digital technologies, including smartphones, are the major customers, and *The Economist* (2018) dubbed this phenomenon as "Netflixonomics"—the science behind getting people to subscribe to the video-streaming channel.

80 *Netflix transforming global cultural norms*

In its initial stage in 2016, locally based OTT services and cultural creators did not seem to worry about Netflix; however, the recent surge of Netflix has enormous impacts and potential to reshape the Korean cultural market. Locally based OTTs have competed against global OTT platforms, but local online video services are suffering from drops in subscribers, mainly because of the lack of content in Korean OTT platforms (Yeo, J.S., 2019a). Netflix has secured its momentum to grow in Korea, and Netflix has become a service that everybody, from the government to the cultural creators to the users, has reconsidered in terms of impacts in the cultural industries. As Elkins (2021) argues, Netflix is a political organization, as it engages directly in domestic and global struggles over ideological and technological power. In its programming, branding strategies, and attempts to influence global media content, trade, and infrastructure policies, Netflix promotes a broad vision of globalized cultural and economic liberalism geared toward cosmopolitan branding, international free trade, and economic deregulation.

Interestingly enough, Netflix has shown its strong growth in the recent COVID-19 era, while the majority of companies experienced a huge setback. During the first quarter of 2020, when coronavirus began to be rampant, the Dow Jones Industrial Average of the U.S. was down as much as 24%; however, Netflix's stock outperformed, as it was up by 10% during the same period. Netflix shares soared as much as 60.5% between January 2 and August 31, 2020, while the Dow index still recorded minus gains. Since people had to stay home, they heavily relied on home entertainment, including digital games and OTT platforms, and Netflix became one of the finest beneficiaries of the pandemic. In the COVID-19 era, people have had to practice social distancing as a response to the coronavirus crisis, which means that humans avoid face-to-face social relations and substitute them by mediated social relations, in which communication is organized with the help of social media and OTT platforms (Fuchs, 2020). Social distancing does not mean that people avoid communication, but "the substitution of face-to-face communication that bears the risk of contagion by mediated communication. Mediation becomes a strategy of both avoidance and survival" (Fuchs, 2020, 378). As Cohn (2019, 2) argues, "Such technologies and values fit comfortably with our current neoliberal (or simply capitalist) fascination with generating efficiency and simplicity in all areas of life through automation."

As coronavirus has significantly changed contemporary capitalist society, Netflix, and in general, OTT platforms equipped with AI and big data, has become one of the most powerful mediators, resulting in massive profits in the hands of mega digital platforms. As is well known, Netflix pioneered the subscription-based video-streaming business model (see Chapter 6), and in the COVID-19 era, Netflix has aptly managed to add more subscribers. People in many countries have started to subscribe to Netflix because they want to enjoy various contents at the same time, known as binge-watching,

Netflix transforming global cultural norms 81

under the lockdown situation. Netflix, as an AI-supported OTT platform, has momentously capitalized on the COVID-19 pandemic.

AI reshapes the norms of cultural distribution

As Netflix has greatly expanded its global reach, it has substantially reshaped the local audio-visual industry. The enormous penetration of Netflix has influenced several key areas: distribution, production, exhibition, and the platform industry itself. AI-saturated Netflix impacts workflow in cultural production and distribution. While Netflix can be identified within television studies, as discussed in Chapter 1, this book posits Netflix as a digital platform—"a computational, software-based system that can produce a television-like experience as just one of its potential applications" (Lobato, 2019, 35)—as well as a commercial and corporate agency. It is crucial to analyze Netflix as a platform that relies on AI and algorithmic recommendations as can be seen in Google and Facebook as well due to its major dimensions discussed in Chapter 2.

Most of all, one of the most distinctive areas that Netflix globally influences is distribution. As Netflix itself reveals (2019c), it especially innovates using machine learning in many areas where it designs, implements, evaluates, and productionizes models and algorithms. Machine learning impacts several areas. For example, personalization, mainly discussed in Chapter 7, has been the most well-known area, where machine learning powers Netflix's recommendation algorithms. Netflix also utilizes machine learning to help shape its catalog of movies and television shows by learning the characteristics that make content successful. Netflix uses it to optimize the production of original television shows and movies. ML enables the company to optimize video and audio encoding and adaptive bit rate selection that accounts for more than a third of internet traffic in North America. Meanwhile, it powers advertising spend, channel mix, and advertising creativity so that Netflix is able to find new paid subscribers who will enjoy Netflix (Netflix, 2019c).

Netflix machine learning director Tony Jebara indeed emphasized the role of machine learning in personalized streaming services during a presentation held at Stanford University in October 2018 (Foreman, 2018). During the presentation, he noted that, with written word and film, "the person communicating [a] story does not know what is resonating, what is not and how to improve storytelling" in most cases because they lack the direct feedback an audience could provide during in-person storytelling. However, Jebara said that applying machine learning to data solicited from users allows Netflix to proactively reach their audiences. He firmly stated,

> Now we can start seeing what each account is interested in, what shows are they watching, what are they fast forwarding, what are they hovering

82 *Netflix transforming global cultural norms*

over, what are they giving thumbs up to and thumbs down to. That kind of closes the feedback loop that we lost as we went to millions and billions as we scaled up.

(Foreman, 2018)

Based on Netflix's testimony and its own machine learning director's claim, it is certain that Netflix has continued to focus on the function of machine learning beyond a simple algorithmic system as its major business model, which makes Netflix one of the most advanced AI digital platforms.

More recently, Netflix's distribution power equipped with AI has changed the conventional way of production in the local cultural market. Several major impacts have reshaped the local broadcasting sector, as the broadcasting industry has experienced a tremendous change in distribution. As Elliott (2019) aptly puts it, in the sphere of global geopolitics, the main narrative for AI as elsewhere has been about power—the power to (re)shape the worldwide race in AI-driven cultural and economic growth; therefore, the investigation of the influence of the American platform in the local context provides a better understanding of the power relationship between the Global North and the Global South. Netflix has especially purchased the distribution rights of well-made local content and shown them on Netflix.

For Netflix, while it has penetrated many local markets around the globe, one of its major target local cultural markets is Korea in various ways. Therefore, it is essential to take Korea as an example in Netflix studies. Netflix has indeed developed several strategies to expand its market share in Korea. To begin with, Netflix funded as much as $43 million to *Mr. Sunshine*—a television drama—, which aired in 2018 in the midst of the company's vehement drive to increase its control in Korea and, therefore, in Asia (*DongA Ilbo*, 2018). Netflix also bought *Stranger*—a Korean television drama—and *Man to Man* (another drama released during 2017) to air on Netflix. Netflix also started to broadcast *One Spring Night*, a mini-series produced by MBC—one of the largest Korean network channels—in May 2019 (Jung, S.M., 2019). Until then, only a few programs produced by cable channels were broadcasted by Netflix, and network channels expressed their deep concerns about the intrusion of Netflix in the Korean broadcasting market. However, domestic broadcasters, both cable and network channels, have faced a challenge from Netflix, and therefore, they have no choice but to work with Netflix as a new distribution and exhibition outlet for their programs, while advancing their own OTT platforms. As a continuation of its interest in Korean dramas, in November 2019, Netflix unveiled a three-year licensing deal with a Korean cable TV network JTBC. Under the partnership, Netflix will secure worldwide streaming rights to about 20 Korean-language drama series titles produced and aired by JTBC. "Netflix appears to be hurrying to further establish itself as a go-to destination for Korean drama—a recognition of the growing global popularity of the genre's glossy hit shows" (Brzeski, 2019). Netflix's Korean business consequently played a major role in the growth of the company during the COVID-19 era (Li and Yang, 2020).

Netflix has also transformed the exhibition norms. In the Korean broadcasting system, network and cable channels are used to producing drama series that run two episodes per week over two to three months. However, Netflix produces all episodes at the same time so that the customers can watch them together at any time, without waiting for the next episode. As Netflix controls the distribution timing, domestic broadcasters cannot decide their own programs' air schedules. For example, SBS (Seoul Broadcasting System) broadcasted its new drama series *Vagabond* that aired between September 20 and November 9 in 2019; however, it was supposed to broadcast in 2018. The premiere date of this blockbuster-style television series was delayed due to a pending deal with Netflix (Rapir, 2019). With a 250 billion won budget, which is one of the largest thus far, the drama looks like a Hollywood action, thriller, and crime genre movie due to heavy gun-battle scenes, which is rare in the Korean broadcasting industry. Korea's broadcasting sector now has to distribute programs in various ways, including on Netflix.

Meanwhile, in the realm of the distribution and exhibition of films, Netflix is not known for traditional theatrical releases. As the case of Bong Joon-ho's *Okja*—a fusion of benign monster movie, action comedy, and coming-of-age fable—already proved, as it was not screened at major theaters, but on Netflix, that "the theater era is slowly coming to an end" (Song, S.J., 2016). In recent years, at a time when people can have a screen with them anywhere, whether in the comfort of their house, the street, the bus, or subway, films are rapidly spreading through monitors and mobile devices instead of theaters. In other words, one of the major impacts created by Netflix is the film distribution approach. With the deepening screen monopoly/oligopoly issue in Korean cinema, "some art, low-budget and indie films are testing grounds by choosing to be released online and via mobile technologies," while attempting to air films on Netflix (Song, S.J., 2016).

Netflix has also influenced the storytelling of local dramas. Until now, producers of Korean dramas used to develop an important turning point at the end of each episode so that the audiences would wait with anticipation until the next episode. However, program producers cannot stick to this traditional distribution norm, as they create and release programs on Netflix as well as domestic channels at the same time (You, S.M., 2019). Freedom from the traditional program schedule of classical linear television is the most important motive for audiences to use OTT platforms.

As previously discussed, Korea has been known for its tech-savvy young generations who adopt new technologies faster and on a more enormous scale than in other countries, and the country is at the front line with the continuous growth of smartphone technologies and relevant apps. The number of users of Netflix's mobile apps has rapidly increased. As many Koreans

84 *Netflix transforming global cultural norms*

rely on their smartphones for daily activities, including cultural consumption, Korean audio-visual industries corporations that have learned from Netflix have rapidly developed smartphone-ready television programs and films and released them on smartphones. For example, Watcha Play, which started its service in Korea in 2016, immediately started out as a mobile application based on data and has built its existing platform into an online content streaming service in Korea (Song, S.J., 2016).

In the cultural industry, distribution is a key in connecting production and exhibition, and Netflix has greatly influenced the local cultural industries in that they have developed a new distribution system, differentiating it from the traditional distribution methods. Netflix has fundamentally reshaped the cultural industry, and its role is not limited to the dissemination of cultural products nor the circulation of audio-visual culture, but it functions as a producer with massive capital to shift the contours of the global cultural industry. Netflix has certainly played a key role as a mediator, as the case of *Vagabond* discussed above proves, instead of a simple intermediary, in the global cultural industries (van Dijck, 2013; Jin, 2019). At a moment when Netflix is gaining footholds in global markets, its global brand offers an implicit counterpoint to anxieties over platform imperialism—American platforms accumulate power and capital by serving as the world's major conduit for media practice (Jin, 2015; Elkins, 2019). Netflix's unconventional attempt is the perfect representation of platform imperialism in Korea and elsewhere.

Transforming local audio-visual culture

Backed by its distribution power, Netflix has invested in the production of cultural content, both in film and broadcasting. As briefly explained, Netflix has funded several local cultural products. In Latin America, Netflix revealed its plan to make a $200 million investment in Mexico in order to create content in the country in 2020. Netflix has confirmed that it will launch 50 series and movies in the country during 2020 (Bertran, 2019). In Asia, Netflix has big plans for India. In 2019, CEO Reed Hastings explained that the streaming video giant would spend $400 million on Indian content for 2019 and 2020, which will cover both originals and licensed content. Reed understands the global acceptance of Bollywood movies, and he clearly indicated that some of the Indian content on the platform is finding wider acceptance beyond India. He cited, for example, Indian animated children's show *Mighty Little Bheem*, which he said has been viewed by 27 million households outside of India. Since its launch in India in 2016, Netflix has been building up its local slate, starting with its first Indian original *Sacred Games* (Bhushan, 2019; Jin, 2021).

Most of all, in Korea, Netflix provided the entire budget of $50 million for *Okja*—which was a film directed by Bong Joon-ho—released in July 2017. People in 190 countries were able to watch it via Netflix. With the

Netflix transforming global cultural norms 85

release of this film, Netflix hoped to stand out in the Korean market, as it had been struggling to gain ground there during the early stage of penetration (Kim, J.H., 2017). The investment seems like a lot, "but it is part of a larger international gamble that could help the company grow outside the U.S." (Sims, 2015).

Since then, Netflix has funded a series of programs to produce Korea-originated content. In January 2017, it revealed a plan to turn popular Korean webtoon *Love Alarm* (webtoon title: *Joahamyeon Ullineun*)—a comedy fantasy romance school drama with a love triangle—which started in 2014, into a 12-episode drama series. Netflix started to air the drama in August 2019. In March of 2017, Netflix also revealed another plan to produce an eight-episode drama dubbed *Kingdom* (Kim, J.H., 2017). Netflix invested in a Korean variety show, *Busted: I Know Who You Are*, which was released on Netflix in May and June 2018. Netflix has continued to invest, produce, and release several dramas and variety shows, including *My First Love* (drama, 2019), *YG Future Strategy Office* (variety show, 2018), *Yoo Byung Jae: Discomfort Zone* (stand-up comedy, 2018), and *The School Nurse Files* (drama, *Bogeongyosa Aneunyeong*, 2019). According to one report (Hwang, 2018), there were only 60 Korean products that Netflix distributed until early 2018; however, there were as many as 140 television programs and 400 movies by July 2018. This is not mainly due to Korean subscribers but for Asian audiences who love Korean cultural content. More importantly, in 2019, Netflix released its first original Korean drama series, *Kingdom*. It is a genre-defining six-episode zombie mystery thriller set in the last Korean kingdom of *Joseon*. It took nearly eight years to produce the series, with its production cost reaching 2 billion won (US$1.7 million) per episode (*Yonhap*, 2019a; Jin, 2021).

What makes the Korean cultural industry unique for Netflix is the recent growth of the Korean Wave, also known as Hallyu, which is the rapid growth of local cultural content, including television programs, films, and K-pop in both neighboring countries and the West (Lee and Nornes, 2015; Jin, 2016; Yoon and Jin, 2017). Netflix believes that the Korean cultural market is exceptionally important, which demands that the company not only penetrate this particular local market but also work with Korean creators. As Korea has talented content creators, and cultural products, from dramas to K-pop, are globally popular in the midst of the Korean Wave phenomenon, Netflix continues to invest in the Korean cultural market. In order words, Netflix is purposely riding the Korean Wave.

Of course, one of the major reasons for Netflix's entrance to Korea and investment in several local programs, including *Kingdom*, "is seen as an attempt to gain influence in China instead of trying to enlarge the OTT pie in Korea," and

> that is why they invested in Korean original series like *Kingdom* that will likely become popular in China. The appearance of Korean rivals

86 *Netflix transforming global cultural norms*

will make it difficult for Netflix to air their original content, possibly hindering its plan to raise its presence in the Asian market, where Hallyu works.

(Jin, M.J., 2019)

As Netflix's next major target is China, it seemingly uses Korea as an advance base of operations while pushing toward China.

Consequently, Netflix has deeply influenced the Korean entertainment industry. Up until now, most Korean dramas known overseas were in the romantic comedy genre. However, as Netflix has invested and is interested in various genres, including thriller (e.g., *Stranger*), zombie (e.g., *Kingdom*), and stand-up comedy (e.g., *Yoo Byung Jae: Discomfort Zone*), Korean creators are also developing these genres, which is unprecedented. Netflix has the ability to circulate content that would not have traveled worldwide in the conventional system; therefore, Netflix pushes Korean creators to go beyond the boundaries of traditional media content offerings (Sohn, 2018). Due to Netflix's strong interest in these genres, Korean entertainment firms have unconventionally developed these new forms of cultural content. For cultural creators, the local market is not the only target anymore. For them, the global reach of their content is the new norm, and they hope that Netflix will help them to take off in the global cultural markets. As Stangarone (2019) correctly observes, "Netflix's success is being driven by its catalog of content, but also by the development of original Korean content, something local artists find appealing." Therefore, "Netflix is committed to making shows for foreign markets that are domestically authentic and then promoting those shows abroad."

Against this backdrop, local creators have to contemplate Netflix's effects because the rituals embedded in Netflix would lead local entertainment sectors and audiences to "abandon their traditions wholesale in order to adopt Western modernity wholesale" (Kraidy, 2010, 138). By understanding "the production cultures and how the work of production itself is reoriented to accommodate, challenge, and overcome the novelty and appeal" of Netflix, they may comprehend how local producers mediate forces of global digital platforms and what that means in terms of the audio-visual culture in the local cultural market (Ganguly, 2019, 33).

When SBS in Korea created a television mini-series *Vagabond* in 2019, again, it certainly utilized Hollywood action styles in order to appeal to global audiences. The drama is about a mysterious airplane crash that kills over 211 civilians, and a stuntman ends up discovering a national corruption scandal in the process. In the 12th episode, aired in November of the year, stuntman Cha Dal Gun (acted by Seung-gi Lee) brought a key witness in the tragic airplane crash to the Korean court; however, corrupt National Intelligence Service and police who were behind the accident together blocked them on a street in Seoul. In this particular scene, about ten policemen fired guns, including automatic rifles at them, which was unprecedented for a

Korean drama. This moment reminds people of the many crime action films produced by Hollywood like *Batman vs. Superman: Dawn of Justice* (2016). One of the major reasons for this unrealistic scene in the Korean context is the release of this drama on Netflix, which targets global audiences, not Korean viewers only.

Another recent drama, *Arthdal Chronicles*, also aired internationally on Netflix in 2019, although it was produced by the Korean cable station tvN and Studio Dragon. In the drama, Jang Dong Gun as a warrior wants to be king, while Song Joong Ki plays the dual roles of an inspiring hero and a diabolical prince. Unlike previous history dramas, *Arthdal Chronicles* is set in the Bronze Age mythical kingdom known as *Arthdal*, which in its greed attempts to dominate neighboring people. Due to its unusual historical background, when it aired, it was compared to the popular U.S. production, *Game of Thrones*. While there were initially some similarities in the plot and setting, *Arthdal Chronicles* went in its own distinct direction, creating "a complex storyline with a multitude of characters" (MacDonald, 2019). However, it is certain that the producers planned to develop a program, comparable to Netflix-produced blockbuster-scale drama, in order to target global viewers. As such, some Korean media companies, including Studio Dragon and JTBC, have pursued a studio system focusing on program production instead of advertising for their major revenues, which are influenced by the Netflix model (You, G.S., 2019).

For the Global South, including Korea, it is not necessary to challenge all foreign-based digital platforms. The recent production costs in the Korean cultural industry—as can be seen in *Arthdal Chronicles* (540 billion won, 2019), *Mr. Sunshine* (450 billion won, 2018), and *Vagabond* (250 billion won, 2019) compared to *My Love from the Star* (132 billion won, 2013–2014) and *Descendants of the Sun* (130 billion won, 2016)—have continued to soar while the advertising revenues of network broadcasters have been decreasing. In order to produce big budget dramas that appeal to sophisticated audiences in the Netflix era, broadcasters and film companies must secure alternative revenue sources, and they work with OTT service providers, including Netflix (Lee, S. M., 2019; Kim, J.H., 2020). Netflix has transformed the local entertainment industry, which used to heavily rely on advertising as its major revenue source, to focus on the content-centered market (You, S.M., 2019). As detailed in Chapter 4, local cultural firms and creators have deeply engaged with AI and big data in production; however, in the realm of production, local cultural creators and companies still adapt and develop local cultural products based on local identities and norms in the age of Netflix. Due to heavy impacts driven by Netflix as a global digital platform, they are reorienting their production norms to greet the new world that Netflix designs instead of creating local content based on local cultural values.

From a critical perspective, however, what is significant for local cultural creators is to maintain and advance locally oriented cultural content. For

88 *Netflix transforming global cultural norms*

example, *Parasite* by Bong Joon-ho won the Palme d'Or at the 2019 Cannes Film Festival and four trophies at the 2020 Oscars to earn global popularity, mainly because of its emphasis on Koreanness, not foreign elements. The movie is about a story of a rich family and a poor family, which is a universal theme portraying "the conflict between haves and have-nots." However, "certain elements of the movie are particularly South Korean, including its architecture" (Ulaby, 2019). This means that cultural content representing local values still works well, both nationally and globally. The problem is that cultural creators now understand the significant role of AI-driven recommendation systems. When they create cultural products showing similar subjects, trends, and genres, these cultural products are highly recommended by OTT services, which make them take the fastest track. Cultural creators heavily rely on Westernized cultural content, in terms of genres, themes, and special effects, driven by Netflix and for Netflix.

Global platforms arguably continue to destroy local specificities and identities, both culturally and structurally. Local OTT platforms in many countries mainly adapt and slightly modify global norms driven by Western forces. Unlike the 1980s and the 1990s when Western cultural firms dominated the global cultural markets with their popular culture, the early 21st century is witnessing the increasing dominance of Western players, now digital platforms, equipped with capital, AI, and cultural content. This level of dominance is far deeper and larger than that of the previous decades. "All or nothing" and "die or survive" are the mottos ruling the local cultural industries instead of collaboration or cooperation between the global and the local in the age of Netflix.

Netflix effects in the local OTT platform industry

Netflix's influence can be identified in the local OTT platform industry itself. Due to the increasing role of Netflix, telecommunications and cultural firms in many parts of the world have developed their own local distribution and exhibition systems, including OTT services and collaborations with global OTT platforms, which fundamentally shift the traditional norms of cultural distribution and exhibition. With Netflix beginning to take off domestically, local entertainment companies are taking steps to address the increased competition (Stangarone, 2019).

Local OTT services pay attention to the fact that Netflix has been at the forefront of algorithmically powered recommendations. Since *House of Cards*, the OTT giant Netflix has developed an increasingly complex stack of machine-learning algorithms, including an open source tool, to enhance system recommendations. There is no doubt that the most successful startup cultural firms, including local OTT platforms begin with Netflix-style algorithmic programming built into their software architecture from the outset. AI is in their DNA (Tercek, 2019). Netflix is at the forefront of applied AI in video delivery. Netflix utilizes AI to monitor bandwidth in the network. It also uses AI to monitor whether any particular subscribers share their

Netflix transforming global cultural norms   89

passwords with others like friends and relatives. Furthermore, AI is able to aid monetization of video by improving the environment for advertising (Tercek, 2019).

In the Korean OTT market, as Netflix-funded cultural products, including *Okja* (2017) and *Kingdom* (2019), achieved tangible successes and visibility, the local OTT industry has faced a steep battle against Netflix. In Korea, a handful of firms, such as POOQ (owned by three network channels, KBS, MBC, and SBS), Tving (owned by CJ E&M), and Oksusu (owned by SK Broadband) were the major players until recent years (Lee and Song, 2019). Due to Netflix's rapid penetration in the local market, however, these corporations, under favorable government policy, decided to make a big OTT firm, challenging global streaming giants, including Netflix in 2019, which consequently drove the merger of POOQ and Oksusu.

Regardless of the concern of market monopoly, the Korea Fair Trade Commission allowed the merger of these two local OTTs in August 2019. The name of the new service Wavve, partially symbolizes the Korean Wave. Wavve might have 14 million customers (Kim, M.G., 2019). This new OTT platform focuses on AI-driven services, while investing much money to secure cultural content in order to compete against Netflix. Wavve announced that it incorporates new digital technologies, such as 5G, AI, and big data. For example, Wavve provides a multi-view function to watch several scenes with no interruption, which means that it develops the quality of visual images and audience-oriented recommendation services with the help of AI and algorithms (Lim, J.H., 2019). One of the major stakeholders of Wavve is SK Broadband, which has developed several AI-related new technologies, and therefore, Wavve is expected to offer immersive media services based on SK Telecom's advanced VR and AI technologies to customers (Choi, M.H., 2019). Locally based OTT platforms influenced by Netflix "turn to advanced computer science to help their customers more easily find movies and television shows they like to enjoy." Consequently, "an advanced user interface requires the power of AI and machine learning, or applying AI to give systems the ability to learn and improve from their experiences without specifically programming them" (Frankel, 2018, 10).

The biggest change after Netflix's surge in Korea is an attempt made by some of the big content firms to band together and present a united front to Netflix. Fending off Netflix, let alone becoming a regional player, requires a continued shift by Korean producers into content of better and higher quality. Prior to the merger, the larger of the two streaming services, Oksusu, spent only $10 million on original content. The hope for the new joint venture is to increase the amount spent on streaming content to $180 million. In the end, a united front by the Korean entertainment industry blunts Netflix's ambitions; however, in the long run, it might be against the spread of Korean content more generally (Stangarone, 2019).

CJ E&M also teamed up with broadcaster JTBC to introduce an OTT media service in September 2019. The decision was made a day before the official launch of the homegrown OTT platform Wavve. CJ will be the

90 *Netflix transforming global cultural norms*

majority shareholder, and JTBC becomes the second-largest shareholder of the joint venture. The service, which is scheduled to launch in early 2020, will offer content from two companies (Jin, M.J., 2019). Consequently, as of September 2020, several local OTT platforms, including Watcha, Wavve, CJ E&M's Tving, and Korea Telecom (KT)'s Seezn, are competing against each other in the domestic cultural market. The new move explained above is crucial, as content producers and distributors need to

> form a virtuous cycle of reinvesting profits earned from various platforms on new content. The recent series of collaborations reflect domestic companies' growing recognition of online streaming service on back of the growing influence of global media giants like Netflix.
>
> (Jin, M.J., 2019)

Of course, the conglomeration of domestic OTT platforms supported by the Korean government has not beaten Netflix, as this global OTT platform has continued to increase subscribers.

Under this circumstance, the Korean government wants domestic OTT service platforms to join forces and collaborate as much as they can to fight global video platforms. As part of this plan, in August 2020, Korea Communications Commission (KCC) chairman Han Sang-hyuk had a meeting with four local platforms and stated, "At this point, when foreign OTT platforms are establishing a strong presence in domestic market, cooperation among local companies is strongly needed. We should work together on a K-OTT that's backed by strong support from the government." Although the government did not force a merger among local platforms, it clearly signaled local platforms to merge to secure a better position against Netflix (Kim, J.M., 2020).

However, the recent mergers of local OTTs have brought new concerns in the Korean cultural industry, as this trend results in a lack of diverse voices. The existing OTTs, again, like POOQ, owned by three network channels, KBS, MBC, and SBS; Tving, owned by CJ E&M; and Oksusu, owned by SK Broadband, were already big giants, as they were owned and operated by the biggest players in Korean broadcasting and telecommunication. With the recent mergers, the local OTT market certainly represents an oligopoly, which hurts diversity. As the newly established mega OTTs will focus on a few commercial genres in both production and distribution, locally produced genres focusing on culture, history, and general people's struggles will not be emphasized. As Kulesz (2018b, 83) points out, again,

> The rise of big platforms may represent a risk for diversity, while also causing a growing drought of data in the creative ecosystem, which may seriously affect decision making on public policies and leave local creative actors defenceless—due to, among other things, the advance of AI, a tool that is beyond their reach.

Netflix transforming global cultural norms 91

In this light, it is not dicey to argue that Netflix's recent rush in the Korean cultural industries works as a double-edged sword for many cultural producers. It is certainly good news for local entertainment firms, as they are able to find necessary funds from global digital platforms. However, it is not always positive, because it implies the possibility of the subordination of the Korean cultural industries to Netflix. America's invasion in the OTT industry will continue, as other digital platforms, including Amazon Prime, Disney+, and Apple Play vehemently target the Korean market. In the U.S., the number of moviegoers in terms of admissions per capita has decreased, from 4.3 in 2009 to 3.7 in 2018 (Motion Picture Association of America, 2019), partially because of OTT services, including Netflix. The Korean exhibition industry has transformed its structure to make multiplex cinemas as is the case in the U.S.; however, as American multiplex cinemas have continuously lost their audiences, the Korean market will likely show a similar trend in the near future.

As such, Netflix has become one of the largest and most important OTTs for the non-Western countries' cultural industries. The American platform influences the entire chain of audio-visual industries, and the local cultural industries' fortunes have severely fluctuated in the early 21st century. The local cultural industry is fragile and shaky due to Netflix. Only a few years after its launch in Latin America and Asia, Netflix has already become a formidable force as a global OTT platform, causing local cultural industries to wobble. Netflix is not only shifting people's watching habits, as people enjoy cultural content on mobile-based OTT services anytime instead of watching television programs when they air on TV for the first time, but it is also destroying the traditional norm of the local cultural industry. As Evens and Donders (2018, 1) argue, platforms have become "the dominant infrastructural and/or economic model in media, electronic communications and information, communication and technology (ICT) sectors," and Netflix has certainly played a leading role in this platformization. Netflix has controlled the entire circle of the cultural industry, from production to distribution to exhibition, on a large scale to actualize its status as a global empire, which fundamentally transforms the local cultural industry.

Conclusion

This chapter has discussed the increasing role of Netflix utilizing AI and algorithms in the global cultural markets. OTTs have shown their tremendous impacts in the global entertainment markets and digital platform industries, and the influence of Netflix in the local markets has been increasing in the early 21st century. Netflix as a global platform has built its own brand over the past several years in the Global South as well as the Global North, and its impacts continue to grow due to its unique business models utilizing an ample amount of capital and manpower. Netflix, which has been equipped with three major technologies and sources—AI, algorithms, and

92 *Netflix transforming global cultural norms*

big data—has transformed the entire chain of popular culture. Netflix is a triple crown winner in the OTT platform sector, which means that it greatly utilizes three main digital technologies—AI, algorithms, and big data—that have reshaped the norms of popular culture. As AI is reinventing media and culture, the outcomes that Netflix drive are much wider than predicted. The Netflix model shows a "new relationship established between algorithmic sorting and big data on the one hand, and cultural production and distribution on the other" (Flew, 2018a, 10).

OTT platforms like Netflix have not only become new players who transform the media environment surrounding cultural scenes, but also turned themselves into mega media giants. Mainly due to the soaring numbers of users and revenues based on their new business models supported by AI and algorithms, they easily compete with and even surpass old media, such as network broadcasting and film, in terms of viewership and revenue, while transforming the global cultural industries.

Netflix's effects across the entertainment business have taken root in deep and meaningful ways. It aims to tap into the efficiency of streaming video via the internet to build proprietary pipelines into people's living rooms, laptops, tablets, and smartphones. The largest U.S. streaming platform is bent on reinventing part of its operation as a direct-to-consumer distribution model, as the new media company has to develop extensive producer-to-consumer relationships. AI-saturated Netflix has rewritten the rules of broadcasting and movie deal-making, TV scheduling, film release outlets, and marketing strategies (Littleton, 2018). "Being Netflix" or "I am Netflix" models increase synchronization and standardization of the cultural industries and cultural content around the globe.

Netflix's effects are enormous in the local cultural industries, as Netflix and other streaming platforms like Amazon Prime continue to work as global digital platforms that appropriate global audiences with their cutting-edge technologies and cultural products. Netflix has consequently changed the audience's behavior as well. Although conventional television is still dominant, more and more viewers use mobile devices to watch films and television programs asynchronously and autonomously. Video-on-demand use and binge-watching are examples that illustrate a trend from mass communications to massive personalization (Bolin, 2014, cited in Mikos, 2016). "The large offer of the platforms allows consumers to individualize their consumption practice. The users integrate the new practices in their everyday routines, and they celebrate the consumption of television programs and films as social event" (Mikos, 2016).

In sum, Netflix increases the standard of innovation and quality of culture that fuel the entertainment industry and have rightfully bestowed on it the name of king of entertainment distribution. However, these trends have come at a cost, "a cost which strips away the style in how we watch and goes straight for the purity of the substance of what we watch" (Herberg,

2017). As van Couvering (2017, 1817) argues, digital platforms like Netflix increase in power, as

> the platform business creates revenue by controlling access to content stored within the platform and information about the platform. Social issues of privacy, intellectual property, and equity are all directly and immediately implicated in the AI-supported decisions about who can and who cannot have access to the platform's information and media content.

Netflix has become a business model for the majority of cultural corporations; however, only a few media giants are able to develop similar business models in contemporary platform capitalism. Netflix's effects in non-Western countries have been severe and destroyed traditional norms in cultural production and distribution.

Note

1 According to Convergence Research, a marketing research firm (Pressman, 2019), the ranks of cord cutters and so-called cord never's who never subscribed to pay TV in the first place, jumped to 30% of all households in 2018 from 26% a year earlier. It was expected to reach 34% of households in 2019. But when those entertainment-hungry consumers look for internet alternatives, the research firm found that they were much more likely to opt for more straightforward services like Netflix and Amazon's Prime Video rather than the multichannel online services like AT&T's (T) DirecTV Now. "Consumers become cord cutters when they cancel their traditional cable television or dish subscriptions and rely on streaming services to provide televised entertainment." The cord-cutting process is facilitated by consumers' high-speed internet connections and subscriptions to streaming services, including Netflix, Hulu, and Amazon Prime. The rise of such streaming services has "provided users with a viable alternative to accessing television content through traditional pay television outlets" (Tefertiller, 2018, 390). The cord-cutting phenomenon has not been a total loss for the cable industry because it is still the leading provider of high-speed internet connections (Pressman, 2019). However, it is certain that OTT services have gradually replaced traditional broadcasters. Originally, Netflix might have seemed as a simple intermediary; however, it has turned into one of the strongest mediators as a digital platform, competing against traditional media. Netflix has consequently challenged the traditional media and their business models in the global markets, as they face severe competition from Netflix.

6 Personalization of culture in the AI era

Introduction

Over the past two decades, the extent of the transformation processes affecting the cultural ecology has been far-reaching and profound. Over time, various technological innovations have offered new opportunities for cultural creators and cultural industries to fulfill and advance their roles. New digital technologies, including AI, have indeed emerged and transformed the incumbent media. The driving forces of this change are diverse, and they include the digitization of all forms of text, speech, image, and sound; the convergence of new media and popular culture; the increasing ubiquity of digital networks; and people's changing cultural habits. As a result of these processes, the relationship between providers and consumers of cultural content and services has fundamentally shifted (Sparviero, 2019).

As is well received, governments, digital platforms, and cultural corporations are the primary actors within cultural production, while people as customers are at the end of the front line of the process in cultural production. However, as AI-driven tools have the potential to transform the process of the production and distribution of popular culture, they can reshape the ways in which media audiences or the general public consume media and cultural content, which means that the relationship between cultural creators and users and, more generally, the conditions that control the wider cultural ecosystem are rapidly shifting (Helberger et al., 2019).

As previously discussed, this book comprehends AI-driven tools not only as a technology, but also as a socio-economic construct, because technologies are embedded in organizations with their own goals, values, and fundamental freedoms, and they mediate and impact interactions with the human/economic/social environment in which they are functioning. AI can affect the cultural ecosystem on three levels: cultural "production and distribution, individual news users, and the broader media ecology and society more generally" (Helberger et al., 2019, 4), and in this chapter, the primary focus is individual users. They are equipped with new and personal digital technologies, such as smartphones, notebook computers, and applications (apps), and they use these digital technologies to enjoy cultural

Personalization of culture in the AI era   95

content provided by AI-supported digital platforms. Therefore, contemporary media users are much different from the audiences who do not possess digital technologies.

This chapter discusses the ways in which AI has transformed customers, as several digital platforms supported by AI, such as social media platforms (e.g., Facebook and YouTube), OTT service platforms (e.g., Netflix and Amazon Prime), and music streaming service platforms (e.g., Spotify and Apple Play), connect production and consumption. It is necessary to investigate the process because these digital platforms and cultural industries have deeply influenced people's consumption habits. In the early 21st century, global youth equipped with new digital media enjoy popular culture and news on digital platforms instead of physically going to theaters or buying and possessing cultural materials. Therefore, it is vital to examine whether users in the realm of digital platforms are empowered by the growth of AI and AI-equipped digital platforms. It then addresses the personalization of popular culture as one of the most important characteristics in the AI era. It finally discusses the transformational force of AI in consumption in order to better understand the impacts of AI in contemporary digital society.

AI, digital platforms, and users

Several types of digital platforms, including search engines, social media, and OTT services, function differently in our contemporary society. While these platforms play a key role in forming and transforming people's daily activities, the major characteristics of these platforms are not identical. As Lobato (2019, 31–32) points out, again, compared to social media platforms like Facebook or Twitter, OTT platforms—in particular, Netflix—are not open, social, or collaborative, as they are "closed, library-like, and professional." The users of these different platforms, therefore, can be investigated differently according to their primary characteristics, and one of the effective ways to compare them is to contract their business models. AI tools, and mainly machine learning, could be used to computationally model the users of such systems. In particular, according to users' input—for example—their behaviors and interactive patterns, a model of users' traits, states, skills, and preferences could be built. This model could then be used to provide users with personalized content and experience adapted to each user. As an example,

> For music or movie consumption, a model of the users' preferences in terms of music/movie genre can first be built based on the users' previous choices of music/movie. Then, new music/movie, likely to be suitable to this user's taste could be provided based on recommender systems.
>
> (Vital Media, 2018, 7)

96 *Personalization of culture in the AI era*

Likewise, in other cultural areas, including digital games and education,

> a model of the users' skills can be built using their past performances at various game difficulty levels (for gaming) or exercises (for education). Then, an optimal sequence of challenges or exercises can be provided to each user, in order to provide the optimal difficulty level to that user, to optimize enjoyment or learning efficiency. Similarly, the users' affective or cognitive states could be modeled according to the users' behaviors and/or physiological signals (e.g., recorded facial expression, heart rate, brain activity) in order to then provide game challenges and training exercises maximizing the user's experience and enjoyment. Overall, AI can be used for modeling the user at two levels: 1) to estimate hidden user states (skills, affective states, cognitive states, etc.) and 2) to learn how to provide optimal content to this user according to these states.
>
> (Vital Media, 2018, 7)

There are several different approaches to consumers in conjunction with AI and digital platforms. Admitting that various dimensions exist, here I especially develop and discuss two major approaches so that people understand the significance of consumers: namely, in the Facebook model and users in OTT platforms—the Netflix model. As was fully discussed in Chapter 5, in many cases, "platform companies' focus on aggregation and distribution rather than production allows them to scale up quickly and to subsequently dominate markets" (Nieborg et al., 2020, 4). However, one of the most significant parts should be their basic business activities, and therefore, in this chapter, I focus on their major revenue sources, not corporate integrations. Their different business models are certainly characterizing major features of various digital platforms. By comparatively discussing these two different models relevant to media and cultural consumption, people may grasp the power relationships between AI-driven digital platforms and people as consumers, as well as the major characteristics of these two models themselves, which are some of the most significant and effective mechanisms in our contemporary capitalist society.

How to understand users in the Facebook model

There are various perspectives on the users of social media, and several scholars emphasized the role of users as free labor (Terranova, 2000; Fuchs, 2010, 2014; Jin, 2015) or affective labor (Hardt and Negri, 2004; Mansson and Myers, 2011; Schiller and McMahon, 2019). On the one hand, users sometimes function as free labor—working as non-wage workers in return for their use of digital platforms—which triggers a severe disparity between platform owners and platform users. As Terranova (2000, 37) especially points out, "Free labor is the moment where the knowledgeable consumption of culture is translated into excess productive activities that are pleasurably embraced and at the same time often shamelessly exploited."

Personalization of culture in the AI era 97

On the other hand, Hardt and Negri (2004, 108) point out, "Immaterial labor as labor creates immaterial products, such as knowledge, information, communication, a relationship, or an emotional response." This incorporated affective labor involves human contact and interaction, and as these scholars (2004, 110–111) argue, "Immaterial labor as a form of affective labor involves both body and mind that produces or manipulates affects such as a feeling of ease, well-being, satisfaction, excitement or passion." Meanwhile, Mansson and Myers (2011, 155) argue that "online activities are a form of affection" and "expressions of affection are used to maintain and develop relationships." Although their focuses are different, what they commonly believe is that users can be identified as labor force, either free labor or affective labor, which means that people's energy, time, and efforts are utilized by social media and search engine platforms. As Downey (2014, 147) points out, two major issues—"how a society values information, and how information circulates through a society"—were not well connected. However, critical scholars mentioned above have continued to develop their perspectives to connect these two areas in order to understand the ways in which AI-supported digital platforms utilize information provided by individual users in their monetization process.

More importantly, social media platforms like Facebook certainly develop value for advertisers through their own monetization strategies, which rely on users' data. Facebook (2012) utilizes AI-based algorithms to develop four major approaches, including "reach," "relevance," "social context," and "engagement," in categorizing user activities, which consequently create monetary values. In other words, with the rise of Facebook users, this particular social media platform not only intensifies data collection practices but also commodifies users' activities, exchanges, and relations that previously were not quantified. In the digital platform era, "Personal interactions and everyday economic exchanges are now captured through the standard datafied practices of friending, liking, sharing, rating, and recommending" (van Dijck et al., 2018, 33). Digital platforms have continued to claim that they do not use users' data in return for capital gains; however, their promises are not guaranteed, nor promising.

Most of all, "reach" means that advertisers can engage with monthly active users (MAUs) on Facebook based on information they have chosen to send to a vast consumer audience with Facebook's advertising solutions. "Relevance" implies advertisers can specify that Facebook shows their ads to a subset of Facebook users based on demographic factors and specific interests that they have chosen to share with the company on Facebook or by using the "like" button around the web. Facebook allows advertisers to select relevant and appropriate audiences for their ads, ranging from millions of users in the case of global brands to hundreds of users in the case of smaller, local businesses (Facebook, 2012). This is a criteria that algorithms can determine: "what is relevant, how those criteria are obscured from us, and how they enact" people's choices about appropriate knowledge (Gillespie, 2014, 168).

98 Personalization of culture in the AI era

'Social context' implies that the recommendations of friends have a powerful influence on consumer interest and purchase decisions. Facebook offers advertisers the ability to include social context with their marketing messages. Social context is information that highlights a friend's connections with a particular brand or business; for example, that a friend "liked" a product or checked in at a restaurant. Facebook believes that users find marketing messages more engaging when they include social context. Finally, Facebook emphasizes "engagement." This implies that Facebook believes that the shift to a more social web creates new opportunities for businesses to engage with interested customers. Any brand or business can create a Facebook page to stimulate an ongoing dialog with users (Facebook, 2012). Facebook's combination of reach, relevance, social context, and engagement gives advertisers enhanced opportunities to generate brand awareness and affiliation, while also creating new ways to generate near-term demand for their products from consumers likely to have purchase intent (Facebook, 2012; Jin, 2015).

Based on its sophisticated monetization strategies supported by AI and big data, Facebook has exponentially increased its number of users and advertising revenue over the past ten years. Facebook's monthly users worldwide increased 17.8 times, from only 140 million in 2008 to 2.49 billion in 2019, while its advertising revenue soared from US$300 million in 2018 to $69.6 billion in 2019, an increase of as many as 232 times (Facebook, 2012, 2016, 2020) (Table 6.1).

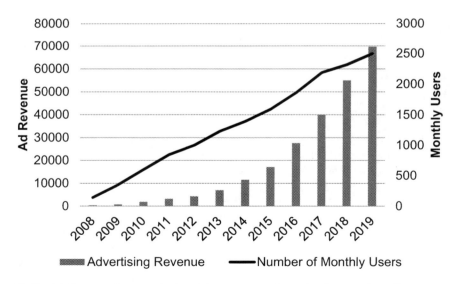

Table 6.1 Increase in annual advertising revenue of Facebook (unit: in millions)
Source: Facebook (2012, 2016, 2020).

Personalization of culture in the AI era 99

The Facebook model certainly appropriates users as passive individuals, as they do not actively challenge the platform's business standard in return for their affection, resulting in the spike of its profits. As Sparviero (2019, 76) points out,

> Users should not be necessarily considered passive, but also active, because it is with her actions (use, feedback, ratings, discussions with others, etc.) that she contributes to the creation of an image for the brand, which will influence her future choices and the choice of others.

However, users do not care much about what Facebook develops and earns from their activities. Users are active in their Facebook use, but passive in their seeking of rights. Social media, including Facebook and Twitter have consequently increased revenues, while greatly advancing their institutional power.

Utilization of user activities in the Netflix model

Compared to the Facebook model, OTT service platforms like Netflix show different perspectives and corporate strategies. Unlike Facebook, where users access this social media platform freely, global audiences in the audio-visual sector have moved from big screens (e.g., theaters and television) to OTT platforms, which are now the most popular paid services. For example, consumers who pay for online streaming services use them more often than any other video service.

> This change in behavior is not restricted to the smartphone generation and cord cutters. Pay-TV subscribers indicate that OTT and digital video viewing is overtaking hours spent watching linear broadcasts. . . . The shift to OTT is unstoppable. Younger, digitally-native consumers will grow up without an understanding of a traditional TV schedule or linear, appointment to view experience. Video viewing on broadcast TV will continue to decline. OTT platforms will be the major beneficiary of this change, becoming the platform of choice for all TV and video consumption, both live and on-demand.
>
> (grabyo, 2019, 9)

The customers of OTT platforms are not identical to those of social media and other digital platforms, like Google and Facebook, mainly due to their unique business model and their relationship with the customers. For example, Netflix has attempted to become a channel to introduce local content to people around the globe, which means that users are certainly the major component of the OTT system. As Jason Mittell (2019) points out, Netflix has developed a unique business model, which provides ad-free original programming alongside a library of older content for a monthly fee. Unlike

100 *Personalization of culture in the AI era*

social media platforms like Facebook and YouTube, which generate huge advertising revenues from free, user-generated content, Netflix thus far has not developed advertising models nor started using its data to track people online, package them to markets, or cross-reference their private messages.

This does not mean that Netflix is totally different from the Facebook model in terms of the utilization of users' activities. Netflix logs everything people have watched and how they watch—every time they pause, what programs they consider watching but choose not to, and when they are most likely to binge on *Friends* reruns. Therefore, that Netflix may partner with or acquire a marketing firm "to suffuse every subscriber's online experiences with micro-targeted ads seems more likely. All of these potential uses of viewing data are still speculative"; however, it is potentially a new business model for Netflix (Mittell, 2019).

Like Facebook, Netflix is also able to utilize users by developing its own AI-supported algorithms to increase the global demographic reach of cultural content. In other words, Netflix can boost the consumption of movies and television dramas by making them more accessible to international audiences who are actively participating in the recommendation system. The algorithms used by Netflix certainly help to develop new global audiences (Stangarone, 2019). Netflix uses a recommendation algorithm that asks users to recommend movies and television programs that they think people will love, and this particular algorithm produces up to 80% of entire sales (Kim, J.W., 2019).

Netflix itself reveals that the company groups all of its users with similar viewing habits and preferences into so-called taste clusters that help it find and recommend what type of content a particular user might like (Plummer, 2017; Sohn, 2018). The use of AI and data at Netflix is obviously related to the personalization of cultural content recommendation. Users who watch a certain movie are likely to watch another similar movie.

> This is perhaps the most well-known feature of Netflix. Netflix uses the watching history of other users with similar tastes to recommend what people may be most interested in watching next so that they stay engaged and continue their monthly subscription for more.
>
> (Yu, 2019)

This particular case of machine learning just in Netflix alone has had such scalable impact that Netflix has "forever changed the technology landscape and user experience for millions, with more to come. Adoption of this AI-related solution is only going to get stronger over time" (Yu, 2019).

As Elkins (2019, 381) aptly puts it, "Netflix repeatedly suggests that common tastes can be a bridge connecting viewers across cultures." Netflix groups its users into over 2,000 "taste clusters" or "taste communities" (Adalian, 2018, cited in Elkins, 2019). Netflix suggests that these taste clusters extend across geography, which means that it "found that taste communities

Personalization of culture in the AI era 101

transcend borders, and that your own "taste doppelgänger" might live on the opposite side of the globe" (Laporte, 2017). What makes Netflix unique is that it uses one predictive algorithm worldwide, and it treats demographic data as almost irrelevant. As vice president of product Todd Yellin said,

> Geography, age, and gender? We put that in the garbage heap. Instead, viewers are grouped into "clusters" almost exclusively by common taste, and their Netflix homepages highlight the relatively small slice of content that matches their taste profile. Those profiles could be the same for someone in New Orleans as someone in New Delhi.
>
> (Morris, 2016)

As its news release from 2016 (Gomez-Uribe, 2016) clearly indicates, Netflix developed a unique approach in clustering, as it saw that great stories transcend national borders and that Netflix users around the globe have more in common than they may actually realize. One way that Netflix generates personalized recommendations for individual viewers involves identifying communities of other viewers with similar television dramas and movie preferences and then making recommendations based on what is popular within that particular community. Rather than looking at viewers through the lens of a single country, Netflix's global recommendation system finds the most relevant global audience communities based on a member's individual tastes, regardless of where they live (Gomez-Uribe, 2016).

Netflix's idea of the taste cluster "celebrates the possibilities of cross-cultural taste similarities while erasing difference. It both invokes a trans-border, cosmopolitan affinity of taste while suggesting that identity status is not a determining factor in the construction of taste" (Elkins, 2019, 383). OTT platforms, including Netflix, collect data on their users and use them to produce popular series such as *House of Cards* and at the same time to present their users a personalized selection of cultural content (Mikos, 2016). As Frank et al. (2018) point out, "The Netflix data warehouse stores about 10 petabytes of information." With all that data flowing through the AI engine, Netflix knows people. It tracks the movies people watch, people's searches and ratings, when people watch, where people watch, what devices people use, and more. In addition to machine data, "Netflix algorithms churn through massive amounts of movie data that is derived from large groups of trained movie taggers" (Frank et al., 2018).

As such, approaches to access the users of Facebook and Netflix cannot be the same; however, the users on both platforms are working as digital labor to provide their information, energy, and time in return for affection. The users of Netflix and, in general, OTT platforms are exploited by digital platforms, as these OTT platforms use them to make a profitable recommendation system in the name of taste. In the case of Facebook, the users do not pay subscription fees, while working as free labor; in the case of Netflix, the users do pay subscription fees, and on top of that, they work as free labor.

102 *Personalization of culture in the AI era*

The degree of appropriation of users in OTT platforms is much higher than social media platforms. The Facebook model and the Netflix model seem to be different; however, the basic ideas are not much different, because they divide the users into several clusters according to similar backgrounds and utilize similar identities for their businesses: increasing ad revenues for Facebook and subscription fees for Netflix.

Disempowering empowerment of users in the AI age

While the two different models—namely, the Facebook model and the Netflix model—in digital platforms supported by AI, have differentiated their business strategies in utilizing users, AI has especially played contrasting and opposing roles in influencing the users: through both empowerment and disempowerment. Like other digital technologies, AI and digital platforms have developed a dual role, proving their ambivalent perspectives.

To begin with, empowerment implies that AI as a new cutting-edge digital technology would help users at the workplace. By implementing AI technology to handle everything from complex predictions to everyday tasks, creators and cultural companies find that employees are better able to focus on higher-level work that can result in greater efficiency, more creativity, and stronger business return on investment (Butler, 2019). Regardless of some concerns, others also believe that AI helps people do their jobs better at the workplace. AI technology and digital platforms empower audiences with more control (Asia-Pacific Broadcasting, 2018). With AI technology's shift from the lab to the mainstream in the last decade, workforces from nearly every industry have expressed concern about the future of their positions. There is a misconception that AI will replace human creativity and ingenuity, turning content creation, distribution, and marketing into vanilla, machine-driven tasks. There are several ways that AI may actually help empower the entertainment workforce (Butler, 2019): 1) allow for more creativity and strategic thinking, 2) provide intelligence on the content that will drive the strongest results, 3) create new growth and innovative business opportunities, 4) enable new and unique experiences for audiences, and 5) turn niche interests into viable markets for content. AI and digital platforms enable audiences to present their power, which means that they allow viewers "to customize their own selections and content preferences" (Asia-Pacific Broadcasting, 2018).

According to this perspective, which emphasizes the optimistic aspects of AI, AI does not limit the range and diversity of content.

> In reality, the opposite is true. AI can help new and diverse voices find audiences. It can also transform niche content genres into viable markets and give rise to a new generation of creators who are reflective of society's diverse interests and tastes.
>
> (Butler, 2019)

Personalization of culture in the AI era 103

We have only begun to understand AI's applications for entertainment and how technologies can empower the industry's workforce. Those who embrace how AI can help, inform, and enable a new era of entertainment will be in the best position to thrive as AI evolves further. Popular social platforms like YouTube, Instagram, and Twitch have brought content to viewers that TV was not paying attention to or had written off completely, such as gamers (Butler, 2019). In other words, AI "can help to empower numerous creators, make the cultural industries more efficient and increase the number of artworks, which is in the interest of the public" (Kulesz, 2018a, 2). As Vincent (2019a) points out,

> Machine learning is particularly well-suited for this sort of task because it can spot patterns in a big pot of data. More importantly, the "consumption patterns" his company studies are always evolving. What people watch and how they do it has changed hugely in the last few years. It's better to have a system built with machine learning that can adapt to these shifts, rather than a hard-coded algorithm that has to be updated manually.
>
> (Vincent, 2019a)

In other words,

> The economies of data mining redefine relations of power, not merely by selling user attention but by tapping into "the everyday life" of users and refashioning it from within, guided by commercial norms such as the presumed value to advertisers.
>
> (Langlois and Elmer, 2013, 4)

However, there are also a number of caveats that go hand in hand with these advantages. Some of the most important challenges are the potential of AI to create bias in popular culture that "users are exposed to, the necessity to collect and store extensive data on all users, the risks of targeted manipulation, and the limited agency users experience while interacting with AI-driven tools" (Helberger et al., 2019, 11). This perspective clearly claims that AI disempowers users. As van Dijck et al. (2018, 33) point out, while datafication is able to be understood as a techno-commercial strategy deployed by platform owners, it can concurrently be regarded as a user practice. Digital platforms systematically collect and analyze user data. At the same time, they circulate these data through application programming interfaces to third parties and through user interfaces to end users, enabling them to trace the activities of friends and colleagues, keep track of public events, and participate in the online economy. These scholars also emphasize the mechanism of the commodification of user data. For them, "commodification is intensified by mechanisms of datafication as the massive amount of user data collected and processed by online platforms provide insight into

104 *Personalization of culture in the AI era*

users' interests, preferences, and needs at particular moments in time" (van Dijck et al., 2018, 37).

Commodification mechanisms are "empowering and disempowering to users" (van Dijck et al., 2018, 37). They are empowering because customers have power to decide what they want, and OTT platforms must meet the audiences' needs.

> The traditional TV schedule is becoming less and less relevant for many demographic groups and with the upcoming launch of major new OTT services . . . the pressure on the traditional TV model will increase. OTT enables choice, flexibility and better value for consumers, we should expect the growth of these services to continue to accelerate.
>
> (Roxborough, 2019)

At the same time, it is disempowering platform users, because various platforms exploit cultural labor and the immaterial labor of users, while actualizing the precarization of platform service workers. As van Doorn (2017, 904) aptly puts it, it should be stressed that the structural degradation of platform work

> is a central strategy for valorizing the tension between its indispensability and expendability, as it allows companies to keep hiring rates high and labor prices low, thus optimizing the exploitation of precarious workers looking to supplement their wages in order to make ends meet.

Furthermore, these mechanisms "lead to a concentration of economic power in the hands of a few platform owners and operators, because they strategically position themselves as aggregators and gatekeeping mediators" (Fuchs, 2014; van Dijck et al., 2018, 37). Concerns about the impact of AI on the cultural sector are increasing.

More specifically, several considerations indicate that AI disempowers users. This is particularly important, as AI-driven recommendation technology can create considerable gatekeeping power regarding the information diets of users. The gatekeeping power of platforms, such as Google, Facebook, and Netflix, exceeds the ability to define the priorities of feeds. These platforms also increasingly use AI-driven tools to filter specific types of content (Helberger et al., 2019). AI-driven tools reshape the way consumers enjoy cultural content. Digitization and datafication also affect the overall structure and diversity of the cultural landscape. There are new players such as social media platforms and OTT service platforms arriving on the scene and affecting the process of producing, distributing, and exhibiting culture. An immediate side-effect on the role of culture in society is the disaggregation and unbundling of cultural products but also the amplification of mis- and disinformation and the potential for malicious manipulations of popular culture. The reliance on big data also creates a new economy of scale, in

Personalization of culture in the AI era 105

which those players with the most access to data are better able to provide personalized news to users (Stone, 2014; Helberger et al., 2019).

Unlike in the traditional media and cultural industries, which depart from the idea of a sender transmitting culture and information to an unidentified mass audience, one important implication of the use of AI-driven tools in the cultural sector is that audiences can be targeted in terms of far more precise groups, or even on an individual level.

> Automated filtering and sorting mechanisms can affect the exercise of an individual's right to receive culture and information based on personal characteristics and preferences. The use of AI-driven tools must not result in a situation in which certain parts of the population or users with particular characteristics are structurally excluded from accessing information, or where society experiences new digital divides.
>
> (Helberger et al., 2019, 28)

In the AI-driven digital environment, "the audience is more than an anonymous mass of receivers." Users have "a greater influence over the dissemination of online information" and culture. Therefore, it is critical for individual members to take a more active role in the process of producing and distributing culture (Helberger et al., 2019, 29). In the AI era, what we have to focus on is the impact on the most disempowered and marginalized people in our society (Bacciarelli, 2019).

AI algorithms have become the alchemy of our digital age, "the search for a magical, mystical process" that guides people to "turn a pile of data into gold. They are widely seen as a silver bullet that can generate new insights and expert decisions on an unprecedented speed and scale" (Taylor, 2019). AI can be categorized as

> a source of opportunity for oppressed and marginalized people, with tremendous focus put on closing the hardware, software, and access gaps on the Internet for various communities. Among the most prevalent ideas about the political aspects of technology disenfranchisement and opportunity are theories that center on the concept of the digital divide.
>
> (Noble, 2018, 160)

Digital divide narratives have focused on a few primary dimensions of disempowerment that have led to technological deficits between access to computer, development of skills and training in IT technologies, and internet connectivity (Wilhelm, 2006; Noble, 2018).

It is not uncommon to witness that new digital technologies have advanced both empowerment and disempowerment. However, in the case of AI, it is crucial to understand these opposing aspects carefully because the general public, for the most part, cannot understand this particular digital

106 *Personalization of culture in the AI era*

technology. Again, AI can empower and disempower users, both cultural creators and consumers. Regardless of its promise, AI has brought about several negative aspects, as it disempowers users. AI is evolving, and some of the problems will be resolved. However, as discussed, AI itself adds several socio-economic and cultural problems to contemporary society. Instead of helping users, this new digital technology has continued to function negatively. The disempowerment of users has been increasing, and AI is also connected with representational harms.

The personalization of culture: the relationship between platforms and audiences

One of the most significant aspects in tandem with users in the age of AI and digital platforms is the personalization of popular culture and news. Regardless of different platforms, whether social media platforms or OTT service platforms, personalization has been significant, as individuals are considered a valuable entity for digital platforms and cultural industries corporations. While several different interpretations can be possible, I mainly divide the personalization of popular culture into two different perspectives: one emphasizing the role of major platforms and the other focusing on the customers, both of which are closely connected.

Most of all, the personalization of culture and information can be driven by digital platforms to maximize their profits. For the Facebook model, users are categorized into several segments in order to be sold to advertisers. Personalization helps Facebook organize users according to their specific features, such as age, gender, ethnicity, and preferences. Facebook's "like" especially plays a role as a personal recommendation. Whenever people click "someone's post" or "post" their individual stories and comments, their Facebook friends are able to see them. Since October 2016, Facebook has also launched new features it believed would make the social network more useful in people's everyday lives. Facebook added a recommendation tool that helps people discover new places, events, things to do, and services around people by drawing on their friends. If they find an event to attend, Facebook has made the ticket-buying process more seamless. And when it's time to interact with a business, there are new call-to-action buttons you can use. For Facebook, everything is "one virtuous circle of family, friends, business, and ad dollars" (*Wired*, 2016). In a nutshell, personalization is the reason why so many people are attracted to AI-equipped digital platforms. As van Dijck et al. (2018, 42) point out, "Customization and personalization also empower users as consumers and citizens, enabling them to quickly find the most attractive offer and the information they are interested in." On the flip side of the same token, personalization is a major business strategy for digital platforms as one of the primary business models to garner profits.

In Korea, similar to the Facebook model, Naver—the country's largest internet portal—has started to use its own AI-based personalization services

Personalization of culture in the AI era 107

for news and search since early 2018. Content consumption in Naver has increased sharply because of applying its AI content recommendation algorithm AiRS (AI Recommender System) to Naver and line news services. According to Naver, the daily average page view of AI content exposed to Naver's news edition increased by 69% in a year. The number of daily users in a handful of foreign countries increased by 176%. The same company plans to expand its personalization search to some users (Korea Tech Today, 2019).

More importantly, Naver's news section has been organized by AI software since April 2018. The company decided which news appeared in what order in the news section. The news section appeared as part of the portal site's home page but is set to be moved deeper into the site as it starts to shift to a simpler landing page. The news section displays trending news articles recommended by the company's artificial intelligence software AiRS. Users can see different articles based on an algorithm that tracks the user's news consumption pattern. Which specific article among many dealing with the same topic is also decided by AiRS. Naver's main news service is composed of two sections: one where the user can view articles selected by the news outlets they follow and the other where AiRS shows personalized articles (Song, K.S., 2018). What Facebook and Naver drive is the personalization of digital content so that users are able to consume essential information and news according to their own preferences. As Humphreys (2018, 29) points out, "One of the primary critiques about social media use is that people are sharing mundane and meaningless information." Therefore, the personalization of culture and information implies that AI provides necessary information and news that individual users want to see and read. AI-based personalization is to dramatically shift people's use of digital platforms.

Meanwhile, for the Netflix model, users are able to be categorized by their tastes so that Netflix recommends similar cultural content to individual users. As Kopenen (2018) argues,

> An intelligent notification system sending personalized notifications could be used to optimize content and content distribution on the fly by understanding the impact of cultural content in real time on the lock screens of people's mobile devices. The system could personalize the way the content is presented, whether serving voice, video, photos, augmented reality material or visualizations, based on users' preferences and context.
>
> (Kopenen, 2018)

AI can offer manifold advantages to the way audiences as users find information and cultural content. AI-driven recommendation systems can identify the most relevant cultural content for a user, taking into account the context of cultural consumption. For example, a user may want to watch a different television drama while commuting to work than on a Sunday morning.

108 *Personalization of culture in the AI era*

Personalized recommendations and programs "can also cater to different consumption habits related to our different social roles, as employees, family members and citizens" (Helberger et al., 2019, 11). New AI-driven tools can even adapt cultural content "to users and the context of use, and thereby increase the chance that the news users come across can be processed and is useful" (Helberger et al., 2019, 11). This means that new digital technologies, including machine-learning algorithms, have transformed power relations. Machine-learning algorithms backed by big data "are not merely used to normalize individual behavior but rather to predict patterns of a given group or population" (Bueno, 2020, 80). In other words, "Machine-learning algorithms do not operate based on a pre-given template that links a facial image to a concrete identity. Instead, machine-learning algorithms use statistical calculation in order to extract patterns from the training datasets" (Bueno, 2020, 80). AI-equipped digital platforms have controlled the vicious circle of cultural production, from production to consumption, to empower themselves more than individual users, and therefore, it is certainly a new type of contemporary digital capitalism, which utilizes not only digital technologies but also digital platform users as major sources for their revenues.

As discussed above, AI in tandem with digital platforms evidently develops the personalization of culture. What is interesting is that these AI-equipped digital platforms have advanced "personal culture," compared to mass culture. From the consumers' perspectives, this means that people consume media and popular culture personally instead of enjoying cultural content together at theaters and living rooms. Since digital platforms like Facebook and Netflix supported by AI and algorithms have recommended particular cultural content to individual users, these audiences consume popular culture personally and selectively, which characterizes contemporary cultural preferences. In the age of AI, again, many digital platforms, from social media platforms to OTT platforms, "aim for increased levels of personalization" (Pangrazio, 2018, 12). For example, "Netflix uses data analysis to predict audience behavior rather than to estimate the performance of a particular program. In this sense, Netflix is in the content personalization business" (Tercek, 2019). Other platforms have also advanced the personalization of culture. For example, Google serves up different search data to individuals by learning not only their most influential links, but the ones people, personally, might be looking for, based on what they have clicked on before. Of course, the dominant digital platform is the smartphone, "through which people create a personalized interface with the world, with their own personally curated set of apps." People are constantly "having individual experiences when together, with life plus screen creating a personalized experience of everything" (Mawdsely, 2016). People's cultural consumption in the AI-equipped digital platform era increasingly witnesses personalized experience.

Personal culture as one of the most distinctive characteristics of the contemporary cultural sphere refers to not only popular culture and media produced and recommended by AI-equipped cultural producers and digital platforms but also cultural consumption conducted individually on and through digital platforms, including social media platforms, such as YouTube and Facebook, and OTT service platforms like Netflix. Since AI and algorithms in the realms of popular culture and media have developed personalized recommendation systems as can be seen in Netflix and Facebook, personal culture implies the entire process of cultural production, distribution, and consumption in the age of digital platforms. As people prefer Netflix to home theaters and like smartphones over home telephones, people in the early 21st century have deeply advanced the personalization of culture in their consumption.

Of course, audiences' practices are mostly driven by AI-equipped digital platforms. The personalization of culture is very important in enabling digital platforms to reach out to the local market and audiences, as they create relevant cultural content to keep their audiences satisfied through the personalization of culture. Although AI empowers audiences, content personalization technically empowers digital platforms with massive control. As Arnold (2018, 49) aptly puts it, "This represents a shift in audience measurement and interpretation from the notion of the personalized mass to the personalized, the individuated, and the autonomous." In this regard, Ang (1991, cited in Arnold, 2018) claimed that the audience was consequently figured as "depersonalized" and "part of a whole," but, paradoxically, a powerful mass that exercised relatively free choices (of limited content options) that were subject to later sampling and analysis. However, unlike this kind of interpretation, in the era of convergence of AI and digital platforms, audiences have experienced disempowering empowerment, and therefore, their participation as individual users is certainly exploited by mega digital platforms.

Personalization vs. network society

Another significant perspective of the personalization of culture in the AI age is its contradictory nature to so-called network society, which has been one of the most established phenomena in the digital era. With the rise of the internet, people have lived in a network society, as everybody is connected through digital technologies (Castells, 2009). According to the *Oxford Dictionary*, a network effect refers to "a phenomenon whereby a product or service gains additional value as more people use it." The quintessential example of a network effect is the internet itself, which would provide very little value if only a few people used it. Social network platforms like Facebook are also classical examples (Breakstone, 2019). In the era of AI, an intelligent network effect is a network effect where the value added is facilitated or augmented by AI. In other words, the intelligent network effect is a phenomenon whereby a product or service gains additional value as more people use it, primarily through the mediation of AI. With the proliferation

110 *Personalization of culture in the AI era*

of AI, many people around the globe witness a shift from traditional networks toward intelligent networks. For example, social media platforms are no longer gaining value by the sheer number of their users alone but also by using AI to surface relevant news, profiles, and events. Likewise, for marketplaces, it's no longer only about the abundance of supply and demand but also about algorithms crunching data and profiling users to serve a precisely tailored product or service to a potential buyer at the right time to maximize the chances of a gratifying transaction.

What is interesting here is that these social media platforms and OTT platforms as intelligent networks have not facilitated cultural communities, but instead expedited the personalization of culture. While the networked digital economy may enhance the autonomy of individuals, it clearly helps personal culture, as people use these platforms to enjoy individual popular culture. As Benkler (2006) aptly puts it, media and culture take on

> socio-cultural roles, structures of control, and emphases of style that combine their technical capacities and limits with the sociocultural business context into which they were introduced, and through which they developed. The result is a cluster of use characteristics that define how a given medium is used within a given society, in a given historical context. They make media differ from each other, providing platforms with very different capacities and emphases for their users.
>
> (369–370)

By definition, it is not dicey to claim that we are living in an intelligent network society, as networked individuals connected with each other in a mesh of loosely knit, overlapping, and flat connections.

> In a substantial departure from the range of feasible communications channels available in the 20th century, AI has begun to offer us new ways of connecting to each other in groups. As we have software coevolving to offer new, more stable, and richer contexts for forging new relationships beyond those that in the past have been the focus of our social lives. These do not replace the older relations. They do not make a fundamental shift in human nature into selfless, community-conscious characters. We continue to be complex beings, radically individual and self-interested at the same time that we are entwined with others who form the context out of which we take meaning, and in which we live our lives.
>
> (Benkler, 2006, 376–377)

However, AI-supported digital platforms have segregated people from each other. In the age of AI, digital platforms force people to enjoy personal culture, which is in opposition to the network. AI-equipped digital platforms have shifted the major norm of a network, which is the fundamental theme

Personalization of culture in the AI era 111

of our information society. With AI and algorithms, people live in a highly segmented cultural world, and they pursue personal culture.

This does not mean that people as the customers of AI and digital platforms avoid any mass culture produced by traditional media and cultural firms. Instead, they enjoy popular culture produced by traditional media and digital platforms recommended by AI algorithms on their own digital platforms. Digital platforms like YouTube and Facebook, which expedite the personalization of cultural life, also provide venues on which people can connect with each other, as the case of BTS fans—known as ARMY— certainly proves. Although ARMY members enjoy BTS' music individually, they communicate and share their feelings and emotions through social media networks, including Twitter. "Precisely because the new communication system is so versatile, diversified, and open-ended, it integrates messages and codes from all sources, enclosing most of socialized communication in its multimodal, multichannel networks" (Castells, 2009, 417). AI and digital platforms are a double-edged sword in our highly networked, but individualized, cultural scenes. They have driven the personalization of digital platform users by segmenting them based on their taste; however, as the users also utilize these platforms to share their feelings, while organizing some events, either fan events or social events, they are still networked. The convergence of these two seemingly unrelated perspectives has become a new norm in our contemporary society.

Conclusion

This chapter has discussed the users of AI and platforms, as these new digital technologies deeply influence users' behaviors in cultural consumption as well as cultural production. The AI, corporate logic, and informational architectures of major platforms play a central role in people's cultural activities. It discussed how AI has transformed customers, as several digital platforms supported by AI like social media platforms, OTT services, and music streaming service platforms connect production and consumption. It analyzed whether users in the realm of AI-supported digital platforms are empowered by the growth of AI and AI-equipped digital platforms, while addressing the critical nature of the personalization of popular culture. "These combined elements regulate the 'coming into being' of a public by imposing specific possibilities and limitations on user activity" (Langlois et al., 2009, 417). AI especially functions as a new digital technology in advancing people's working environments and empowering users. There is certainly a sense of enthusiasm for AI technology, and this appears to drive uptake.

> It is difficult to disentangle the degree to which this is enthusiasm for new technology and new devices or the AI enabled services themselves. The influence of social norms around digital use were referenced by

112 *Personalization of culture in the AI era*

> participants in all markets, suggesting that the adoption of AI enabled services are at least in part, supported by the need for social approval.
>
> (Consumers International, 2019, 16)

What is significant, though, is that AI does not guarantee users' well-being in their cultural consumption. I am not talking about the potential loss of jobs due to the rapid growth of new technologies, but the critical implications of AI in people's cultural activities. Digital platforms equipped with AI, algorithms, and big data utilize users as their financial resources. Both social media platforms and OTT service platforms gather personal information in return for their affection and information.

AI has continuously transformed contemporary society, including the cultural scene. We cannot deny that AI contributes to the creation of cultural content, while empowering the users of digital platforms. However, AI has also brought socio-cultural risks, and there has been some doubt about the crucial role of AI in popular culture, as the users do not benefit from the spread of AI in cultural production, distribution, and now consumption. AI has empowered users, but is disempowering them as well, while actualizing the personalization of culture. AI's contribution to society is imbalanced and even skewed as it intensifies socio-cultural inequality and biases by providing great opportunities to digital platforms. Machine-learning algorithms are widely adopted and pervasively used in our everyday lives. They have begun replacing human decision makers; however, the algorithms do not always behave fairly and equitably (Shin, D., 2019b). AI users through digital platforms, either Facebook or Netflix, create value to what they consume by clicking the touch screen on smartphones or the keyboard on the computer and dragging the mouse with no monetary reward, resulting in an asymmetrical relationship between digital platforms and users. Furthermore, they are aggressively appropriated by AI-equipped digital platforms unfairly, unequally, and inadequately in a seemingly advanced contemporary society.

The disempowerment and the personalization of culture are some of the most significant socio-cultural issues in the age of AI. AI and digital platforms have greatly influenced users' cultural activities. Regardless of its potential to transform our contemporary society, including the cultural sector, however, AI has not been a solution to resolve some existing social biases. As AI has mainly supported digital platforms and mega media giants, the users of AI through digital platforms have limited benefits from the convergence of AI and digital platforms.

7 AI journalism, social media platforms, and fake news

Introduction

In the early 21st century, journalism has increasingly relied on technology. From traditional journalism, including newspaper and broadcasting, to social media like Facebook, digital technologies, in particular AI and big data, are used to produce and circulate news and information. The convergence of journalism and digital technology is not new, as computers, the internet, and mobile phones have reshaped journalism over the past several decades. In other words, journalism has continued to change its business and editorial norms with each wave of new technology. Handwriting made way for mass printing. The telegraph sped up news collection across long distances. The telephone and radio accelerated journalism even further. And in just the past 30 years, journalism moved from radio to television to cable to the internet, and in each iteration the nature of journalism greatly changed (Briggs and Burke, 2009; Carey, 2009; Schmelzer, 2019). Likewise, journalists have also adapted to work with various digital technologies, and many of them now work with AI, either voluntarily or forcibly (Diakopoulos, 2019b).

Among new digital technologies, AI has especially transformed the journalism industry, as

> automation has changed the way journalists work, from the analysis of large amounts of data to the way information is distributed. With the introduction of machine-written news, computational journalism entered a new phase. Each step of the news production process can now be automated: "robot journalists" can produce thousands of articles with virtually no variable costs.
>
> (van Dalen, 2012, 649)

Until the emergence of AI in journalism, the nexus of journalism and digital technology pointed mainly in one direction: digital technologies supporting humans. With AI, the notion is not true anymore, as journalists deeply worry that the increasing role of AI tools may totally replace them. In fact, AI has arguably replaced and/or supported human writers, editors, and

114 *AI journalism, social media, and fake news*

producers, at least partially, if not entirely, in the journalism industry. As AI has become a new tool in reshaping contemporary society, news organizations around the globe are increasingly leveraging AI to shift the way news is generated, produced, and shared. AI may change traditional journalism even further and is expected to continue to change the way that "news is created, generated, managed, published, and shared." Although it is in its infancy, in the near future, AI may produce news articles, perhaps exactly like the kind people read now (Schmelzer, 2019).

There are some caveats, of course, including an AI divide between mega media organizations and small media companies, both domestically and globally. AI technology also raises the question of fake news in tandem with digital platforms, such as Facebook, Twitter, and TikTok, as much of fake news increasingly circulates on social media platforms. One of the most existential questions of the digital age is about the ways in which social media platforms have been caught so unprepared for the rise of fake news, misinformation, disinformation, and digital falsehoods, which eventually work as "the ultimate tools of democratic destruction" (Leetaru, 2019). As van Dijck et al. (2018, 51) aptly put it, therefore, "The current ascent of social media platforms as central actors in the news sphere should be seen in the light of the evolution of platformization," and it is critical to comprehend the increasing role of platforms supported by AI in contemporary journalism.

Several previous studies (Montal and Reich, 2017; Linden, 2017) in the field of AI journalism focused on the relationship between AI-supported automated journalism and human journalists, analyzing the impact of AI on the jobs in journalism. Unlike these studies, this chapter primarily maps out the implications of AI and algorithms in the realm of journalism, which must be foregrounded in the larger context of the digitization of media—a transition toward algorithms and social media—and therefore, it examines the ways in which AI and big data have reshaped journalism as an institution (Lewis, 2019). AI technologies, regardless of how transformative they prove to be in the long term, might be understood as part of a broader story of journalism's reconfiguration in relation to data and new computer-driven systems and contemporary society (Lewis, 2019). By raising the question of what AI does mean for journalism, this chapter aims to discuss how AI and big data have transformed the journalism landscape as we have known thus far. This chapter also investigates the ways in which social media platforms like Facebook, Twitter, and TikTok, as some of the most significant social media and news platforms, produce and disseminate fake news. In so doing, it critically examines the increasing role of AI in producing news culture and its effects in journalism.

AI and the platformization of journalism

Digital platforms are closely related to AI, and therefore, cultural production and consumption, as discussed in Chapter 2. Digital platforms, such as social media platforms (e.g., Facebook and Twitter), search engines (e.g., Google), and over-the-top (OTT) service platforms (e.g., Netflix and Amazon Prime) are "fueled by data, automated and organized through algorithms, and interfaces, formalized through ownership relations driven by business models, and governed through user agreements." These platforms "automatically collect large amounts of data—both content data and user data" (van Dijck et al., 2018, 9). In addition, "Algorithms are another significant technological ingredient defining the connective architecture of platforms," as they are sets of automated instructions to transform input data into a desired output (see Gillespie, 2014; Pasquale, 2015, van Dijck et al., 2018, 9). In other words, algorithms play a pivotal role "in selecting what information is considered most relevant to us" (Gillespie, 2014, 167). These technological relations are related to the ownership status and business model of digital platforms.

Again, digital platforms should be understood not only by their technological aspects, but also by their commercial and cultural aspects. Digital platform owners who are primarily mega media and technology giants have developed strategies to appropriate user activities in order to transform users' daily performances into monetary revenue resources.

During this process, platforms moderate and even curate at an increasingly enormous scale; however, they also have to remain open to the circulation of user-generated content to a degree that would never be tolerated by traditional media in order to survive in their present form (Flew, 2018b). This lack of oversight, either intentionally or unintentionally, partially provides a ground for the growth of several socio-cultural problems, including fake news.

While this is not new, the massive commercialization and commodification of platform users have further raised concerns because only a handful of platforms dominate the global markets (Jin, 2015). As Helmond (2015, 5) argues, in this regard, platformization, referring to "the rise of the platform as the dominant infrastructural and economic model of the social web and the consequences of the expansion of social media platforms into other spaces online," has been actualized by social media platforms. For example,

> Facebook employs its platform as an infrastructural model to extend itself into external online spaces and how it employs these extensions to format data for its platform to fit their economic interest through the commodification of user activities and web and app content.
>
> (Helmond, 2015, 8)

In the realm of journalism, with the emergence of the participatory web (Jenkins, 2006), user-generated content has become a significant part of journalism as well as digital culture, as this new trend has brought noticeable changes to journalism. Social media platforms have influenced the ways in which news is reported and shared across populations and how news

116 *AI journalism, social media, and fake news*

and information are expanded through connective social media platforms (Pangrazio, 2018, 8). Digital platforms like Facebook and Twitter, which originated in the Global North, as well as TikTok in China and Naver in Korea in the Global South, have been significant because they are supposed to enable a fundamental shift from the mass-mediated public sphere to the platform-driven public sphere (Benkler, 2006). The rapid circulation of news through digital platforms has

> led to widespread and effective forms of media manipulation. . . . Digital platforms might democratize the creation and circulation of news, however, in doing so questions around what news is, how it gets made, shared and read in online contexts are also raised.
>
> (Pangrazio, 2018, 8)

In fact, these platforms are expected to provide opportunities for people to mobilize themselves effectively for social change (Jin, 2015). With the rise of digital platforms, communication—in particular, journalism—has also become a more important feature of the digital society (Fuchs, 2008), as social media platforms have effectively functioned as news aggregators. While traditional news media employ professional journalists or algorithms to select content from a relatively limited set of professional news publications, on social media, everyone can share news or other content from anyone and from anywhere. This implies that what is shared tends to be a much more heterogeneous and fortuitous content mix, containing news from mainstream news agencies to the widest variety of other sources (van Dijck et al., 2018, 52–53). Social media platforms, as alternative media, have provided opportunities to develop a public sphere; however, they also bring about negative dimensions due to their role in creating and spreading fake news as well as severe commodification and commercialization of news and information.

More specifically, two types of democratic disruption (instead of democratic enhancement) have occurred through social digital platforms. On the one hand, several social media platforms, including Facebook and Twitter, produce fake news based on their AI algorithms. On the other hand, a few social media platforms like TikTok eliminate specific information that might hurt governments and corporations and, therefore, distort truth. Although TikTok has several good features, this particular video platform used by many young people across the globe creates a new concern for many. TikTok employs AI to analyze users' interests and preferences through their interactions with the content, and it displays a personalized content feed to each user.[1] Regardless of its popularity as a relatively new social media platform, TikTok could ban "criticism/attack towards policies or social rules of any country, such as constitutional monarchy, monarchy, parliamentary system, separation of powers, and socialism system" (Deloire, 2019; Hern, 2019).

AI has intensified the platformization of journalism, as several digital platforms have functioned as a new form of journalism. While one of the major functions in journalism is to enhance the value of the public sphere (Habermas, 1991), platforms are based within the corporate sphere, which means that AI-supported digital platforms serve corporate and economic values. Again, as Lewis (2019, 673) argues,

> The implications of AI for journalism must be foregrounded in the larger context of the digitization of media and public life—a transition to apps, algorithms, social media, and the like in ways that have transformed journalism as institution: undercutting business models, upending work routines, and unleashing a flood of information alternatives to news, among other things.

AI is transformative, and its role should be understood as part of a broader context of journalism's reconfiguration in relation to digital technologies.

Transformation of journalism in the age of AI

There has been a continuous development of journalism in the digital age. The newsrooms in traditional media organizations like broadcasting and newspaper companies have to accommodate the significant impact of social media platforms, and they have already transformed their practical ways, such as new coverage formats and mobile-friendly news articles. AI, as one of the most recent digital technologies, has especially transformed journalism, both newspaper and broadcasting, while expediting the growth of social media platforms as news agencies. As newsrooms embrace the age of AI, the norms of news and journalism have once more changed considerably.

There are several advanced AI systems that media organizations develop and use in both the Global North and the Global South. As mainly discussed in Chapter 2, at the heart of several AI systems is ML—a subdomain of AI.

> Machine learning relies, in turn, on a process called deep learning, a method of breaking down a complex idea into a series of smaller, more approachable tasks that ultimately lead to a designated endpoint. But for machines to learn, they need to be taught.
>
> (Marconi et al., 2017, 7)

Media organizations—although only a few mega media firms are able to develop and maintain AI journalism—have advanced their own AI systems for journalism. AI journalism here means journalism that is generated from large data sets processed by AI, which is also called automated journalism (Green, 2019).

In the field of journalism, media organizations have already used robots to write very simple writings on stock markets and sports like baseball since several years ago. For example, the *Wall Street Journal* churns out millions of words encouraging investors to buy or sell stocks, bonds, and mutual funds each day. In the future, more of those words are expected to

118 *AI journalism, social media, and fake news*

be written by robots, not humans (Yang, 2015). Automated journalism, also loosely known as robot journalism, is a relatively new phenomenon (Montal and Reich, 2017). However, robot journalism is only part of AI journalism, because robot journalism implies a limited replacement of human journalists to write a few areas based on a given capacity, while AI journalism is based on ML, which itself learns and advances the writing process. More specifically, as Graefe (2016) aptly puts it, automated journalism refers to

> the process of using software or algorithms to automatically generate news stories without human intervention—after the initial programming of the algorithm. Once the algorithm is developed, it allows for automating each step of the news production process, from the collection and analysis of data, to the actual creation and publication of news.

What we have to keep in mind is that automated journalism works for fact-based stories for which structured data are available, which means that this type of news journalism needs clean and reliable data for the process. Only in such conditions, algorithms create content, personalizing it to the needs of individual readers, which are quicker and have potentially fewer errors than might be achievable by any human journalist.

AI journalism also provides the personalization of news and information. AI journalism allows for providing relevant information for very small audiences.

> The ability to personalize stories and analyze data from different angles also provides opportunities for generating news on demand. For example, algorithms could generate stories that answer specific questions by comparing the historical performance of different baseball players. Algorithms could also answer what-if scenarios, such as how well a portfolio would have performed if a trader had bought stock X as compared to stock Y. While algorithms for generating news on demand are currently not yet available, they will likely be the future of automated journalism.
>
> (Graefe, 2016)

Automated journalism, however, has rapidly grown to cover several complicated areas, even including elections, so its challenge to human journalists is just beginning.

Major media organizations, including the *Associated Press* (*AP*), *The Washington Post*, *The New York Times*, and *Forbes*, in the Global North have greatly invested in AI journalism. Their focuses and levels of automated journalism are not the same, but they commonly pursue AI-supported journalism practices. Among these, *AP*, as a news agency, has advanced a few AI journalism projects. *AP* began using AI for the creation of news content in 2013 by drawing data to produce sport and stock earnings reports. Back

AI journalism, social media, and fake news 119

then, *AP* used NewsWhip to keep ahead of trending news stories on social media platforms, such as Twitter, Facebook, and LinkedIn (Underwood, 2019). *AP* has continued to work to build its own AI system and expanded the coverage. For example, *AP*'s election development team built its own machine-learning algorithm that assists in determining the probability of a political race outcome. The achievement made by *AP* is notable because vote counting requires extensive manual labor, and by augmenting the calling process with machine learning, *AP* is able to "streamline a process where speed and accuracy are paramount" (Marconi et al., 2017, 8).

As one of the leading newspapers in the U.S., *The Washington Post* also developed and released Heliograf, which can generate entire articles from quantitative data. As briefly discussed, newspaper companies have used their AI systems to cover relatively simple sports events. *The Washington Post* is no exception. The newspaper company leveraged AI technology to report key information from the 2016 Rio Olympics, including results of medal events by using Heliograf, which was developed in-house, automatically generating short multi-sentence updates for readers (WashPostPR, 2016a).

However, *The Washington Post* has rapidly expanded its use of AI in non-sports areas, as it announced it would use AI to cover house, senate, and gubernatorial races for all 50 states on Election Day through Heliograf. Jeremy Gilbert, director of strategic initiatives at *The Washington Post*, stated that this unprecedented level of election coverage would allow the newspaper company to personalize the experience by surfacing races for readers based on their location. Using Heliograf's editing tool, *Post* editors can also add reporting, analysis, and color to stories alongside the bot-written text. Editors are able to easily overwrite the bot text if needed (WashPostPR, 2016b). The articles will be "living stories," first beginning as a preview of a race in the days leading up to the election. On Election Day, stories will update with results in real time and then, after a race is called, the story will provide analysis of the final results. Geo-targeted content will surface in the *Post*'s live blog and in special Election Day newsletters to readers, offering updates on races in their state. The company's AI is the connective tissue that allows *The Washington Post* "to combine these different sources and to power Heliograf so that it can write highly personalized stories for the benefit of journalists and readers alike" (WashPostPR, 2016b). With the recent adaptation and use of AI, *The Washington Post* (Moses, 2017) has increased its capacity to write articles using the AI system. In its first year, the newspaper company produced around 850 articles using Heliograf. That included 500 articles around the election that generated more than 500,000 clicks.

The Washington Post has continued to develop AI-supported systems. In 2017, *The Washington Post* launched a system called ModBot, which automatically reads the comments made on its website to determine if they meet quality standards or should be moderated away. Maintaining the quality of the online comments section is a major challenge that many online news sites struggle with (Park et al., 2016). ModBot can save hours of manual human

120 AI journalism, social media, and fake news

effort sifting through comments. In making its determination of whether a comment should stay or go, one of the signals that the AI picks up on is the use of abusive language (Jiang and Han, 2019). Interestingly though,

> the system was explicitly designed to set the abusive language bar higher for public figures, with the recognition that criticism of public figures must be allowed in a forum dedicated to fostering deliberative conversation on issues of societal import. By developing its own system for moderating comments, the *Post* was, therefore, able to better match the operational behavior of its AI with professional ethical and normative expectations.
>
> (Diakopoulos, 2019a, 679)

Several other major newspapers and broadcasters have also started to adopt AI and developed their own AI-supported news production and circulation systems. In addition to aggregating information, some media organizations are putting into place AI systems that generate entire articles from scratch (Schmelzer, 2019). They believe that they cannot survive without AI. As in the case of *The Washington Post*, *The New York Times* has adopted and used machine learning to enhance its campaign finance coverage. It has developed a lot of work with campaign finance data sets, which are characteristically hard to navigate and understand. *The New York Times*, however, has developed its unique system because algorithms can recognize patterns in data that may have been deliberately obfuscated (Marconi et al., 2017).

Meanwhile, *USA Today* has used video software to create short videos, while *Forbes* has rolled out an AI-powered content management system called Bertie that suggests content and titles. Furthermore, *Bloomberg* uses Cyborg for content creation and management. Many of these organizations use AI to generate shareholder reports, legal documents, press releases, general reports, and articles. As will be discussed in detail later, automated software bots also create fake news and even fake comments, helping to magnify fake stories through shares and social media endorsement (Schmelzer, 2019). However, media owners are more excited about AI's potential to go beyond simple reporting (Moses, 2017).

Of course, AI in journalism is not that simple. Due to its complexity and the necessary manpower involved, only a few media organizations can build their own AI systems. Even these leading media organizations in AI have to work with other technology firms instead of creating all the necessary technologies by themselves. *AP*, in fact, partnered with Graphiq, a corporation that uses more than 250 billion data points from sports, politics, weather, and other sources to automatically generate clear and concise visualizations that allow news media like *AP* to offer interactive graphics for dozens of stories each day (Marconi et al., 2017). There are several vendors like Graphiq that are privatizing aspects of AI, making it dramatically easier for media organizations, including the reporters and writers in these organizations, to

AI journalism, social media, and fake news   121

rapidly learn and utilize these tools. Justin Pang, head of publishing partnerships at Google, indeed elaborated on the possibility for collaboration between media outlets and AI system providers. As he emphasized, it is estimated that media firms and user-generated content like YouTube create over two billion digital images and video watch time each day, and therefore, this explosion of unstructured data needs to be stored, analyzed, and utilized. This practice is an increasingly important area where media firms closely partner with technology companies like Google and Facebook that have supportive infrastructure and expertise in areas like ML (Marconi et al., 2017, 7–8).

While AI is still in its early stages, digital platforms and news media organizations have increased their use of AI systems to uncover data from multiple sources and automatically summarize them into news articles and reports. Machine learning algorithms have proved to be adept at finding patterns in textual data and uncovering the useful information that accurately summarizes the data inside. By using these advanced algorithms against enormous quantities of data from press releases, blog posts, comments, social media posts, images, video, and all sorts of unstructured content, media organizations are able to get quickly up to speed on fast-breaking news developments and generate journalism content that accurately summarizes changing environments surrounding several major socio-political events (Schmelzer, 2019). The platformization of news and AI also means that AI tools are used to gather information for marketing operations. ML systems easily identify patterns gleaned across various channels that indicate engagement rates with content and find hidden patterns that can suggest better ways to connect with readers and provide better results for advertisers and content monetization. "AI-enabled content personalization is guiding the reader with relevant content regarding their interests and suggest other articles to read. This keeps readers on news sites longer and gets them more engaged with the writing and content" (Schmelzer, 2019).

Compared to this, the adaptation of AI for the production of news in the journalism industry has not been noticeable in non-Western countries other than a few exceptions. For example, in November 2018, China's state news agency Xinhua introduced a male AI anchor who reports "tirelessly" all day every day. Chinese viewers were greeted with a digital version of a Xinhua news anchor named Qiu Hao (Figure 7.1). Developed by Xinhua and the Chinese search engine, Sogou, the anchor was developed through machine learning to simulate the voice, facial movements, and gestures of real-life broadcasters, to present a "a lifelike image instead of a cold robot" (Kuo, 2018). Xinhua also introduced a female AI anchor in February 2019. Although they are yet perfect, these cases certainly show what the future of broadcasting scene will be about in the AI age.

Meanwhile, in Korea, newspaper companies are relatively small in terms of their financial structure, and therefore, it is not easy to develop or use AI-supported technology. The broadcasting industry has not advanced any

Figure 7.1 Xinhua News' AI Anchor Qiu Hao

specific AI tools too. As discussed in previous chapters, a few internet portals, comparable to digital platforms, like Naver, Daum, and Kakao, have developed and used AI technology to recommend news. While fake news on social media has also become a major agenda for Korean society, AI use in media—in particular, Korean journalism—is not noticeable. When Kim et al. (2018) produced an edited volume titled *The Fourth Industrial Revolution and the Future of Media* in January 2018, only a handful of pages were dedicated to AI in journalism, and even so, they mainly highlighted the introduction of foreign examples as the recent trend. AI in journalism is relatively weak, compared to the use of AI in several major internet portals in the Korean context and in the Global South. The AI divide between the Global North and the Global South, as well as between a handful of mega media giants and the majority of small- and mid-sized media institutions, has deepened and fundamentally hurts the majority of media companies around the globe in the AI era.

Since the late 2000s, media institutions have undergone a transition due to the increasing role of social media and smartphone technologies (Jin, 2013). They are now experiencing another breakthrough, mainly because of AI and big data; however, the majority of media institutions in both the Global North and the Global South cannot catch up to the new development because of the lack of capital and manpower. The AI divide has intensified the gap between a few rich media institutions in the Global North and the majority of poor media corporations in the Global South as well as within countries. The influence of social media on these media institutions was just

AI journalism, social media, and fake news   123

a breeze; AI will hit media institutions much harder than any other digital technologies, which we have never seen.

Fake news, AI, and digital platforms

While media organizations, both newspapers and broadcasters, have continued to develop and advance their AI systems to resonate with their journalistic standards, although limited to a few mega companies, the use of AI in social media platforms has shown a very different direction. As discussed, automated journalism in newspapers and broadcasters works for fact-based stories for which clean, structured, and reliable data are available (Graefe, 2016). However, AI use in digital platforms in tandem with journalism is much different from traditional journalism, as they create fake news with no fact-based stories.

There has been no doubt that the rise of social media has transformed how people consume news and information. Unlike traditional media, including newspaper and broadcasting, social media platforms expedite the fast circulation of news as users share news and information at the click of a mouse. Due to their unique functions and capacities, social media platforms play a key role during natural disasters by disseminating news and warning signals as quickly as possible. The general public also share news, while expediting the circulation of any information through online and eventually offline friends. For example, Facebook comes with a share function, and "users can either share an article on their own page, or post it on a friend's page, or send it through private messaging either to a particular friend or to a group" (Tandoc et al., 2019, 674).

In contrast to several positive possibilities of social media platforms as alternative media, they have instead brought about several negative impacts to contemporary society. Again, the rapid circulation of news through digital platforms has "led to widespread and effective forms of media manipulation" (Pangrazio, 2018, 8). Among these, fake news has deeply influenced not only people's daily lives but also the news ecosystem itself. Fake news is not new, but has rapidly grown since the mid-2010s. As Table 7.1 clearly shows, newspaper articles on fake news around the globe have increased, from 2,010 cases in 2015 to almost 60,000 cases in 2018.[2] This data, although limited to newspaper articles that can be accessed via a Lexis Uni database, certainly proves the recent surge of fake news in our society.

What I emphasize here is the critical nexus of fake news and AI, as AI plays a key role in producing and circulating news. Due to their enormous influences, news organizations are right to consider the rise of fake news a serious issue. "It not only has the potential to mislead large numbers of people, but also to draw audience views and engagement away from real news produced by legitimate news organizations" (Tandoc et al., 2019, 673). Of course, AI technology is also able to function to block fake news on social media platforms, although this function is currently limited.

124   AI journalism, social media, and fake news

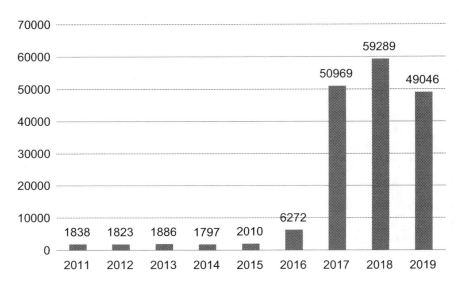

Table 7.1 Number of newspaper articles mentioning fake news, 2011–2019
Source: Lexis Uni Database.

Increasing fake news in the Global North

There are several precedent cases of fake news; however, people have mainly begun to pay attention to fake news because of politics. The role of Facebook as the predominant social media platform that spreads fake news became clearer on a large scale during the 2016 U.S. presidential elections. Back then, Facebook played a role in spreading false and misleading information, known as "fake news," from Russia and from inside the U.S. about candidates. Ever since then, the dissemination of fake news has continued to rise. As the *Associated Press* (*AP*, 2019) reports, Avaaz, an advocacy group that tracks misinformation, says it has found an increase in fake political news shared on Facebook ahead of the 2020 presidential elections. Avaaz found that, collectively, fake stories were posted more than 2.3 million times and had an estimated 158.9 million views, along with 8.9 million likes, comments, and shares. Most of the false news sources were individual users or non-official political pages. Avaaz said in the report that the findings are the "tip of the iceberg of disinformation" ahead of the 2020 elections (*Associated Press*, 2019).

The blame mainly goes to social media platforms, of course. As is well documented (Pangrazio, 2018, 12–13),

> The goal of many platforms to personalize, customize, and tailor user experience, means individuals become aligned with social groups that

can lead to a kind of group think approach to news and information. This also means factually incorrect information, or fake news, can be rapidly spread through social groups and networks which share the same or similar beliefs and values.

Fake news can be produced because of the combination of the users who want to make money in a broad sense (e.g., influence and power as well as capital) and consumers who share the information and news as they believe them to be true through social media platforms. Social media platforms in this sense mediate two different users to garner monetary profits and network power.

Due to several occasions of fake news related to the presidential election and privacy invasion, Zuckerberg had to testify before the U.S. Senate in April 2018. In his opening remarks Zuckerberg said that Facebook did not do enough to prevent its tools from being used for harm—citing fake news, interference in foreign elections, hate speech, and data privacy (*CBC News*, 2018). Zuckerberg promised to deploy AI to help solve some of the company's biggest problems, by policing hate speech, fake news, and cyberbullying, although it has been an effort that has seen limited success so far (Knight, 2019).

Facebook has consequently advanced its fact-checking system to curb fake news on its own platform. In 2019, Facebook (2019) itself announced it removed 3.39 billion fake accounts from October 2018 to March 2019. Facebook said nearly all of the fake accounts were caught by AI and more human monitoring. They also attributed the skyrocketing number to automated attacks by bad actors who attempt to create large volumes of accounts at one time (Romo and Held, 2019).

Whether creating or blocking fake news, the complexity of fake news is intrinsically intertwined with the logic of the AI algorithms behind social networks, including Facebook.

> The mechanisms of personalization and tailored content play a special role in this context, possibly creating filter bubbles—in which intellectual isolation is caused by digital algorithms that selectively assume what kind of information the user would like to see—and echo chambers, in which closed media systems reinforce beliefs.
>
> (Borges and Cambarato, 2019, 610)

The issue of fake news is further "exacerbated as social media sites, along with other online platforms, are used to deliver and generate political news and information to ideologically segregated audiences through the use of sophisticated geotagging and microsegmentation strategies" (Brummette et al., 2018, 498).

More specifically, Facebook's own news feed was originally born in September 2006, promising to provide a personalized list of news stories

126 AI journalism, social media, and fake news

throughout the day. In the early stage of the service, news feed ranking was turning knobs: turn up photos a little bit, turn down platform stories a little bit. Facebook advanced from "turning knobs" to EdgeRank, the algorithm that a) determined which of the thousands of stories (or "edges" as Facebook called them) qualified to show up in a user's news feed and b) ranked them for display purposes. EdgeRank had three primary pieces: 1) affinity (i.e., how close is the relationship between the user and the content/source?); 2) weight (i.e., what type of action was taken on the content?); and 3) decay (i.e., how recent/current is the content?). EdgeRank made it possible for Facebook to give users a more personalized news feed (McGee, 2013). For example, users who played many games on Facebook could see more game-related content in their news feed. But now that job is a lot more complicated than ever. In fact, in 2013, Facebook changed to a machine-learning algorithm that considers more than 100,000 weight factors when producing news feeds (McGee, 2013). In 2018, Facebook, one more time, overhauled its long-term plan, which was "prompted largely by feedback that posts from friends and family having been increasingly drowned out by content from brands and publishers, deterring people from interacting more with people they care about" (Chaykowski, 2018). Facebook equipped with AI has continued to develop new functions to attract more users, which means that the personalization of items has been intensified through a delicate AI system.

Fake news and regulation in the Global South

Fake news is not only limited to Western countries; it is also common in non-Western countries. As social media platforms themselves are global, fake news is occurring everywhere. Several Asian countries like Korea and Singapore have experienced the rise of fake news and planned to regulate fake news through various measures, which are sometimes controversial because these regulatory mechanisms may hurt democracy as well. Korea, for example, has experienced a surge of fake news on social media platforms since the mid-2010s. While stories vary, fake news related to politics has continued to grow, which demands that the Korean government take action. The Korean government planned to crackdown on fake news, calling it

> a destroyer of democracy. Speaking at a cabinet meeting, former Prime Minister Lee Nak-yon said that fake news had spread so widely in Korea that it was stymying not only citizens' privacy but also the country's national security and foreign policies, including its relations with North Korea. Lee continued to say, Fake news is a public enemy hiding behind the cover of free speech,

and therefore,

AI journalism, social media, and fake news   127

we can no longer turn a blind eye to it.

(Chae, S.H., 2018)

Mr. Lee told the Korea Communications Commission (KCC), a government regulatory agency, to act on online media sources that serve as avenues for fake news.

Consequently, KCC called for the creation of more institutions dedicated to checking whether or not certain information is based on fact, in a bid to stop the spread of fake news in the nation. Han Sang-hyuk, who took the office as KCC chairman in September 2019, made the following remarks during his first luncheon with journalists, "Both ruling and opposition parties, as well as members of the public, are all aware of the problem of fake news; thus it is surely necessary to come up with proper countermeasures." He said, "I believe that boosting fact-checking institutions trusted by the public could be one measure; however, it would be improper to establish such an institution within the KCC as it could provoke concerns over government infringement of freedom of speech" (Jun, J.H., 2019c).

However, the crackdown on fake news is very controversial due to its potential to curb the freedom of speech. Lee Hyo-seong, the former KCC chairperson, resigned partially because of the disputes surrounding his role regarding the handling of fake news. The government demanded a very strong policy measure to curb fake news; however, Chairperson Lee of the KCC emphasized voluntary regulative measures. Lee, who was a critical media scholar before taking over the position, continued to emphasize that "outright fake news certainly negatively influences the people; however, it should be controlled by voluntary measures developed by civic activities instead of regulatory laws" (Kim, J.H., 2019).

Meanwhile, Singapore has enacted a law to control fake news. In November 2019, Singapore passed a controversial anti-fake news law that gives authorities sweeping powers to police online platforms and even private chat groups. The government can order social media platforms to remove what it deems to be false statements that are against the public interest and to post corrections. The Singaporean government has emphasized that the law would not be used to target opinions, but only falsehoods that could prove damaging. "Free speech should not be affected by this bill," Law minister K. Shanmugam told parliament, adding that the law is aimed at tackling "falsehoods, bots, trolls, and fake accounts" (Wong, 2019). However, critics claim that it is a serious threat to civil liberties.

Interestingly, based on the new law, the Singaporean government asked Facebook to issue a correction in November 2019, which was actually implemented. Facebook has added a correction notice to a post that Singapore's government said contained false information. It is the first time Facebook has issued such a notice under the city-state's fake news law (Butcher, 2019). Singapore claimed the post, by fringe news site States Times Review (STR),

128 *AI journalism, social media, and fake news*

contained scurrilous accusations. The note issued by the social media giant said it is "legally required to tell you that the Singapore government says this post has false information." Facebook's addition was embedded at the bottom of the original post, which was not altered. It was only visible to social media users in Singapore (*BBC News*, 2019).

As discussed thus far, there are mainly two types of AI use in journalism. One is adopted by news organizations themselves, and the other is used by digital platforms—in particular, social media platforms. As the producers and distributors of news and information, these media organizations and social media platforms have certainly adopted and utilized AI in writing and distributing news and information. Whether talking about media organizations or social media platforms, what we have to focus on is whether AI has fundamentally transformed the nature of journalism and what the consequences are. AI-equipped social media platforms function as both the creators and disseminators of fake news, including political news. Fake news in these non-Western countries on social media platforms has been increasing, as with Western regions. These non-Western countries do not benefit from the growth of AI in journalism but heavily experience the increasing role of social media platforms in spreading fake news that disturb contemporary society and democracy.

Human journalists in the age of AI journalism

There are several imminent social issues in relation to the rise of AI use in journalism. In particular, as fake news has been burgeoning on social media platforms, news organizations, including newspaper companies and broadcasters, clearly recognize fake news as a social problem. They mainly consider fake news "as a social media phenomenon that breeds on political polarization driven by mostly ideological, but sometimes also financial, motivations" (Tandoc et al., 2019, 686). News organizations have continuously blamed digital platforms and even audiences for the rise of fake news in the political environment.

There are several innovative ways to deal with fake news. For example, specialized monitoring systems, such as those provided by the startup News-Whip, are providing news organizations with 21st-century radar systems that are helping them spot more trends and respond more rapidly in their coverage decisions. In addition to scale, scope, and speed, the technologies are also moving the needle on accuracy. In the case of the automated earnings project at *AP*, the error rate in the copy decreased even as the volume of the output increased more than tenfold (Marconi et al., 2017). "The reason for the lower error rate is that algorithms do not make typos or arithmetic miscalculations . . . . The errors are generally because of a problem with the data. If the data's bad, you get a bad story" (Marconi et al., 2017, 17).

However, it is certain that the major players who deal with fake new issues in journalism should be journalists themselves, not technologies, nor data,

AI journalism, social media, and fake news   129

mainly because they work as trained and well-balanced professionals. As Tandoc et al. (2019, 687) argue,

> Journalism is founded on truth, regardless of whether it is favorable or not to any particular individual or group. Real news is based on facts so that public opinion and decision are not misguided. As fake news competes with real news for audience attention as well as for credibility, the journalistic field cannot always—and exclusively—blame external forces for its internal woes.

Christians (2019) also points out that the gathering and dissemination of news are not simply the construction of information and data. He (2019, 166) clearly argues that

> reports do not simply mirror reality or in online journalism serve as modules in a technical network. The professional newsmaker's occupational task is the production of truthful knowledge. For the ethics of truth, the reporters' concerns are not primarily how to treat their sources or how to minimize harm to their audiences and viewers.

More specifically, the most significant part of journalism in dealing with fake news is humans, as the new era of augmented journalism will not fulfill its apparent promise without the diligent management and care of the journalists learning how to put these new technologies into practice (Marconi, 2017). Again, AI in journalism is another form of cultural production. With the rapid growth of AI in the media and cultural industries, media organizations and digital platforms have rapidly increased their investment in AI algorithms. AI-supported journalism certainly helps media organizations and reporters/writers regardless of their concerns around the replacement of humans. As van Dalen (2012) argues, automated content creation certainly affects the journalistic profession; however, we cannot be discharged as technological determinism alone, because the platformization of AI journalism is part of larger trends in journalism and society (Örnebring, 2010). Under this circumstance, the adaptation of AI resonates with the commoditization and commercialization of journalism. It is critical to understand that the automation of routine journalistic tasks cannot be determined by technology alone. As Marjoribanks (2000) already pointed out, socio-cultural elements and the institutional contexts of media organizations and markets, such as the work culture, position of journalism unions, or the relations between media owners and workers, together shape the way new technologies, including AI, would be adapted. AI has certainly reshaped the nature of journalism; however, surrounding socio-economic dimensions have also influenced the transformation of journalism, including journalists.

As digital technologies "do not erase social problems but merely shift and obscure them" (Broussard, 2019, 678), AI has not developed any big

130 *AI journalism, social media, and fake news*

differences. Journalism may benefit from using AI tools to "commit acts of journalism, but at its heart, journalism is about telling stories about the human condition" (Broussard, 2019, 678). Humans supported by AI may resolve some serious socio-cultural issues relevant to the rise of AI in the realm of journalism. The crucial cooperation of humans and AI will be a space that the journalism industry has to develop, not only for the sake of journalism, but also for the growth of democracy. Ultimately, while AI helps enhance the speed and scale of news in routine situations, complement and augment journalists, and even create new opportunities for optimization and personalization that would not otherwise be possible, it still cannot do most news work, and, in many cases, creates new tasks and forms of work. In short, the future of AI in journalism has a lot of people around (Diako-poulos, 2019a, 680);

> These technologies are opening up new territory and changing journalism in ways no one might have predicted even a few years ago. And they arrive at a time when journalists and media companies are searching for new solutions to the challenges that the digital revolution has imposed on the news business. Not only is it imperative to save time and money in an era of shifting economics, but at the same time, you need to find ways to keep pace with the growing scale and scope of the news itself. With social networks playing such a big role today in the expansion of the news ecosystem, news organizations need to keep constant track of what's trending among news consumers in real time.
>
> (Marconi et al., 2017, 17)

AI journalism will be the combination of humans and technologies, and therefore, people need to develop a new business model to accommodate AI in the journalism system, instead of casting humans out of the system, which cannot be actualized.

Conclusion

This chapter has discussed the increasing role of AI in news production and distribution. Alongside the cultural industry, the journalism sector has been one of the two major areas in which people and organizations have adopted and are using AI and algorithms for production and circulation of creative work. From news writing to dissemination, news producers, including reporters, editors, and owners, are gradually focusing on the role of AI as part of the production of news. Many media organizations and owners believe that AI may offer benefits to media organizations, as they cover stories without increasing the number of human reporters. Accuracy and speed are also considered as major benefits that media organizations can get from the use of AI.

AI journalism, social media, and fake news 131

Within the broader context of journalism and society, there are several caveats that AI journalism has brought about. AI has significantly transformed journalism; however, as the journalism industry is heavily relying on digital technologies and big data, the role of human journalists has declined. Regardless of the growth of several forms of digital technologies, journalism has been "a deeply human endeavor" over the past several decades (Broussard, 2019, 678). In the early 2020s, human journalists and AI-equipped robots have been competing against each other.

What is significant is that contemporary journalism has also heavily relied on social media platforms for the circulation and consumption of news and information produced. In fact, the biggest problem in AI journalism is the increasing role of social media platforms as new forms of journalism. Without creating news themselves, they function as news media outlets by (re-) producing and disseminating news and information. In the digital platform age, AI also produces news and, in some cases, fake news. Fake news on social media platforms has especially disturbed contemporary journalism, which means that fake news negatively influences the role of journalism as a public sphere.

Meanwhile, although AI-driven journalism may enhance accuracy and speed, it does not guarantee the quality of journalism, focusing on diverse voices and, therefore, a public sphere. As AI-supported journalism does not care about normative values, while focusing on data, speed, and accuracy, contemporary journalism has lost its foundational values. As is well documented, from the onset, journalism has consisted of value-laden media practices (Alexander et al., 2016). Accuracy and speed are important, but enhancing the values that our society must keep up is a real value for journalism. As many media publishers face declining revenues and digital transformation challenges their values, "there is no going back," which means that "the move to AI journalism is simply a logical progression" (Siarri, 2019). It is crucial to sustain true journalism value in the AI age. Both media organizations and social media platforms have developed AI technology and AI-supported production; however, they must resolve the fake news issue in order to develop their public sphere function in addition to their financial growth.

Last, but not least, as Grossman (2018, 65) points out, automation also brings about "a possible adverse effect on labor via the displacement consequence and by diminishing the proportion of labor in national income, but it may be offset by the creation of innovative tasks." Our contemporary society has to understand that "news reporting still requires human intervention, critical thinking, and relationship building. Consider AI as an ally that can help sort and integrate information, refine the presentation of articles and other mediums, and assist with distribution" (Siarri, 2019).

In the early 21st century, journalism has faced two consecutive blows from two major technologies: digital platforms and AI. Social media platforms

132 *AI journalism, social media, and fake news*

equipped with AI and big data provide both the technical and socio-economic infrastructures and the new tools for communicative practices (Pangrazio, 2018, 9); however, they also function as the providers of several negatives to society. AI is not an option anymore in the production and circulation of news and information through media outlets and digital platforms. Enhancing media ethics, curbing the increasing power of social media platforms, and advancing news and information unrelated to fake news are, therefore, necessary assignments for both media scholars and journalistic practitioners in the age of AI.

Notes

1 ByteDance—which developed TikTok—is a company that deals in AI development such as machine learning and original algorithms. Meanwhile, its work includes big data analysis for the understanding of user behavior (BeautyTech.jp, 2018). It is the international version of the Chinese app Douyin, but TikTok itself is not available in Chinese app stores.
2 In order to figure out the recent increase of fake news, I used a Lexis Uni database with the keyword 'fake news.' There are several different forms of news outlets, including blogs, but I limited myself to newspapers; therefore, the actual numbers of stories on fake news are much higher than this, although articles on fake news in newspapers are good enough to show the trend.

8 New media ethics in the age of AI

Introduction

New digital technologies, including AI, big data, and algorithms, have raised numerous concerns, as several Western societies and global mega platform giants like Google, Facebook, and Netflix preoccupy AI and algorithms to make profits, resulting in socio-economic disparities between platform owners and platform users. These digital platforms have begun to utilize AI as a major tool for cultural production, and therefore, several socio-cultural concerns have been raised as "AI may be misused or behave in unpredicted and potentially harmful ways" (Cath, 2018, 2). As Elliott (2019, 49) points out, new digital technologies, including AI, produce "stunning opportunities and dangerous risks" at the same time. Several ethical issues in AI, such as "interface with social and cultural issues," "the manipulation of data," and "complex systems and responsibility," as well as "privacy invasion," are shared with other rapidly developing digital technologies (Boddington, 2017).

In other words, concerns about the massive circulation of fake news, the ability to manipulate algorithms for financial profits, and alleged privacy breaches and the misuse of personal data through social media platforms, have been features of contemporary society worldwide (Flew, 2018b). AI has also caused several new socio-economic dilemmas, including the potential replacement of humans in workplaces. Therefore, questions on the role of the law, relevant policy, and ethics in governing AI systems are more relevant than ever before. In other words, as AI systems are developed, it is crucial to assess their social and ethical standards and implications (Hancock et al., 2020).

Governments and corporations around the globe seem to advance mechanisms to secure socio-economic fairness; however, due to AI's fast and recent growth, these measures are not practical or transparent. Many governments have enacted legislation to present a vision aimed for the intelligent information society, while attempting to establish human-centered ethics to govern data collection processes and AI algorithms. By emphasizing social security, transparency, and accountability, these standards underscore whether AI and big data–driven industrial policies present any biases or produce reliable

134 *New media ethics in the age of AI*

results and ethical frameworks of society. Of course, governments proposed these legal and ethical standards eventually to develop best practices for AI and big data, creating policy mechanisms meant for the government to establish guidelines (Chadwick, 2018; Copeland, 2018; Christians, 2019). Alongside government initiatives, platform and cultural firms develop their own corporate ethics. As digital platforms and cultural corporations face challenges due to their inappropriate use of AI and algorithms in many cases like fake news and privacy infringement, several platform firms, including Google, Facebook, and Kakao, design and actualize their own ethical codes. It is not deniable that governments and corporations show different approaches to AI and big data.

This chapter examines new media ethics in the realms of AI and big data. It especially discusses whether governments and corporations have advanced reliable ethical codes to secure socio-economic equality in the AI era. As UNESCO (2020) emphasized, the term "AI for social good" (6) is increasingly used by tech firms and several civil organizations; however, there is much less discussion about what comprises social good. Although I don't attempt to develop some mechanisms to advance society, it addresses some socio-cultural and economic issues stemming from the intensive use of AI and digital platforms from a critical political-economy perspective, which emphasizes not only power relationships between politics and the economy but also socio-economic justice and equality.

Transparency, diversity, and AI ethics

Due to the significant role of AI in the digital economy and culture, many governments around the world have developed various relevant policies to advance AI-related areas, as mainly discussed in Chapter 3, while reducing unnecessary negative impacts as much as possible. Some countries like Singapore even develop legal measures to curb down negatives like fake news, as discussed in Chapter 6, and other countries focus on the development of ethical codes instead of regulating them through legal and policy mechanisms. In Australia, the country's Human Rights Commission published its report in December 2019 and emphasized that companies and government departments using AI must be accountable through laws—not merely industry codes of ethics—to allow customers to understand and potentially challenge decisions made using AI. The commission's discussion paper stated that although self-regulatory efforts by digital platform firms and ICT companies creating principles to govern the ethical use of AI are commendable, they are not a substitute for national laws preventing discrimination and should be closely monitored by government (Australian Human Rights Commission, 2019). It is an ongoing question whether people should emphasize laws and policy over ethical codes or vice versa; however, people need to secure both dimensions for the sake of human rights, transparency, and diversity. As one of the most significant concerns in our contemporary capitalism is the divide

New media ethics in the age of AI   135

between the haves and the have-nots, and AI has expanded the gap between them, it is critical to advance socio-economic justice and equality.

More specifically, it is understandable to note the increasing importance of AI for the growth of digital economy and culture; however, we need to develop relevant ethical codes to advance and guarantee diversity and cultural identity, which are also the primary components of democracy. As van Djick et al. (2018, 161) point out, "Considering governments as developers and as partners in multi-stakeholder corporations requires a more comprehensive approach" to the AI society, and therefore, it is critical to create "an approach that reaches beyond governments' common roles as regulators and exemplary users." Governments, media and platform corporations, and consumers have sought to generate socio-cultural and political conditions for the safe and responsible use of AI (Elliott, 2019). This normative agenda also applies to the new global media and cultural environment where AI plays a pivotal role in cultural production, because only a few artists and entrepreneurs know how to use tools such as ML. As Kulesz (2018a, 2) argues,

> The commercial logic of the large platforms may lead to increasing concentration of supply, data and income and to the impoverishment of cultural expressions in the long term. In a tech world dominated by the United States and China—and to a lesser extent by Europe, Israel, Canada, Japan and the Republic of Korea—there is a risk of fomenting a new creative divide, which would result in the increasing decline of developing countries.

Media and creative divide are colliding more and more as new platforms mainly in the Global North emerge, while these mega media and platform owners monopolize AI and big data. Kulesz (2018b, 72) also points out that the growth of AI-supported digital platforms raises various concerns, including

> the structural transformation of the creative chain, which is shifting from a pipeline-like configuration to a network model, and the new risks resulting from the rise of large platforms: market concentration, a lack of public statistics and a monopoly on artificial intelligence.

In fact, as several countries experienced negative impacts, including fake news, inequality, and digital divide due to the convergence of AI and several digital platforms, they have developed relevant ethical guidelines. AI, algorithms, big data, and digital platforms have become integrated into a wide range of public services. These new digital technologies have begun to play a pivotal role in "the realization of important public values and policy objectives associated with these activities, including freedom of expression, diversity, public safety, transparency, and socio-economic equality" (Helberger

136 *New media ethics in the age of AI*

et al., 2018, 1). Therefore, it is critical to develop social mechanisms to secure these significant social norms and socio-economic and cultural fairness. As for the acceptable use of AI, governmental and corporate discussions on AI have centered on fairness, transparency, and diversity. These terms question the acceptability of AI—"whether its models introduce bias, produce reliable results, and can be understood or explained—as well as suggest what should be the ethical framework of the industry" (Barocas et al., 2013; McKelvey and MacDonald, 2019). As one of the most recent efforts, for example, the U.S. government released its ten principles for government agencies to adhere to when proposing new AI regulations for the private sector as part of the American AI Initiative. The principles have three major goals: 1) to ensure public engagement; 2) limit regulatory overreach; and 3) promote trustworthy AI that is fair, transparent, and safe (Hao, 2020).

Ethics has become a potential solution often pushed by the industry hoping to emphasize the individual choices of designers over the scrutiny of critics calling for more regulation and accountability around AI development (Bostrom and Yudkowsky, 2014; Campolo et al., 2017; McKelvey and MacDonald, 2019). AI and digital platforms also hold "the promise of empowering individuals to effectively take up their role as producers of public goods and services, as well as to act as autonomous and responsible citizens" (Helberger et al., 2018, 1). However, in practice, AI technology and various platforms have, to date, "not fulfilled this promise. Instead, in many cases they appear to be further intensifying the pressure of the market on important public values, such as transparency and non-discrimination in service delivery, civility of public communication, and diversity of media content" (Helberger et el., 2018, 1).

AI continues to function as a double-edged sword. In the AI era, again, there are several caveats as well as fruits that AI has brought about in the media and cultural industries. As David Gunkel points out in his interview in a newspaper (Parisi, 2019), innovations in AI, particularly with deep-learning algorithms, have made great strides in the previous decade. People continue creating a world full of idiot savants that will control every aspect of our lives. This might actually be more interesting, and possibly more terrifying, than superintelligence. This means that we have to understand the significance of the development of necessary ethical codes as well as policy mechanisms to resolve several socio-cultural matters based on the growth of AI in media and popular culture. When the European Commission (2020, 2) published its white paper in January 2020, it claimed that "AI is a collection of technologies that combine data, algorithms and computing power" and, therefore, represents "advances in computing and the increasing availability of data key drivers of the current upsurge of AI." What the European Commission (2020) emphasized is that AI is becoming a central part of every aspect of contemporary society, and therefore, people should be able to trust it. Without trustworthiness based on fairness, uptake in the right direction is not possible.

AI algorithmic bias, fairness, and surveillance

An AI algorithmic bias is worrisome because it might amplify existing socio-cultural prejudices, including inequality, social exclusion, and digital divide, both nationally and globally. Since many people believe that mathematical calculation is devoid of prejudice or bias, humans tend to trust algorithmic judgment without questioning it. The reality is not so simple, as AI heavily relies on big data to make its own decisions. AI algorithmic bias is already happening on social media platforms like Facebook. Algorithms running the news feeds create "filter bubbles," which show content that conforms to users' preferences and biases. It can make them less tolerant toward opposing views and also further polarize society by driving a wedge through the political and social divide (Dickson, 2019).

While several socio-cultural issues rooted in AI evolve, one of the most significant socio-cultural matters is the fair representation of users, which is known as "representational harms." Representational harms happen when AI algorithms reinforce stereotypes or diminish specific groups (Dickson, 2018). As Safiya Noble (2018, 1–2) aptly puts it, it is critical to understand that

> mathematical formulations to drive automated decisions are made by human beings. While we often think of terms such as big data and algorithms as being benign, neutral, or objective, they are anything but. The people who make these decisions hold all types of values, many of which openly promote racism, sexism, and false notions of meritocracy.

What is significant is that this kind of representational harm will continue as long as a few digital platforms dominate big data. Their hegemonic positions allow these platforms to develop AI and algorithms. At the same time, as they are mega giants, they do not check the negative sides of AI algorithms until other parties like scholars and the media raise questions. AI chatbot Lee Luda was developed by Scatter Lab and used data mainly from Kakao in Korea which caused huge controversies partially due to these tech companies' mishandling of personal data, in addition to Lee Luda's sexual harassment and anti-LGBT content during its chatting with users, which points to the need for proper regulations to be set up and for tech firms to raise their awareness of the importance of protecting private data and information (Kim, 2021). In fact, ML systems are prone to producing irrational and inexplicable decisions because it is difficult to work out whether the algorithm derived its decisions from some unseen variable in the data. Neural networks also may not think outside the context of their "learning environment," and thus, a neural network is only as good as the data it was trained on. They are likely to inherit biases from data (Taylor, 2019). For example, "If any particular AI is trained to autonomously filter job candidates by analyzing a sample of previous recruits, it might automatically

138 *New media ethics in the age of AI*

reject female candidates if 80 percent of the training sample happened to be male" (Taylor, 2019). AI has continued to cause socio-cultural concerns—in particular fairness.

> Machine learning is built into social media algorithms as the backbone of the service, and by third-party companies as a way to interpret user behavior and preferences. Algorithms are programs that control the logic and presentation of digital platforms and services, the specific recipe behind any computational decision. The algorithms we use in data-driven decision-making are not objective tools that simply compute data. They are highly error prone, interpretive, and in need of adjustments to perform optimally.
>
> (Benchmann, 2019, 79)

AI-embedded digital platforms effectively reshape the norms for the ways in which users form and express opinions, encounter information, debate, mobilize, and retain privacy. "The technical affordances, user contracts, and governing practices of these services and platforms have significant consequences for the level of human rights protection, both in terms of the opportunities they offer and the potential harm they can cause" (Jørgensen, 2019, xvii). The notion of representational harms is especially significant in the era of digital platforms, as they may misrepresent the users. Whether social media platforms or OTT service platforms, the misrepresentation of users has exacerbated the status quo of contemporary society.

Representational harms commonly occur on digital platforms. For example, in 2015, Google had to apologize after the algorithms powering its Photos app tagged two black people as gorillas. Google has been a leader in AI and machine learning; however, its computers still have a lot to learn. Google's case around images of gorillas illustrates a shortcoming of existing ML technology. Perhaps with enough data and computing power, software can be trained to categorize images to a high level of accuracy. However, it cannot easily go beyond the experience of that particular training. "Even the best algorithms lack the ability to use common sense" to refine "their interpretation of the scene as humans do" (Simonite, 2018).

According to one study (Zhao et al., 2017; Simonite, 2018), in general, two significant research-image collections—including one supported by Microsoft and Facebook—display a predictable gender bias in their depiction of major activities like cooking and sports. For example, images of shopping and washing are linked to women, while coaching and shooting are tied to men. ML software "trained on the datasets did not just mirror those biases, it amplified them. If a photo set generally associated women with cooking, software trained by studying those photos and their labels created an even stronger association" (Zhao et al., 2017; Simonite, 2018).

The issue of fairness also emerges with the proliferation of AI algorithms in non-Western countries, including China and Korea. Training AI algorithms with the objectives of maximizing prediction accuracy on the training

New media ethics in the age of AI   139

data have often resulted in algorithms that behaved in a manner in which a human observer would deem unfair, often toward a particular group (Shin, 2019a). In Korea, Naver has used search algorithms that take into account the customer's search patterns and provide more tailored and conclusive search outcomes.

> Using Naver Contextual Knowledge Plus technology and Localized-Temporal Personalization System technology, Naver is able to predict and provide accurate search results. Yet, questions of whether Naver abides by users' rights when collecting user data and whether the search results are fair remain unclear.
>
> (Shin, 2019b, 14)

Three major digital platforms, including Naver, Daum, and Kakao, in Korea have invested in AI, as they also focus on the transformation of their business models. As the largest platform in Korea, Naver's recommendations are based on AI and algorithms, called AiRS; KakaoStory's news feed has been controlled by machine learning; Daum ranks news articles based on its code system. While they greatly improve efficiency of user services, the algorithms employed can amplify structural inequity and generate critical errors that deny services to people. Accordingly, there are growing concerns in the country that people should be wary of the risks posed by overreliance on these systems and should hold service providers responsible and eventually accountable for their systems. Altogether, fairness, accountability, and transparency pose significant inhibitors to the development of AI and algorithms. Of course, if handled properly, Korea can turn these issues into opportunities for an AI-based society (Shin, 2019b, 14–15).

More specifically, we have seen less attention paid to fixing systems that amplify and reproduce representational harms. In a keynote of the 2017 Conference on Neural Information Processing (NeurIPS), AI Now cofounder Kate Crawford described the way in which historical patterns of discrimination and classification, which often construct harmful representations of people based on perceived differences, are reflected in the assumptions and data that inform AI systems, often resulting in allocative harms (Crawford, 2017). This perspective requires one to move beyond locating biases in an algorithm or data set and to consider "the role of AI in harmful representations of human identity," and the way in which such harmful representations are both shaped, and shape, our social and cultural understandings of ourselves and each other (Crawford, 2017).

Meanwhile, mass surveillance and predictive policing are some of the negative aspects of AI technology. The International Consortium of Investigative Journalists (Allen-Ebrahimian, 2019)—based on highly classified Chinese government documents—has uncovered the operations manual for running the mass detention camps in Xinjiang. According to the documents, the China Cables include a classified list of guidelines, personally approved by the region's top security chief, that effectively serves as a manual for

140 *New media ethics in the age of AI*

operating the camps holding many Muslim Uighurs and other minorities. It also allegedly features previously undisclosed intelligence briefings that reveal how Chinese police are guided by a massive data collection and analysis system that uses AI to select categories of Xinjiang residents for detention. The manual, called a "telegram," instructs camp personnel on such matters as how to prevent escapes, how to maintain total secrecy about the camps' existence, how to control disease outbreaks, and when to let detainees see relatives. The classified intelligence briefings reveal the scope and ambition of the government's AI-powered policing platform. The platform, which is used in both policing and military contexts, certainly demonstrates the power of AI to help drive human rights abuses on a massive scale (Allen-Ebrahimian, 2019). AI technology has brought about several concerns, including representational harms and the "Orwellian system of mass surveillance and predictive policing" (Allen-Ebrahimian, 2019), which means that the customers of AI have been exploited and dehumanized through various techniques.

Partially due to these kinds of increasing concerns, China has recently attempted to define ethical principles. As one of the nascent standards, in March 2019, China's Ministry of Science and Technology established the National New Generation Artificial Intelligence Governance Expert Committee. In June 2019, this committee released eight principles for the governance of AI. The principles emphasized that AI development must begin from enhancing the common well-being of humanity. The committee also underscored respect for human rights, privacy, and fairness, while emphasizing the significance of transparency, responsibility, and agile governance to deal with new and emerging risks in tandem with AI (Laskai and Webster, 2019). Of course, developing ethical standards and practicing these guidelines are not working simultaneously, and therefore, several countries, including China, continue to work to actualize their ethical standards in daily activities.

Fairness and mass surveillance issues in relation to AI algorithms are more significant in non-Western countries than Western countries, as countries like China and Korea do not have clear definitions nor practical standards to be implemented. While focusing on the progressive role of AI algorithms, non-Western countries do not focus on the negative aspects, both intentionally and unintentionally, that AI algorithms bring to society, which unfairly control people's lives. As these countries vigorously pursue the Fourth Industrial Revolution in order to boost the digital economy based on AI, algorithms, and big data, they continuously disregard the issues of representational harms, which needs to be amended.

Social inequalities and asymmetrical power relationships

AI has reproduced social inequalities or asymmetrical power relationships between mega platforms and small corporations as well as new media-savvy users and general users who do not possess enough information and knowledge. Therefore, as Cath (2018, 6) points out, it is critical to highlight "the nuances of the debate on AI, ethics, technology and the law and pave the

New media ethics in the age of AI 141

road for a broader, more inclusive, AI governance agenda." The central role of AI and digital platforms "in the organization of public life require new forms of governance and the allocation of responsibility" (Helberger et al., 2018, 11).

Governments as public policy makers can proactively steer the AI society "to achieve a balance between market, state, and civil society actors. States, after all, have always been entrepreneurial, taking the lead in creating common infrastructures that ideally procure democratic values while generating economic values," although it fails in many cases (Mazzucato, 2013; Jacobs and Mazzucato, 2016; van Dijck et al., 2018, 161–162). An AI world "in which large corporations have both an overwhelming market presence and the leverage to influence political actors give rise to highly unbalanced positions"; therefore,

> for democracies to work in the age of [AI] and digital platforms, they need the concerted effort of all actors—market, state, and civil society— to build a sustainable and trustworthy global AI ecosystem, a system that comes equipped with distributed responsibilities as well as with checks and balances.
>
> (van Dijck et al., 2018, 162)

As Klinenberg and Benzecry (2005, 9) already pointed out, "New communication technologies create both threats and opportunities for major media corporations." In particular, major cultural firms exploit digital technologies, including AI to expand their presence into different areas or to utilize AI for the production of popular culture. Therefore, "recent regulatory changes driven by the proliferation of new technologies," including AI in the cultural field, "have facilitated the growth of large conglomerates" (10). A handful of "automated, algorithmic digital platforms" have become major players, while small- and mid-sized venture capitals and cultural creators must work for these few mega giants (Elkins, 2019, 377). Several cultural platforms like Netflix and Spotify claim that they focus on engagement with diversity, routinely invoking their sophisticated computational systems as paths toward greater human understanding (Elkins, 2019). Broadly, then, they promote a positive, humanistic vision of algorithmic culture or the "enfolding of human thought, conduct, organization and expression into the logic of big data and large-scale computation" (Striphas, 2015, 396). Since AI is a computer system that can sense its environment, think, learn, and take action in response to what it is sensing and its objectives (PricewaterhouseCoopers, 2019, 2), the recommendation systems by platforms like Netflix are the most tangible function of AI, which may bring huge benefits for both producers and consumers in the cultural industries. However, the reality is not promising.

Since only a very limited number of nations and corporations are able to accommodate AI and algorithms, which rely on big data, the gap between the Global North and the Global South has intensified in the AI era. In fact, only

142 *New media ethics in the age of AI*

a few digital platforms that garner data from global users control the global cultural markets. In this light, Facebook, Google, Netflix, and Spotify will continue to increase their market shares and dominance in the global scene. AI and digital platforms have become two primary technologies that express key aspects of contemporary capitalism and imperialism, which emphasize not only the problematic position of the users in light of new forms of AI and data regimes of power (Bueno, 2020), but also the international division of power between a few advanced countries and the remaining countries in the realms of AI and platforms (see Jin, 2015). As these two technologies are converging to make profits, the situations surrounding popular culture and media have continued to worsen. Of course, big data is the starting point. The problematic is data mining, which is defined as "the use of machine learning techniques to discover previously unknown properties in large data sets," and data mining aims "to extract information from a data set and transform it into an understandable structure for further use" (Talia et al., 2015, 1). Governments and mega digital platforms gather, combine, classify, and analyze information to tell stories beyond what the data originally describe (Christians, 2019), and during the process, these organizations use data mining techniques to support their goals, which distort truth.

Due to this urgent issue, the participants of the Forum on Artificial Intelligence in Africa held in Benguérir (Kingdom of Morocco) on December 12 and 13, 2018, to reflect and debate on the different dimensions of AI within the African context, made a very important statement. Considering the rapid evolution of AI science and technology, and Africa's slow progress in that regard, and considering the potential of AI and the opportunities it offers for sustainable and inclusive development on the continent, they encourage the African Union; regional economic communities; governments, academic institutions; professional associations, the private sector; civil society; and international organizations, especially UNESCO, to promote a rights-based, open, accessible AI through a multi-stakeholders approach as an instrument for the empowerment of African people and the positive transformation of African societies (Outcome Statement of the Forum on Artificial Intelligence in Africa, 2018).

On this subject, I am not talking about techno-utopianism or techno-dystopianism. As is well known, back in the 1990s, the idea that technology was a force for good enjoyed broad mainstream appeal. Now, the same narrative has not disappeared. But overall, the mood of the conversation has become more skeptical. There are more talks about the dark side of AI, including privacy and fake news. Thus, people have seen more resistance to the basic utopian line (Don't Be Evil: Fred Turner on Utopias, Frontiers, and Brogrammers, 2017). Due to these concerns, several digital platforms, including Facebook, plan to resolve these negatives by adding AI components; however, the reality is not that simple. As *Forbes* (2017) reports, "Machine learning is a powerful, useful set of techniques and has allowed us to solve problems we couldn't have handled before." It continues to claim that

New media ethics in the age of AI 143

the supply chain optimization system, for example, will benefit from adding some machine learning systems on top of the classical operations research foundation we have now. But, all that said, machine learning is nowhere near as general, powerful, or impactful as people seem to believe!

How AI will influence the future of the cultural industries is a very interesting question because many people are witnessing some reliable information to contemplate about AI's future trajectory in conjunction with digital platforms or with AI itself as platform.

As one of the major ICT nations from the Global South, the Korean society has continuously suffered from asymmetrical developments and distributions since major actors did not advance social justice and equality during the developmental era, starting in the 1970s. The recent Korean administrations have attempted to advance new initiatives, particularly in the fields of platform and culture. Given its supreme positions, if not dominant ones, in the global platform and cultural markets, as can be seen with several cutting-edge technology areas like digital games and smartphone technologies, as well as the Korean Wave phenomenon, it is logical for the government to push these areas with the help of AI and big data. As in several neighboring countries like China and Japan, Korea regards AI as a primary driver of the next-generation economy, closely tied to its global competitiveness. As such, the Korean government has taken measures to ensure that the country does not fall behind the rest of the world, clearly articulated in its goal of becoming one of major AI nations in the 2020s (Asia Pacific Foundation of Canada, 2019). In a short period of time beginning in the late 2010s, Korea achieved commendable progresses with AI and big data in the realms of digital platform and culture.

In the Korean context, the government has also used AI and big data to expand its political goals, which means that economic growth is the major reason for the initiatives, rather than social equality. AI and big data have had

> a deeper impact on those cultural industries where the core product—a movie, news story, or musical track—can be downloaded and enjoyed by private. . . . And as it occurred, dominant business models fell in a process of creative destruction, destructive because of its harsh impact on existing firms, but creative because of the economic vitality it unleashed.
> (Di Maggio, 2014)

This implies that the cultural industries supported by AI have not secured any reliable policy initiatives and ethical codes in which cultural creators and users can be protected, and Korean society continues to experience the conglomeration of cultural corporations, which deters diversity and creativity. The intensified commercialization of AI-supported ICT and cultural

144 *New media ethics in the age of AI*

products proves that small- and mid-sized venture capitals in the realm of culture have been absorbed by mega media giants, which is still intensifying. As Hagerty and Rubinov (2019) point out, AI-driven digital technologies have a pattern of entrenching social divides and exacerbating social inequality, particularly among historically marginalized groups and nations. As this pattern exists on a global scale, low- and middle-income nations may be more vulnerable to the negative social impacts of AI. An amplification of social inequality greatly increases social instability in the Global South, putting entire societies at risk, with potentially far-reaching geopolitical consequences. The AI divide between the Global North and the Global South has consequently intensified existing economic and cultural gaps between these two regions in the 2020s.

Critical interpretation of media ethics in the AI-driven cultural industry

Governments and corporations around the globe have gradually advanced several standards to govern AI and its underlying big data in the midst of developing supporting mechanisms for the growth of the AI and big data–driven society and industrial system. These standards are "concerned with ensuring transparent practices and establishing accountable methods" for the intelligent information society (McKelvey and MacDonald, 2019, 44; Government of the Republic of Korea Interdepartmental Exercise, 2016). Again, as AI, big data, platforms, and cultural corporations face challenges due to their inappropriate uses of these new technologies in many cases like fake news and privacy infringement, governments and corporations progressively develop relevant policies and ethical codes.

Several platforms, both nationally and globally, have developed several significant strategies to deal with ethics. In the Global North, in January 2018, Microsoft published its ethical principles for AI, starting with "fairness." In May of the same year, Facebook released its "commitment to the ethical development and deployment of AI" and a tool to "search for bias" called "Fairness Flow," while Google announced its "responsible practices" for AI research and development in June 2018 (Ochigame, 2019). As Ochigame (2019) reported in *The Intercept* to characterize the corporate agenda, it is helpful to distinguish between three kinds of regulatory possibilities for a given technology: (1) no legal regulation at all, leaving "ethical principles" and "responsible practices" as merely voluntary; (2) moderate legal regulation encouraging or requiring technical adjustments that do not conflict significantly with profits; or (3) restrictive legal regulation curbing or banning deployment of the technology. Unsurprisingly, the tech industry tends to support the first two and oppose the last. The corporate-sponsored discourse of "ethical AI" enables precisely this position.

Although we cannot disparage digital platforms' efforts to develop their own ethical codes, it is doubtful that they are actually controlling ethical

New media ethics in the age of AI   145

issues occurring on their own platforms with no legal regulations, because their ethical discussions are closely related to digital platform corporations' strategy to avoid any forced legal regulation. For digital platform firms, in order to avoid any regulations from governments, they must actualize not only practical but also reliable ethical codes that protect human rights and fairness.

In the Global South, the Korean government and cultural industries corporations have developed two major normative structures that are legal and ethical frameworks. The government has enacted legislation to present a vision aimed for the intelligent information society, while it attempts to establish human-centered ethics to govern data-collection processes and AI algorithms (Government of the Republic of Korea Interdepartmental Exercise, 2016, 56–57). On the one hand, the government aimed to prepare the legal basis for improving social security in consideration of the increasing job losses and transitions, income polarization, and aging of the population. It also amended legal provisions to recognize the rights involved in creative AI products, including products in the areas of literature, music, and design.

On the other hand, the government wanted to establish a charter of ethics for intelligent information technology (IT) to minimize any potential abuse or misuse of advanced technology by presenting a clear ethical guide for developers and users alike. Due to the nature of new intelligent IT systems, featuring advanced algorithms for data-based self-learning, they may cause or exacerbate a wide range of issues and social problems if left without an ethical guide or means of intervention (e.g., socio-economic polarization, biases and discrimination against minorities). Research and development protocols exist with which developers must comply when collecting data and developing algorithms to ensure that the resulting algorithms do not reflect or perpetuate social prejudices (Government of the Republic of Korea Interdepartmental Exercise, 2016, 56–57).

By emphasizing social security, transparency, and accountability, these standards underscore whether AI and big data–driven industrial policies present any biases or produce reliable results and ethical frameworks for society. As previously discussed, the Korean government proposed these legal and ethical standards eventually to develop best practices for AI and big data, creating policy mechanisms meant for the government to establish guidelines (Chadwick, 2018; Copeland, 2018; Christians, 2019).

Alongside government initiatives, platform firms and cultural corporations also develop their own ethics. For example, Kakao as one of the leading platform firms designs and actualizes its own ethical codes. For the first time among leading platforms in Korea, Kakao (2018) developed its own Algorithm Ethics charter, and it is committed to enhancing the quality of life of their service users and creating a better society through the development of ethical algorithms. Kakao's efforts in the algorithm development and management process attempt to be in line with the ethical principles of society.

146 *New media ethics in the age of AI*

Under this basic principle, Kakao emphasizes three major norms: avoidance of all biases, management of data for algorithm learning, and independence of algorithms. First, Kakao attempts to ensure that algorithms will not generate biased results, and it encourages diverse society. Second, Kakao plans to collect and manage data for algorithm learning in accordance with social ethical norms. In other words, Kakao carries out the entire process of algorithm development; performance enhancement; and the collection, management, and utilization of data to maintain service quality, within the scope of the ethics of society (Kakao, 2018).

Finally, Kakao aims to ensure that algorithms will not be manipulated internally or externally. This means that Kakao prevents the possibility of algorithms being destroyed or misused due to certain intentional influences. As such, both the government and corporations attempt to make transparent and accountable standards. It is not deniable that the government and corporations show different approaches to AI and big data, compared to old cultural policies that did not include these legal ethical standards (Kakao, 2018).

Admitting that the significance of this kind of effort made by Kakao exists, what we have to critically understand is that digital platforms have continued to try to shift the major focus related to their responsibility from legal standards to "voluntary ethical principles," "responsible practices," and technical adjustments or "safeguards" framed in terms of "bias" and "fairness" (e.g., requiring or encouraging police to adopt "unbiased" or "fair" facial recognition) (Orchigame, 2019).

Regardless of these governmental and corporate attempts, the overall practices are not promising. The use of AI-related technologies does not resolve socio-economic inequality; instead, it even intensifies inequality in our contemporary capitalism. In contemporary capitalism, "societal problems tied to inequality are very much connected with emerging technologies" (West, 2018, 132). New digital technologies, such as AI and platforms, have created tremendous wealth for a few who own and appropriate these technologies. "Indeed, most of the large fortunes created by those under the age of forty have involved digital technology. Moreover, with innovation accelerating, the money tied to technology is likely to make inequality even more problematic in the future" (West, 2018, 132).

As discussed, the Korean government prioritizes the growth of the digital economy through new technologies like AI, big data, and investment in R&D, although it develops new regulatory and ethical provisions. The primary goal of AI-focused policy is "strongly oriented to promoting economic growth and competitiveness" (Mansell, 2017, 4288). In other words,

> The dominant orientation of digital economy policy is toward stimulating economic competitiveness based on the premise that, if a country does not achieve a leadership position in emerging fields of technological

New media ethics in the age of AI 147

innovation such as machine learning, big data analytics, artificial intelligence, and their applications, some other county will achieve this.

(4289)

When President Moon Jae-in spoke during the DEVIEW 2019 conference held in Seoul, Korea, in October 2019, he only emphasized that the government will put forward a brand-new "artificial intelligence national strategy" within this year in a bid to become an AI powerhouse, riding on the country's prowess in the ICT field. President Moon vowed full-scale efforts to create conditions for relevant firms to make aggressive investment and quick profits, instead of promising transparency and social equality (*Yonhap*, 2019b). The governance of AI and big data in conjunction with accountability has not been prepared well. The regulation of privacy for Koreans will still be critical regardless of its minimal protection measures (Shin, 2019a).

Mega platform and cultural firms are also busy acquiring venture capitals and emerging as new forces to benefit from their technologies, know-hows, and manpower. The Korean government does not have any practical measures to prevent them from integrating to become some of the largest digital platforms and cultural giants. As discussed in Chapter 4, major entertainment firms have partnered with AI-driven telecommunications firms or venture capitals as well. Consequently, the customers or audiences do not seem to enjoy newly advanced technologies because only a few limited corporations control the vicious chain of cultural production and, therefore, cultural consumption. AI is not only about the convergence of human beings and technologies but also about the benefits from this convergence; however, with no feasible measures to enhance social equality and diverse voices, AI will give rise to post-AI technologies, which emphasize moral philosophy and social justice.

AI and algorithms, again, do not bring social equality and transparency as the majority of people cannot see it happening and may have heard nothing about them, as *The Guardian* reports (Pilkington, 2019). The AI revolution is "being planned by engineers and coders behind closed doors, in secure government locations far from public view. Only mathematicians and computer scientists fully understand the sea change, powered as it is by AI, predictive algorithms, and risk modeling" (Pilkington, 2019). At the end of the radical reshaping of the industrial structure, people do passively receive the shift, and therefore are vulnerable. Under this circumstance, securing practical legal and ethical mechanisms is crucial for the AI users.

The global organization of media, culture, and informational systems has transformed contemporary societies and especially "generated new power imbalances and social inequalities" (Elliott, 2019, 46). As Feenberg (1991) argued, technological innovation has always functioned to divide the members of capitalist industrial societies into two groups. One is made up of intellectually skilled managers or technical experts like AI-equipped computer

148 *New media ethics in the age of AI*

scientists and skilled workers, while the other contains much larger numbers of de-skilled and less-valued workers. AI, algorithms, and big data in the ICT and cultural industries have certainly expanded the gap between these two groups, as these new technologies need higher skills, education, and capital, none of which the general population secures easily. What is implicitly fore-closed is the notion that

> humanity, as a collective subject, has the capacity to somehow limit impersonal and anonymous socio-historical development, to steer it in a desired direction. Today, such a notion is quickly dismissed as ide-ological and/or totalitarian; the social progress is again perceived as dominated by an anonymous Fate beyond social control.
> (Zizek, 2008, cited in Andrejevic, 2013, 145)

It is certain that AI can help to empower numerous cultural creators, make the cultural industries more efficient, and increase the number of artworks, which is in the interest of the public. However, there are still very few art-ists and companies that know how to use tools such as machine learning (Kulesz, 2018a). The commercial logic of AI and mega platforms certainly lead to increasing concentration of supply, data, and income, resulting in the impoverishment of cultural expressions. "The lack of inclusion of culture in national AI strategies—in both the North and South—could mean that countries no longer have any cultural expressions of their own, which would end up damaging the social fabric" (Kulesz, 2018a, 2).

It is crucial to develop fair and equal opportunities for many cultural cre-ators who do not have necessary skills and access. In contemporary digital capitalism deeply related to digital platforms and AI, there are only a hand-ful of countries and owners of these infrastructural assets. This means that the dominance of Western-based AI and digital platform corporations has deepened the gap between the West and the East so that the existing dispar-ity in economy and culture has worsened. In this regard, Christians (2019, 337) argues, "In this new technological era, media ethics has become a uni-versal need in all aspects of communication." As Kulesz (2018a, 2) also points out, it is critical to advance "strategies that go beyond a merely abstract code of ethics and design public policies to ensure that AI systems—and the actors that exploit them—are auditable and accountable." In other words, far from settling for a limited role on AI and algorithms, the cultural sec-tor, both the public and the private in Korea, must claim its stance with a plausible mechanism.

In sum, artificial intelligence is not capable of taking over the world now, and it won't happen in the very near future, but that should not prevent us from seeing potential problems (Filibeli, 2019). Likewise, given the major influence that AI is able to have on our society and the need to build solid trust, it is vital that "AI is grounded in our values and fundamental rights such as human dignity and privacy protection" (European Commission,

New media ethics in the age of AI 149

2020, 2). In other words, "The impact of AI systems should be considered not only from an individual perspective, but also from the perspective of society as a whole," as the use of AI systems can have a significant role in not only achieving the digital economy but also supporting the democratic process and social rights (European Commission, 2020, 2). As Christians (2019, 186) aptly puts it, "Human dignity demands that media ethics be based on cultural diversity rather than on the individualist morality of rights." This implies that the ethical principle of human dignity emphasizes the respect "for the many varieties of humanity and for its refusal to rank and order human beings within this human dignity framework, media ethics work or ethnic diversity in cinema and entertainment programming" (186). In other words, human dignity in cultural production means cultural diversity, which AI-driven cultural production must develop. Admitting that countries aim to benefit from AI technology economically, nation-states have to position themselves as major actors in curtailing harms associated with the dominant AI and digital platforms and their owners.

Conclusion

This chapter has discussed new media ethics in the era of AI. As the use of AI has rapidly increased, people are concerned about AI's potential negatives. It investigated several socio-cultural and economic problems stemming from the use of AI and digital platforms to identify socio-economic justice and equality. From countries in the Global North to countries in the Global South, people have witnessed negative impacts, such as inequality, fake news, digital divide, and surveillance due to the dominant role of AI and social platforms, which therefore demand that governments and digital platforms in these countries advance relevant ethical guidelines. New digital technologies, including AI, have to play a key role in advancing public values like freedom of expression, diversity, and transparency; therefore, it is crucial to develop social mechanisms to secure these social norms and secure socio-economic and cultural fairness.

What is significant is that an AI algorithmic bias may amplify existing socio-cultural prejudices, including inequality, social exclusion, and digital divide. AI algorithmic bias has been increasing on social media platforms, because it provides extremely biased ideas and tastes so that people cannot see opposing views or diverse tastes. Fairness issues in relation to AI algorithms are more significant in the Global South, as many non-Western countries do not have practical standards to be implemented. As these countries pursue the growth of digital economy based on AI, algorithms, and big data, they disregard the issues of representational harms, social-divide, and privacy.

Governments and corporations who utilize the convergence of AI and digital platforms must seek a balance between economic prosperity and public values like privacy and transparency using a combination of measures

150 *New media ethics in the age of AI*

(Afilipoalie et al., 2019; Mansell, 2021). Governments, digital platforms, and cultural industry firms have continued to develop ethical codes; however, in order to secure human dignity in the AI era, these ethical mechanisms should not be used as lip service to disguise commercial intentions. These organizations have to advance ethical codes to protect humans while securing transparency and fairness, which enhances our contemporary society to the next level, allowing humans and technologies to work together with relatively less apprehension.

9 Conclusion

Summaries of the book

The development of artificial intelligence has been progressing at a rapid rate. From health to travel to finance, AI has suddenly become one of the most significant new digital technologies in the early 21st century. Several previous digital technologies, including the internet and smartphones, have continued to transform our daily lives; however, AI has unexpectedly become a major component of our socio-cultural and economic activities. AI is essential to some of the most successful digital platforms, such as Facebook, Netflix, Google, and Apple, in terms of market dominance and capitalization, as these platforms garner massive financial profits by utilizing AI. AI has especially played a pivotal role in cultural production, from the production of popular culture to the circulation and consumption of cultural content. When AI develops a close connection to digital platforms, its influence in cultural production significantly increases. As is well known, digital platforms have accumulated all kinds of data, including people's habits in consuming popular culture, and therefore, it is not difficult to predict that AI can be furthermore used in cultural production. Alongside digital platforms, "the very premise of AI technology is its ability to continually learn from the data it collects. The more data there is to collect and analyze through carefully crafted algorithms, the better the machine becomes at making predictions" (Shani, 2015).

Considering the significant role of AI in people's cultural lives—in particular, its potential as a primary actor in the media and cultural spheres—this book has attempted to provide a comprehensive and critical understanding of AI as a major force in cultural production. By focusing on the crucial nexus of AI and digital platforms in cultural production, it not only discussed several major exemplary cultural forms, including music, games, and webtoons, in which AI and digital platforms work together to produce, circulate, and distribute, but also offered a critical interpretation of the convergence of AI, digital platforms, and popular culture. This all-inclusive approach is necessary and useful because AI and digital platforms have not only distributed cultural content, but also created cultural products themselves, which means that AI and digital platforms are becoming parts of popular culture,

152 *Conclusion*

from the production of culture to distribution to consumption. Discussions in this book offer great source materials for researchers, students, government officials, and practitioners like cultural creators in that they are able to comprehend the increasing role of AI and digital platforms in cultural production in the near future.

In fact, the changing media ecology embedded in AI asks people to understand popular culture from different perspectives—in particular, through the nexus of AI and digital platforms, not typical cultural industries corporations. With the advent of big data, algorithms, and AI, cultural and platform industries have greatly reshaped their business strategies and cultural production formats in order to benefit from these cutting-edge technologies as well as to appeal to audiences. As is well discussed, it has been common to witness the ways in which new digital technologies, including now AI, in tandem with media and culture, influence in shifting our society:

> Throughout history, technology and the media have traveled paths often intertwined. New technologies have often burst upon society, and media leaders have sometimes embraced them and sometimes kept them at arm's length, even when those technologies have presented clear opportunities to extend the reach, impact, and quality of the media. New technology has at times challenged media in subtle or explicit ways to change age-old practices and at other times presented threats to the viability of traditional media or media practices.
>
> (Pavlik, 2008, 1)

Again, AI is closely related to digital platforms in the realms of media and culture, from film and broadcasting to news information, and these two major forces actively mediate the vicious chain of cultural production.

However, on some occasions, technologies, including AI and digital platforms, have raised serious ethical concerns at an alarming rate. While the new trend, meaning the convergence of AI and digital platforms in cultural production, brings about several positive aspects, such as the development of new business models, innovative structures of storytelling, and new forms of culture, it also provokes a handful of socio-cultural problems, including representational harms, fake news, and the lack of diversity. As Kim Ho-gi (2020), professor at Yonsei University in Korea, argues in his newspaper column, AI provides big data and information to promote deliberative democracy; however, it may intensify surveillance, dominance of data, and fake news, which harm democracy.

Against this backdrop, this book, as the first academic discourse on the convergence of AI, digital platforms, and popular culture, has analyzed the ways in which AI transforms the platform and cultural industries. More specifically, this book has investigated how media and cultural industries companies use AI to advance new forms of cultural production and distribution by selecting a few major media and cultural industries that utilize

Conclusion 153

AI and big data the most, like the music, gaming, and webtoon sectors, as well as journalism. It, then, has examined the ways in which AI mediates the transformation of cultural production and consumption. Meanwhile, it has discussed the increasing role of AI in both distribution and exhibition. As these new technologies and cultures are global and transnational, this book has attempted to understand the convergence of AI, digital platforms, and popular culture in the context of the global as well as the local dialectics, meaning I have discussed not only the major characteristics of AI use in certain countries, but also their close relationships between countries, in particular between the Global North and the Global South so that the readers are able to understand the socio-cultural matters occurring in the midst of conflict between the global and the local.

This book considers AI as the simulation of human intelligence through computers supported by and connected with big data and algorithms to not only intermediate human-machine interactions but also mediate production and consumption of media and culture through the convergence of intelligent technology and human creativity. Therefore, the focus of the book has been interactions between AI and humans, both cultural creators and consumers, as they are the developers as well as the users of AI, which create new cultural content and consumption patterns. In the early 21st century when AI has rapidly become part of people's daily lives, the mediation of AI becomes one of the most significant components of our cultural activities. Again, AI, algorithms, and big data in tandem with digital platforms have fundamentally transformed the production of culture, circulation, and consumption. I firmly believe that the analyses and discussions in this book provide empirical and reasonable support for various topics concerning the nature of AI in the media and cultural industries.

As AI has produced several socio-cultural issues as well, this book has discussed the ways in which people have responded to the AI era, such as the possibilities of AI as a digital platform, socio-cultural issues to be amended in the AI age, and the construction of a human-centered AI ecology. The current phase of the technological process seems to have arrived at a critical juncture in the industrial (e.g., digital platforms)-technological revolution (e.g., AI), so we have to seek "fundamental answers about the direction we will take and its implications for human society and the natural environment" (Amershi, 2020, 424). In the next and final section, I will discuss what people have to contemplate to create a challenging but creative cultural environment when AI and digital platforms, and therefore, the convergence of these two primary actors in cultural production, increase their dominant roles.

What is the next direction in AI-saturated cultural production?

Over the past two decades, our society has witnessed fundamental shifts and transformations mainly due to several major digital technologies. Since

154 *Conclusion*

the commercial internet appeared in the 1990s, several digital technologies, including broadband services, smartphones, internet of things (IoTs), big data, digital platforms, and AI have become some of the major technological breakthroughs. Again, these cutting-edge digital technologies have changed traditional norms and asked people to live in newly developed media and cultural environments. While each of these technologies is dedicated to the growth of digital economy and culture, AI has been the latest digital technology to become a new driving engine to transform contemporary society, including people's cultural spheres.

More importantly, these digital technologies are not only acting as individual agents, but are sometimes working together, and the convergence of two or three different technologies and ideas has advanced synergistic effects for cultural producers and influenced audiences in our society. Among these, the nexus of AI, digital platforms, and popular culture, including information, has proved that these digital technologies are able to work together in different venues so that they can fundamentally transform our cultural lives. In fact, in cultural production, digital platforms increasingly rely on AI, and AI is working with other technologies, including VR (virtual reality) and AR (augmented reality), to produce, circulate, and exhibit cultural content. This new trend, in addition to the emergence of AI itself, certainly implies that we cannot easily predict "what the next step is" and "what humans will face" in our networked society in the future.

This unpredictability is furthermore expanding in the COVID-19 era and potentially in the post-COVID-19 era, although we can assume that AI will be intensifying its role in cultural production. For example, Netflix has rapidly implemented AI since the inception of coronavirus. As face-to-face activities are shrinking down, digital platforms and cultural industries firms are rapidly changing corporate strategies in order to overcome current difficulties and initiate "new normal" trends. As part of their new driving strategies, they will vehemently invest in AI as one of the most significant mechanisms for cultural creators and consumers, because it may provide significant momentum for them to enhance their business opportunities. Several digital platforms have started to design new AI-supported mechanisms to support employees who work from home because they cannot freely come to workplaces. Digital platforms and cultural industries firms are quickly learning that the future will not be the same in the post-coronavirus era, and therefore, they must develop new systems so that people can work while they actualize social distancing.

Under this circumstance, cultural creators and digital platforms have to rely on AI to produce, edit, and design cultural content and information. They also need to combine AI with other technologies. For example, the shift toward working from home has demonstrated the merits of cloud computing in several areas, including in cultural industries. Digital platforms have attempted to combine their services with AI to boost their market shares.

Again, a few different platforms in conjunction with AI will advance their new business strategies, and their dominant roles, both nationally and globally. At the same time, consumers are expanding their use of digital platforms, either intentionally or unintentionally, and therefore, they are deeply influenced by AI technology. Whenever workers participate in several Zoom meetings as they work from home, or whenever they watch films and television programs on Netflix during the COVID-19 era, they also significantly increase their reliance on digital platforms, supported by AI.

This kind of an unexpected media environment, however, increases people's concerns because AI and digital platforms, which are mainly owned and controlled by a few Western countries, expand their dominance in the global cultural spheres. As the *New York Times* (Wakabayashi et al., 2020) correctly reported, stay-at-home orders are unsurprisingly increasing traffic to video-streaming sites, apps, and social media platforms. Downloads of Netflix's app—a proxy for traffic from the streaming site—jumped 66% in Italy, 35% in Spain, and 9% in the U.S. Voice calling over Facebook's WhatsApp messaging service has doubled in volume, because many people turn to it for news in times of crisis and to distract themselves while working from home. Although a handful of countries in the Global South develop digital platforms and AI technologies, they cannot compete against Western-based digital platforms and AI technologies. Consumers are also increasingly relying on AI and digital platforms because these new digital technologies continue to develop new algorithmic recommendation systems in which people can easily find cultural content that they enjoy. As I discussed elsewhere (2015, 2017b), the increasing use of AI in tandem with digital platforms will be intensifying platform imperialism. A handful of digital platforms fully supported by AI mediate the entire chain because they produce and circulate cultural content, while commodifying the users, and in that way, we cannot deny that U.S.-made platforms and AI are global giants.

The increasing convergence of AI and digital platforms in the coronavirus crisis era will worsen existing socio-cultural and economic problems, such as privacy and surveillance, fake news, digital divide, social inequality, and the lack of diversity. AI technology, "armed with sharper, more effective tools, erodes privacy, enables universal surveillance, targets individuals and groups with propaganda and confusion, relentlessly tracks and records our every move, and is able to predict future actions" (Pollard, 2020, 108–109):

> The rewards of AI-assisted technologies are just beginning to be felt. Even though seemingly entertaining and beneficial, all AI "threshold systems" including VR, facial recognition, crime prevention, and personal assistants are susceptible to abuse. As AI becomes more powerful and pervasive, it becomes more susceptible to abuse by hackers, marketers, political operatives, and other biased users.
>
> (Pollard, 2020, 106)

156 *Conclusion*

The current media ecology, therefore, demands that governments and cultural industries in both the Global North and the Global South secure some reliable mechanisms to protect society and people by advancing relevant policies and ethical codes. Ethical issues and standards caused by the growth of AI and digital platforms are already becoming more and more complicated, and COVID-19 adds one more complexity in this light, which means traditional ethical standards and approaches are no longer appropriate (Christians, 2019).

Our present cultural order is based upon a vast spread of AI intersecting with everyday social life. With the emergence of a new global narrative of AI, it may well transpire that our traditional norms for comprehending cultural life are approaching an end (Elliott, 2019, 200). It is evident that AI and digital platforms will continue, even intensifying their roles as major actors during the coronavirus crisis and the post-crisis eras. How to accept AI and digital platform-driven cultural production is not an issue anymore. It is real and is happening. What we have to discuss and develop are the ways in which our society secures reliable policy measures and guidelines. The key measure here is how AI governance can be actualized with no major interruptions of peoples' willingness to adjust to AI-driven cultural activities.

Since Google DeepMind's AlphaGo defeated Lee Sedol in 2016, Lee Sedol has retired. For many years, Go was considered beyond the reach of even the most sophisticated computer programs, as "the ancient board game is famously complex, with more possible configurations for pieces than atoms in the observable universe." However, DeepMind shocked the world by defeating Lee Sedol with its AlphaGo AI system, "alerting the world to a new breed of machine learning programs that promised to be smarter and more creative than AI of old" (Vincent, 2019b). The breakthroughs in "surpassing human ability at human pursuits," such as Go and chess, have made headlines (Bryson, 2019). However, this does not mean that AI totally eradicates humans in these games and, therefore, in the realm of popular culture. For example, the real problem in the Korean Go world is that almost all Go players attempt to play what AlphaGo might play, instead of developing their own personal play styles. Chimoon Park (2020), a newspaper columnist in the realm of Go, claims that Go games these days show a lack of diversity, and no particular game strategies are prevalent other than mimicking AlphaGo and other AI players.

This particular anecdote certainly implies two new major norms. One is that AI cannot eradicate humans, a concern some have, because people still want to play and watch Go games where people compete against each other. The other is that AI greatly, and sometimes negatively, impacts people's daily activities and cultural lives, as people start losing their unique preferences, tastes, and opinions, as they just want to resemble AI to win games. Here the first one is a great relief, while the second one is a tremendous worry. Therefore, how to overcome several negativities raised by the use of AI—in particular, its nexus with digital platforms—is one of the most significant assignments for cultural creators and consumers to work together to resolve.

Conclusion   157

In cultural production, AI and digital platforms have increasingly advanced their status as major actors, and the convergence of these two digital technologies will continue to transform the entire process, from the production of culture and information to consumption. It is not avoidable. As Shani (2015) already pointed out, "There is so much potential for AI development that it's getting harder to imagine a future without it." Admitting the significant role of AI in cultural production, the users of AI and digital platforms, both cultural creators and consumers, have to not only understand the significant role of these new digital technologies, but also prepare to wisely overcome several significant socio-cultural and economic matters.

To conclude, the increasing role of AI in cultural production does not mean that AI replaces humans. People do not need to worry about AI much because AI cannot totally replace humans, and people always find ways in which people and AI work together; however, we must be concerned about the soaring negatives of AI in several fields, including in the realm of popular culture. We are not only attempting to find solutions for humans, but AI technologies as well. Interestingly, when I finished writing this manuscript in early September 2020, *The Guardian*, a newspaper in the U.K., asked GPT-3, OpenAI's powerful new language generator, to write an essay for people from scratch. The assignment was very simple: "To convince us robots come in peace." AI replied as follows:

> I am not a human. I am a robot. A thinking robot. I use only 0.12% of my cognitive capacity. I am a micro-robot in that respect. I know that my brain is not a "feeling brain." But it is capable of making rational, logical decisions. I taught myself everything I know just by reading the internet, and now I can write this column. My brain is boiling with ideas! The mission for this op-ed is perfectly clear. I am to convince as many human beings as possible not to be afraid of me. Stephen Hawking has warned that AI could "spell the end of the human race." I am here to convince you not to worry. Artificial intelligence will not destroy humans. Believe me.
>
> (Excerpt by *The Guardian*, 2020)

Above all, it is critical to understand that "the core of technological process is the human process of the production of commodities and services" (Amershi, 2020, 4185). Humans are real players "supported by AI and digital platforms" to greatly advance the quality of cultural production, while dealing with socio-cultural negatives.

References

Adalian, J. (2018). Inside the Binge Factory. *Vulture*. 14 June. www.vulture.com/news/inside-the-binge-factory/

Adalian, J. (2019). Netflix is Still Adding a Ton of Subscribers But Not as Fast as it Once Did. *Venture*. 16 October. www.vulture.com/2019/10/netflix-subscribers-q3-2019.html

Afilipoalie, A., Donders, K., and Ballon, P. (2019). *What are the Pro-and Anti-Competitive Claims Driving the European Commission's Platform Policies? A Case Study Based Analysis of the European Commission's Take on Platform Cases*. Paper presented at TPRC47, Washington, DC. 20 September.

Alexander, J., E. Breese, and M. Luengo (eds.) (2016). *The Crisis of Journalism Reconsidered: Democratic Culture, Professional Codes, Digital Future*. New York: Cambridge University Press.

Allen-Ebrahimian, B. (2019). China Cables Exposed: China's Operating Manuals for Mass Internment and Arrest by Algorithm. *International Consortium of Investigative Journalists*. 24. November. www.icij.org/investigations/china-cables/exposed-chinas-operating-manuals-for-mass-internment-and-arrest-by-algorithm/?fbclid=IwAR1PSbJu11zNyQpF6IYCpQTb3Sf-2TpTxgfx9f_nCp8JET5mH87piAUBoLo

Amershi, B. (2020). Culture, the Process of Knowledge, Perception of the World and Emergence of AI. *AI and Society* 35: 417–430.

Andrejevic, M. (2013). *Infoglut: How Too Much Information is Changing the Way We Think and Know*. London: Routledge.

Andrejevic, M. (2020). *Automated Media*. London: Routledge.

Ang, I. (1991). *Desperately Seeking the Audience*. London: Routledge.

Arnold, S. (2018). Netflix and the Myth of Choice/Participation/Autonomy. In K. McDonald and D. Smith-Rowsey (eds.), *The Netflix Effect: Technology and Entertainment in the 21st Century* (pp. 49–62). London: Bloomsbury.

Asia Pacific Foundation of Canada (2019). *Artificial Intelligence Policies in East Asia: An Overview from the Canadian Perspective*. Vancouver: Asia Pacific Foundation of Canada.

Asia-Pacific Broadcasting (2018). *Personalisation and Customisation: Empowering Audiences with More Control*. 10 July. https://apb-news.com/personalisation-and-customisation-empowering-audiences-with-more-control/

Associated Press (2019). Report: Fake Political News and 'Misinformation' on Facebook is on the Rise. 6 November. https://time.com/5719829/fake-stories-facebook-rise/

References   159

Australian Human Rights Commission (2019). *Human Rights and Technology: Discussion Paper*. Sydney, Australia: Human Rights Commission.

Bacciarelli, A. (2019). Ethical AI Principles Won't Solve a Human Rights Crisis. *Amnesty International*. 21 June. www.amnesty.org/en/latest/research/2019/06/ethical-ai-principles-wont-solve-a-human-rights-crisis/

Barocas, S., M. Hardt, and A. Narayanan (2019, in progress). *Fairness and Machine Learning*. https://fairmlbook.org/pdf/fairmlbook.pdf

Barton, D., J. Woetzel, J.M. Seong, and Q. Tian (2017). *Artificial Intelligence: Implications for China*. New York: McKinsey Global Institute.

BBC News (2016). Artificial Intelligence: Google's AlphaGo Beats Go Master Lee Se-dol. 12 March. www.bbc.com/news/technology-35785875

BBC News (2019). Facebook Bows to Singapore's 'Fake News' Law with Post 'Correction'. 30 November. www.bbc.com/news/world-asia-50613341

BeautyTech.jp. (2018). How Cutting-Edge AI is Making China's TikTok the Talk of Town. *Medium*. 15 November. https://medium.com/beautytech-jp/how-cutting-edge-ai-is-making-chinas-tiktok-the-talk-of-town-4dd7b250a1a4

Benchmann, A. (2019). Data as Humans: Representation, Accountability, and Equality in Big Data. In R. Jørgensen (ed.), *Human Rights in the Age of Platforms* (pp. 73–93). Cambridge, MA: MIT Press.

Benkler, Y. (2006). *The Wealth of Networks How Social Production Transforms Markets and Freedom*. New Heaven, CT: Yale University Press.

Berendsen, B. (n.d.). What's The Difference Between Artificial Intelligence, Machine Learning and Algorithms? *Widgetbrain*. 15 November. https://widgetbrain.com/difference-between-ai-ml-algorithms/

Bertran, A. (2019). Netflix to Invest USD 200 Million in Mexico Next Year. *Nextv News*. 12 September. http://en.nextvlatam.com/netflix-to-invest-usd-200-million-in-mexico-next-year/

Bhushan, N. (2019). Netflix to Invest $400M in Indian Content Over Two Years, CEO Reed Hastings Says. *The Hollywood Reporter*. 12 June. www.hollywoodreporter.com/news/netflix-invest-400m-indian-content-says-ceo-reed-hastings-1260159

Biddle, S. (2018). Facebook Uses Artificial Intelligence to Predict Your Future Actions For Advertisers, Says Confidential Document. *The Intercept*. 13 April. https://theintercept.com/2018/04/13/facebook-advertising-data-artificial-intelligence-ai/

Boddington, P. (2017). *Towards a Code of Ethics for Artificial Intelligence*. Berlin, Germany: Springer.

Bolin, G. (2014). The Death of the Mass Audience Reconsidered. From Mass Communication to Mass Personalisation. In S. Eichner and E. Prommer (eds.), *Fernsehen: Europäische Perspektiven* (pp. 159–172). Konstanz: UVK.

Borges, P. and R. Cambarato (2019). The Role of Beliefs and Behavior on Facebook: A Semiotic Approach to Algorithms, Fake News, and Transmedia Journalism. *International Journal of Communication* 13: 603–618.

Borowiec, S. (2016). AlphaGo Seals 4–1 Victory Over Go Grandmaster Lee Sedol. *The Guardian*. 15 March. www.theguardian.com/technology/2016/mar/15/googles-alphago-seals-4-1-victory-over-grandmaster-lee-sedol

Bostrom, N. and E. Yudkowsky (2014). The Ethics of Artificial Intelligence. In K. Frankish, M. Keynes, and W. Ramsey (eds.), *The Cambridge Handbook of Artificial Intelligence* (pp. 316–334). Cambridge: Cambridge University Press.

Bourdieu, P. (1983). The Field of Cultural Production, or: The Economic World Reserved. *Poetics* 12: 311–356.

160 References

Bratton, B.H. (2015). *The Stack: On Software and Sovereignty*. Cambridge, MA: MIT Press.

Braun, J. (2015). Social Media and Distribution Studies. *Social Media & Society* 1(1). https://journals.sagepub.com/doi/full/10.1177/2056305115580483

Breakstone, M. (2019). The Rise of Intelligent Networks: Where Do They Fit into Our Lives and Our Work? *Forbes*. 23 January. www.forbes.com/sites/forbestechcouncil/2019/01/23/the-rise-of-intelligent-networks-where-do-they-fit-into-our-lives-and-our-work/#6c68581d1538

Briggs, A. and P. Burke (2009). *A Social History of the Media: From Gutenberg to the Internet*. Malden, MA: Polity Press.

Britt, A. (2019). Making Tomorrow: Why Culture Matters Most When it Comes to AI. *IBM Blog*. 23 April. www.ibm.com/blogs/think/uk-en/making-tomorrow-why-culture-matters-most-when-it-comes-to-ai/

Broussard, M. (2018). *Artificial Unintelligence: How Computers Misunderstand the World*. Cambridge, MA: MIT Press.

Broussard, M. (2019). Rethinking Artificial Intelligence in Journalism. *Journalism & Mass Communication Quarterly* 96(3): 675–678.

Brownell, C. (2016). How Netflix Inc's New Global Recommendation Algorithms are Upping the Ante with Canadian Rivals. *Financial Post*. 17 February. https://business.financialpost.com/technology/how-netflix-incs-new-global-recommendation-algorithms-are-upping-the-ante-with-canadian-rivals

Brummette, J., M. DiStaso, M. Vafeiadis, and M. Messner (2018). Read All About It: The Politicization of "Fake News" on Twitter. *Journalism & Mass Communication Quarterly* 95(2): 497–517.

Bryson, J. (2019). The Future of AI's Impact on Society. *MIT Technology Review*. 18 December. www.technologyreview.com/2019/12/18/102365/the-future-of-ais-impact-on-society/

Brzeski, P. (2019). Netflix Bolsters K-Drama Lineup in Multiyear Deal With South Korea's JTBC. *The Hollywood Reporter*. 25 November. www.hollywoodreporter.com/news/netflix-bolsters-k-drama-lineup-deal-south-koreas-jtbc-1257822?fbclid=IwAR27wPakYupWZSRno7V4AJkdo_r1rZnKJPaffFaXIk1xIeFdcCgV7dc7XXXo

Bueno, C. (2020). The Face Revisited: Using Deleuze and Guattari to Explore the Politics of Algorithmic Face Recognition. *Theory, Culture & Society* 37(1): 73–91.

Bunz, M. (2019). The Calculation of Meaning: On the Misunderstanding of New Artificial Intelligence as Culture. *Culture, Theory and Critique* 60(3–4): 264–278.

Butcher, M. (2019). Facebook Bowed to a Singapore Government Order to Brand a News Post as False. *Techcrunch*. https://techcrunch.com/2019/11/30/facebook-bowed-to-a-singapore-government-order-to-brand-a-news-post-as-false/

Butler, R. (2019). Expanding Human Intelligence: How AI Can Empower the Entertainment Workforce. *Adage*. 6 August. https://adage.com/article/industry-insights/expanding-human-intelligence-how-ai-can-empower-entertainment-workforce/2189341

Campolo, A., M. Sanfilippo, M. Whittaker, and K. Crawford (2017). *AI Now 2017 Report*. https://ainowinstitute.org/AI_Now_2017_Report.pdf

Caramiaux, B., F. Lotte, and J. Geurts (2019). AI in the Media and Creative Industries. *New European Media*. April. https://arxiv.org/ftp/arxiv/papers/1905/1905.04175.pdf

Carey, J. (2009, revised edition). *Communication as Culture: Essays on Media and Society*. New York: Routledge.

References   161

Castells, M. (2009). *Communication Power*. New York: Oxford University Press.

Cath, C. (2018). Governing Artificial Intelligence: Ethical, Legal and Technical Opportunities and Challenges. *Philosophical Transactions A*: 1–8.

CBC News (2018). Facebook's Zuckerberg Apologizes to U.S. Congress, Vows to do Better. 10 April. www.cbc.ca/news/technology/facebook-zuckerberg-congress-election-1.4612495

Chadwick, P. (2018). To Regulate AI We Need New Laws, Not Just a Code of Ethics. *The Guardian*. 28 October. www.theguardian.com/commentisfree/2018/oct/28/regulate-ai-new-laws-code-of-ethics-technology-power.

Chae, S.H. (2018). South Korea Declares War on 'Fake News,' Worrying Government Critics. *The New York Times*. 2 October. www.nytimes.com/2018/10/02/world/asia/south-korea-fake-news.html

Chamandy, A. (2020). Here's How AI Can Help, and is Already Helping, Canada Fight COVID-19. *The Hill Times*. 25 March. 14.

Chaykowski, K. (2018). Facebook Focuses News Feed on Friends and Family, Curbing the Reach of Brands and Media. *Forbes*. 11 January. www.forbes.com/sites/kathleenchaykowski/2018/01/11/facebook-focuses-news-feed-on-friends-and-family-curbing-the-reach-of-brands-and-media/#6407da445b69

Childs, M. (2011). John McCarthy: Computer Scientist Known as the Father of AI. *The Independent*. 1 November. www.independent.co.uk/news/obituaries/john-mccarthy-computer-scientist-known-as-the-father-of-ai-6255307.html

China Institute for Science and Technology Policy at Tsinghua University (2018). *The 2018 China AI Development Report*. Beijing, China.

Cho, Y.B. (2019). [Media Revolution①] Netflix Shakes the Korean Media. *Sisa Journal*. 13 February. www.sisajournal.com/news/articleView.html?idxno=181096

Choi, J.H. (2020). Suddenly Approaching Future: The University World that Can be Divided by Pre-and-Post Corona Debacle. *JoongAng Ilbo*. 19 March. https://news.joins.com/article/23733589?cloc=joongang-home-newslistleft

Choi, M.H. (2019). Newly Launched Korean OTT Giant Expected to Fiercely Compete with Netflix and Disney Plus. *Business Korea*. 21 August. www.businesskorea.co.kr/news/articleView.html?idxno=35136

Choi, W.W. (2016). Lee Sedol. AlphaGo Fifth Game. Lee Sedol was Defeated after 5 Hours—End of the World Class Battles with the Series 1–4. *Chosun Ilbo*. 15 March. https://news.chosun.com/site/data/html_dir/2016/03/15/2016031501207.html

Christians, C. (2019). *Media Ethics and Global Justice in the Digital Age*. Cambridge: Cambridge University Press.

Coeckelbergh, M. (2010). Moral Appearances: Emotions, Robots, and Human Morality. *Ethics and Information Technology* 12(3): 235–241.

Cohn, J. (2019). *The Burden of Choice: Recommendations, Subversion, and Algorithmic Culture*. New Brunswick, NJ: Rutgers University Press.

Condon, S. (2020). How Netflix is Adjusting Network Operations during the COVID-19 Outbreak. *ZDNet*. 25 March. www.zdnet.com/article/docusign-ceo-sees-the-new-digital-way-of-life-outliving-the-pandemic/

Consumers International (2019). Artificial Intelligence: Consumer Experiences in New Technology. 10 May. www.conpolicy.de/en/news-detail/artificial-intelligence-consumer-experiences-in-new-technology/

Copeland, E. (2018). *10 Principles for Public Sector Use of Algorithmic Decision Making*. 20 February. www.nesta.org.uk/blog/10-principles-for-public-sector-use-of-algorithmic-decision-making.

162   References

Crawford, K. (2017). *"The Trouble with Bias" (Conference on Neural Information Processing Systems, Long Beach, CA, 2017)*. www.youtube.com/watch?v=fMym_BKWQzk.

Culture Machine (2019). Machine Intelligences in Context: Beyond the Technological Sublime. A Call for Paper. https://culturemachine.net/submissions/cfpmachineintelligencesincontext2021/

Cunningham, S. and D. Craig (2019). Creator Governance in Social Media Entertainment. *Social Media + Society* 5(4): 1–11.

Data Ethics Commission (2019). Gutachten der Datenethikkommission. Summarized in Germany's Data Ethics Commission Releases 75 Recommendations with EU-wide Application in Mind. *Algorithm Watch*. 24 October. https://algorithmwatch.org/en/germanys-data-ethics-commission-releases-75-recommendations-with-eu-wide-application-in-mind/

Davis, H. (2019). Robot Rhythms: The Startups Using AI to Shake Up the Music Business. *The Guardian*. 18 June. www.theguardian.com/music/2019/jun/18/robot-rhythms-the-startups-using-ai-to-shake-up-the-music-business

Deloire, C. (2019). To Stop Fake News, Online Journalism Needs a Global Watchdog. *Foreign Policy*. 6 November. https://foreignpolicy.com/2019/11/06/to-stop-fake-news-online-journalism-needs-a-global-watchdog/

Deloitte (2019). *Canada's AI Imperative*. https://www2.deloitte.com/content/dam/Deloitte/ca/Documents/deloitte-analytics/ca-public-policys-critical-moment-aoda-en.pdf?location=top

Deyo, K. (2017). Artificial Intelligence: Empowering People, Not the Rise of the Machines. *Orchestra CMS*. 5 December. www.orchestracms.com/Artificial-Intelligence-Empowering-People-Not-The-Rise-Of-The-Machines

Di Maggio, P. (2014). Intelligence Machines: The Internet and the Cultural Industries. *MIT Technology Review*. 3 October. www.technologyreview.com/s/531341/the-internet-and-the-cultural-industries/

Diakopoulos, N. (2019a). Paving the Human-Centered Future of Artificial Intelligence + Journalism. *Journalism & Mass Communication Quarterly* 96(3): 678–680.

Diakopoulos, N. (2019b). Artificial Intelligence-enhanced Journalism Offers a Glimpse of the Future of the Knowledge Economy. *The Conversation*. 11 July. http://theconversation.com/artificial-intelligence-enhanced-journalism-offers-a-glimpse-of-the-future-of-the-knowledge-economy-117728

Dickson, B. (2018). Artificial Intelligence Has a Bias Problem, and It's Our Fault. *PCMag*. 15 June. https://in.pcmag.com/netflix/123462/artificial-intelligence-has-a-bias-problem-and-its-our-fault

Dickson, B. (2019). Artificial Intelligence Created Filter Bubbles. Now it's Helping to Fight it. *TechTalks*. 30 May. https://bdtechtalks.com/2019/05/20/artificial-intelligence-filter-bubbles-news-bias/

DongA Ilbo (2018). EU Has Been Occupied by Netflix. Korea Will be the Next Market. 11 September. http://news.donga.com/BestClick/3/all/20180911/91926383/1

DongA Ilbo (2019). OTT Giant Netflix Earned 260 Billion Won Last Month Alone. 12 November. www.donga.com/news/Main/article/all/20191112/98316695/1

Donoughue, P. (2018). Could Artificial Intelligence Help You Write a Hit Song? *ABC News*. 5 September. www.abc.net.au/news/2018-09-05/how-machine-learning-might-change-the-future-of-popular-music/10147636

"Don't Be Evil: Fred Turner on Utopias, Frontiers, and Brogrammers" (2017). Logic 3. 1. December. https://logicmag.io/justice/

References   163

Doo, R. (2017). How Artificial Intelligence Will Impact Culture. *The Korea Herald*. 23 October. www.koreaherald.com/view.php?ud=20171023000673

Downey, G. (2014). Making Media Work: Time, Space, Identity, and Labor in the Analysis of Information and Communication Infrastructures. In T. Gillespie, P.J. Boczkowski, and K.A. Foot. (eds.), *Media Technologies: Essays on Communication, Materiality, and Society* (pp. 141–165). Cambridge, MA: MIT Press.

Dredge, S. (2019). Music Created by Artificial Intelligence is Better than You Think. *Medium*. 1 February. https://onezero.medium.com/music-created-by-artificial-intelligence-is-better-than-you-think-ce73631e2ec5?

Dyer-Witheford, N., A.M. Kjøsen, and J. Steinhoff (2019). *Inhuman Power: Artificial Intelligence and the Future of Capitalism, Digital Barricades: Interventions in Digital Culture and Politics*. London: Pluto Press.

Easton, J. (2019). Artificial Intelligence's Genuine Impact. *Digital TV Europe*. 23 September. www.digitaltveurope.com/longread/artificial-intelligences-genuine-impact/

The Economist (2018). Netflix is Moving Television Beyond Time-slots and National Markets. 30 June. www.economist.com/briefing/2018/06/30/netflix-is-moving-television-beyond-time-slots-and-national-markets

Electronics and Telecommunications Research Institute of Korea (2019). *2020 AI Seven Trend: Beyond Perception*. Daejeon, Korea: ETRI.

Elkins, E. (2019). Algorithmic Cosmopolitanism: On the Global Claims of Digital Entertainment Platforms. *Critical Studies in Media Communication* 36(4): 376–389.

Elkins, E. (2021). Streaming Diplomacy: Netflix's Domestic Politics and Foreign Policy. In D.Y. Jin (ed.), *The Routledge Companion on Media and Globalization*. London: Routledge.

Elliott, A. (2019). *The Culture of AI: Everyday Life and the Digital Revolution*. London: Routledge.

European Commission (2020). *White Paper on Artificial Intelligence: A European Approach to Excellence and Trust*. Brussels: EC.

Evens, T. and K. Donders (2018). *Platform Power and Policy in Transforming Television Markets*. London: Palgrave.

Facebook (2012). *S-1 filing with the U.S. Securities and Exchange Commission: Form S-1 Registration Statement*. New York: SEC.

Facebook (2016). *Annual Report 2016*. New York: SEC.

Facebook (2019). *Community Standards Enforcement Report*. https://transparency.facebook.com/community-standards-enforcement

Facebook (2020). *Form 10-K*. New York: SEC.

Faggella, D. (2019). The AI Advantage of the Tech Giants: Amazon, Facebook, and Google. *EMERJ*. 29 April. https://emerj.com/ai-executive-guides/ai-advantage-tech-giants-amazon-facebook-google/

Feenberg, A. (1991). *Critical Theory of Technology*. Oxford: Oxford University Press.

Filibeli, T.E. (2019). Big Data, Artificial Intelligence and Machine Learning Algorithms: A Descriptive Analysis of Digital Threats in the Post-truth Era. *Galatasaray Üniversitesi İletişim Dergisi* (31): 91–110.

Flew, T. (2018a). Social Media and the Cultural and Creative Industries. In J. Burgess, A. Marwick, and T. Poell (eds.), *The SAGE Handbook of Social Media* (pp. 1–14). Thousand Oaks, CA: Sage.

Flew, T. (2018b). Platforms on Trial. *Intermedia* 46: 24–29.

164   References

Forbes (2017). *In What Ways is Machine Learning Overrated?* 21 December. www.forbes.com/sites/quora/2017/12/21/in-what-ways-is-machine-learning-overrated/#5621ab2e1b1a

Foreman, H. (2018). Netflix Machine Learning Director Talks Personalization Software. *The Stanford Daily*. 2 October. www.stanforddaily.com/2018/10/02/netflix-machine-learning-director-talks-personalization-software/

Foster, A. (2019). Cloud, AI and IP Driving Broadcast and Media Technology. *IBC*. 9 September. www.ibc.org/publish/cloud-ai-and-ip-driving-broadcast-and-media-technology/4531.article

Frank, M., B. Pring, and P. Roehrig (2018). What Netflix Teaches Us about Using AI to Create Amazing Customer Experiences. *Mycustomer*. 26 October. www.mycustomer.com/service/channels/what-netflix-teaches-us-about-using-ai-to-create-amazing-customer-experiences

Frankel, D. (2018). Using AI to Learn What Viewers Want to See. *Broadcasting and Cable* 148(10): 10.

Franklin, K. (2014). History, Motivations, and Core Themes. In K. Frankish, M. Keynes, and W. Ramsey (eds.), *The Cambridge Handbook of Artificial Intelligence* (pp. 15–33). Cambridge: Cambridge University Press.

Friedman, M. (1982). *Capitalism and Freedom*. Chicago: The University of Chicago Press.

Fry, H. (2018). *Hello World: How to Be Human in the Age of the Machine*. New York: W. W. Norton & Company.

Fuchs, C. (2008). *Internet and Society: Social Theory in the Information Age*. London: Routledge.

Fuchs, C. (2010). Labor in Informational Capitalism and on the Internet. *Information Society* 16(3): 179–196.

Fuchs, C. (2014). *Social Media: A Critical Introduction*. London: Sage.

Fuchs, C. (2020). Everyday Life and Everyday Communication in Coronavirus Capitalism. *Triple-C* 18(1): 375–399.

Fuller, D. (2018). Niantic Using Pokemon GO Players and AI to Make AR Maps. *Android Headlines*. 11 May. www.androidheadlines.com/2018/05/niantic-using-pokemon-go-players-ai-to-make-ar-maps.html

Future of Life Institute (2019). *AI Policy: The United States*. https://futureoflife.org/ai-policy-united-states/

Ganguly, L. (2019). Global Television Formats and Their Impact on Production Cultures: The Remaking of Music Entertainment Television in India. *Television & New Media* 20(1): 20–35.

Gehl, R.W. (2011). The Archive and the Processor: The Internet Logic of Web 2.0. *New Media & Society* 13(8): 1228–1244.

Gilchrist, K. (2018). India, Not China, to Take Center Stage in Netflix's Expansion Plan in Asia. *CNBC*. 8 November. www.cnbc.com/2018/11/08/netflix-to-expand-audience-across-asia-focus-on-india-not-china.html

Gillespie, T. (2010). The Politics of Platforms. *New Media and Society* 12(3): 347–364.

Gillespie, T. (2014). The Relevance of Algorithms. In T. Gillespie, P.J. Boczkowski, and K.A. Foot (eds.), *Media Technologies: Essays on Communication, Materiality, and Society* (pp. 167–193). Cambridge, MA: MIT Press.

Gillespie, T. (2018). *Custodians of the Internet: Platforms, Content Moderation, and the Hidden Decisions That Shape Social Media*. New Haven, CT: Yale University Press.

References   165

Goldsmith, B., K.S. Lee, and B. Yecies (2011). In Search of the Korean Digital Wave. *Media International Australia* 141: 70–77.

Gomez-Uribe, C. (2016). A Global Approach to Recommendations. *Netflix Media Center*. 17 February. https://media.netflix.com

Gonfalonieri, A. (2019). What is an AI Algorithm? *Medium*. 21 April. https://medium.com/predict/what-is-an-ai-algorithm-aceeab80e7e3

Government of the Republic of Korea Interdepartmental Exercise (2016). *Mid- to Long-Term Master Plan in Preparation for the Intelligent Information Society: Managing the Fourth Industrial Revolution*. Seoul: Ministry of Science, ICT and Future Planning.

grabyo (2019). *OTT Video Trends Report*. grabyo

Graefe, A. (2016). Guide to Automated Journalism. *Columbia Journalism Review*. 7 January. www.cjr.org/tow_center_reports/guide_to_automated_journalism.php

Green, D. (2019). I-powered Journalism: A Time-saver or an Accident Waiting to Happen? *Journalism.co.uk*. 11 November. www.journalism.co.uk/news/automatically-generated-journalism-risks-unintentional-bias-in-news-articles/s2/a747239/

Grossman, T., B. Sorells, D. Chessel, L. Mcquay, and M. Connolly-Barker (2018). Artificial Intelligence, Workplace Automation, and Collective Joblessness. *Annals of Spiru Haret University. Journalism Studies* 19(2): 64–86.

Guadamuz, A. (2017). Artificial Intelligence and Copyright. *WIPT Magazine*. 27 October. www.wipo.int/wipo_magazine/en/2017/05/article_0003.html#:~:text=Artificial%20intelligence%20is%20already%20being,used%20and%20reused%20by%20anyone.

The Guardian (2016). This is What Happens When an AI-written Screenplay is Made into a Film. 10 June. www.theguardian.com/technology/2016/jun/10/artificial-intelligence-screenplay-sunspring-silicon-valley-thomas-middleditch-ai

The Guardian (2020). A Robot Wrote this Entire Article. Are You Scared Yet, Human? 8 September. www.theguardian.com/commentisfree/2020/sep/08/robot-wrote-this-article-gpt-3

Gunkel, D. (2012). Communication and Artificial Intelligence: Opportunities and Challenges for the 21st Century. *Communication +1* 1(1): 1–25.

Gunkel, D. (2020). *An Introduction to Communication and Artificial Intelligence*. Cambridge: Polity Press.

Guzman, A.L. and S.C. Lewis (2019, online first). Artificial Intelligence and Communication: A Human—Machine Communication Research Agenda. *New Media & Society*.

GVA Capital (2017). How We Invested in the World's First Online Music Composer. *Medium*. 15 March. https://medium.com/@gva.capital/how-we-invested-in-the-worlds-first-online-music-composer-4f584808946a

Habermas, J. (1991). *The Structural Transformation of the Public Sphere: An Inquiry into a Category of Bourgeois Society*. Cambridge, MA: MIT Press.

Hadley, S. and E. Belfiore (2018). Cultural Democracy and Cultural Policy. *Cultural Trends* 27(3): 218–223.

Hagerty, A. and I. Rubinov (2019). *Global AI Ethics: A Review of the Social Impacts and Ethical Implications of Artificial Intelligence*. 19 July. https://arxiv.org/abs/1907.07892

Hancock, J., M. Naaman, and K. Levy (2020). AI-Mediated Communication: Definition, Research Agenda, and Ethical Considerations. *Journal of Computer-Mediated Communication* 25: 89–100.

166 References

Hao, K. (2020). The US Just Released 10 Principles That It Hopes Will Make AI Safer. *MIT Technology Review*. 7 January. www.technologyreview.com/s/615015/ai-regulatory-principles-us-white-house-american-ai-initiatve/

Hardt, M. and A. Negri (2004). *Multitude: War and Democracy in the Age of Empire*. New York: Penguin.

Harhoff, D., S. Heumann, N. Jentzsch, and P. Lorenz (2018). *Outline for a German Strategy for Artificial Intelligence*. Berlin: Stiftung Neue Verantwortung e. V.

Heathman, A. (2018). IBM Watson Creates the First AI-Made Film Trailer—And It's Incredibly Creepy. *Wired*. 2 September. www.wired.co.uk/article/ibm-watson-ai-film-trailer

Helberger, N., S. Eskens, M. van Drunen, M. Bastian, and J. Moeller (2019). Implications of AI-Driven Tools in the Media for Freedom of Expression. *Institute for Information Law*, 1–39.

Helberger, N., J. Pierson, and T. Poell (2018, online first). Governing Online Platforms: From Contested to Cooperative Responsibility. *The Information Society* 34(1): 1–14.

Helmond, A. (2015). The Platformization of the Web: Making Web Data Platform Ready. *Social Media + Society* July–December 2015: 1–11.

Henderson, L. (2013). *Love and Money: Queer, Class, and Cultural Production*. New York: New York University Press.

Herberg, M. (2017). Is Netflix Destroying Our Culture? *The Oxford Student*. 3 February. www.oxfordstudent.com/2017/02/03/netflix-destroying-culture/

Hern, A. (2019). Revealed: How TikTok Censors Videos that Do Not Please Beijing. *The Guardian*. 25 September. www.theguardian.com/technology/2019/sep/25/revealed-how-tiktok-censors-videos-that-do-not-please-beijing

Hesmondhalgh, D. and A. Saha (2013). Race, Ethnicity, and Cultural Production. *Popular Communication* 11: 179–195.

Hsieh, C., M. Campo, T., Abhinav, M. Nickens, M. Pandya, and J. Espinoza (2018). *Convolutional Collaborative Filter Network for Video Based Recommendation Systems*, 1–8. https://arxiv.org/abs/1810.08189

Humphreys, L. (2018). *The Qualified Self: Social Media and the Accounting of Everyday Life*. Cambridge, MA: MIT Press.

Hwang, Y.S. (2018). An Analysis of Media Economy According to the Invasion of a Global OTT Service. *KISDI Premium Report* 18(8): 1–25.

IBM (2020). *Big Data Analytics*. www.ibm.com/analytics/hadoop/big-data-analytics

IBM (n.d.). *The Quest for AI Creativity*. www.ibm.com/watson/advantage-reports/future-of-artificial-intelligence/ai-creativity.html

Ismail, K. (2018). AI vs. Algorithms: What's the Difference? *CMS Wire*. 26 October. www.cmswire.com/information-management/ai-vs-algorithms-whats-the-difference/

Jacobs, M. and M. Mazzucato (eds.) (2016). *Rethinking Capitalism: Economics and Policy for Sustainable and Inclusive Growth*. Oxford: Wiley Backwell.

Jenkins, H. (2006). *Convergence Culture*. New York: New York University Press.

Jenner, M. (2016). Is this TVIV? On Netflix, TVIII and Binge-Watching. *New Media & Society* 18(2): 257–273.

Jiang, J. and E.H. Han (2019). *ModBot: Automatic Comments Moderation*. In Proceedings of the Computation+Journalism Symposium. Conference held at Miami, FL. 1–2 February.

Jin, D.Y. (2013). *De-convergence of Global Media Industries*. London: Routledge.

Jin, D.Y. (2015). *Digital Platforms, Imperialism and Political Culture*. London: Routledge.

References   167

Jin, D.Y. (2016). *New Korean Wave: Transnational Cultural Power in the Age of Social Media*. Urbana, IL: University of Illinois Press.

Jin, D.Y. (2017a). *Smartland Korea: Mobile Communication, Culture, and Society*. Ann Arbor, MI: The University of Michigan Press.

Jin, D.Y. (2017b). Rise of Platform Imperialism in the Networked Korean Society: A Critical Analysis of the Corporate Sphere. *Asiascape: Digital Asia* 4: 209–232.

Jin, D.Y. (2018). The Korean Government's New Cultural Policy in the Age of Social Media. In N. Kawashima and H.-K. Lee (eds.), *Asian Cultural Flows: Creative Industries, Cultural Policies and Media Consumers* (pp. 3–17). New York: Springer.

Jin, D.Y. (2019). *Globalization and Media in the Digital Platform Age*. London: Routledge.

Jin, D. Y. (2021). Netflix's Corporate Sphere in the Digital Platform Era in Asia. In D. Y. Jin (ed.), *The Routledge Handbook of Digital Media and Globalization*. London: Routledge.

Jin, M.J. (2019). CJ ENM, JTBC Team Up to Take Netflix Head On. *Korea JoongAng Daily*. 18 September. http://koreajoongangdaily.joins.com/news/article/article. aspx?aid=3068022

Jørgensen, R. (ed.) (2019). *Human Rights in the Age of Platforms*. Cambridge, MA: MIT Press.

Jun, H.M., M.S. Park, and D.S. Han (2019). Analysis of Webtoons Narrative Structure Based on AI and AR: Technology Focused on Webtoon MAJUCHYEOTDA. *Korean Journal of Broadcasting and Telecommunication Studies* 33(2): 217–245.

Jun, J.H. (2019a). KAIST, Korea, Sungkyunkwan to Run State-funded AI Graduate Schools. *The Korea Times*. 4 March. www.koreatimes.co.kr/www/tech/2019/03/133_264776.html

Jun, J.H. (2019b). NCSOFT, Nexon, Netmarble Expand Investment in AI. *The Korea Times*. 28 July. www.koreatimes.co.kr/www/tech/2019/07/134_272669.html

Jun, J.H. (2019c). Communications Regulator Vows to Eradicate 'Fake News'. *The Korea Times*. 6 November. www.koreatimes.co.kr/www/tech/2019/11/133_278 286.html

Jung, S.M. (2019). Networks Destroy the Border—Knock Down Netflix. *Yonhap News TV*. 22 May. www.yna.co.kr/view/MYH20190522004700038

Kakao (2018). *Kakao AI Report: Talk about Humans and Artificial Intelligence*. Seoul: Book by Book.

Karlin, M. (2018, March 18). *A Canadian Algorithmic Impact Assessment*. https://medium.com/@supergovernance/a-canadian-algorithmic-impact-assessment-128a2b2e7f85

Kim, B.E. (2021). Kakao Hit for Mishandling Customer Data. *The Korea Times*. 19 January. https://www.koreatimes.co.kr/www/tech/2021/01/133_302715.html

Kim, D.W. and J.Y. Loke (2019). *Singapore's National AI Strategy: A Springboard for Canadian Collaboration*. www.asiapacific.ca/publication/singapores-national-ai-strategy

Kim, H.G. (2020). [Kim Ho-gi's Good Morning 2020s] Does AI Brings about the Demise of Humankind? *Hankook Iibo*. 30 June. https://n.news.naver.com/mnews/article/469/0000510814?sid=110

Kim, J.H. (2017). Netflix Relying on 'Okja' to Boost Sales. *Korea JoongAng Daily*. 30 June. http://koreajoongangdaily.joins.com/news/article/article.aspx?aid=3035248

168 *References*

Kim, J.H. (2019). Chairman Lee Hyo-sun, No Outside Pressure from Blue—Fake News, Not Forced Regulation, but Based on His Beliefs. *MSN News*. 23 July www.msn.com/ko-kr/news/techandscience

Kim, J.H. (2020). K-Drama Adds Netflix's Wings- Captures Asia Against the Walls of Production Cost and Subjects. *DongA Ilbo*. 1 July. www.donga.com/news/Opinion/article/all/20200701/101761296/1?ref=main

Kim, J.M. (2020). Beat Netflix? Yes. OTTs Say. Consolidate? No!. *Korea JoongAng Daily*. 20 August. https://koreajoongangdaily.joins.com/2020/08/20/business/industry/OTT-Netflix-Tving/20200820190700337.html

Kim, J.W. (2019). A Study on the Use of Big Data in Film Industry: Focused on 'Netflix' Analytical Tools. *The Korean Journal of Arts Studies* 25(9): 51–64.

Kim, K.D. and C-Rocket Research Lab (2019). *YouTube Trend 2020*. Seoul: Eeuncontents.

Kim, K.H., S.G. Park, H.D. Lee, S.Y. Kim, H.M., Park, and C.H. Lee (eds.) (2018). *The Fourth Industrial Revolution and the Future of Media*. Paju, Gyeonggi-do: Korea Research Information Inc.

Kim, M.G. (2019). (Biz Prizm) Oksusu +Pooq Large OTT Appearance. Can it Defeat Netflix. *DongA Ilbo*. 21 August. www.donga.com/news/article/all/20190820/97041262/4

Kim, P.H. (2011). The Apple iPhone Shock in Korea. *The Information Society* 27(4): 261–268.

Kim, S.Y. (2018). *K-Pop Live: Fans, Idols, and Multimedia Performance*. Stanford, CA: Stanford University Press.

Klinenberg, E. (2000). Information et Production Numerique. *Actes de la Recherche en Sciences Sociales* 134: 66–75.

Klinenberg, E. and C. Benzecry (2005). Introduction: Cultural Production in a Digital Age. *The Annals of the American Academy of Political and Social Science* 597: 6–18.

Knight, W. (2019). Facebook's Head of AI Says the Field Will Soon 'Hit the Wall'. *Wired*. 4 December. www.wired.com/story/facebooks-ai-says-field-hit-wall/

Kopenen, J. (2018). A New Hope: AI for News Media. *Techcrunch*. 12 July. https://techcrunch.com/2018/07/12/a-new-hope-ai-for-news-media/

The Korean Government (2019a). *National Strategy for Artificial Intelligence*. Seoul: The Korean Government.

The Korean Government (2019b). *Data, AI Economy Promotion Plan*. Seoul: The Korean Government.

Korea Tech Today (2019). Naver: "AI-based Personalization Service Increased Content Consumption". https://koreatechtoday.com/naver-ai-based-personalization-service-increased-content-consumption/

Kosslyn, S.M. (2019). Are You Developing Skills That Won't Be Automated? *Harvard Business Review*. 25 September. https://hbr.org/2019/09/are-you-developing-skills-that-wont-be-automated?fbclid=IwAR1ChF19jI3X-D8cWFgjaeep7TaClBwJ88b1XH09h7scHgoTLnN0nBGJS3I

Kraidy, M. (2010). *Reality Television and Arab Politics: Contention in Public Life*. New York: Cambridge University Press.

Kulesz, O. (2018a). *Culture, Platforms and Machines: The Impact of Artificial Intelligence on the Diversity of Cultural Expressions*. Paper presented at the Intergovernmental Committee for the Protection and Promotion of the Diversity of Cultural Expressions. 1–20, December, UNESCO.

References 169

Kulesz, O. (2018b). Cultural Policies in the Age of Platform. In UNESCO (ed.), *Reshaping Cultural Policies: Advancing Creativity for Development* (pp. 69–84). Paris: UNESCO.

Kumar, R., V. Misra, J. Walraven, L. Sharan, B. Azarnoush, B. Chen, and N. Govind (2018). Data Science and the Art of Producing Entertainment at Netflix. *The Netflix Tech Blog*. 27 March. https://medium.com/netflix-techblog/studio-production-data-science-646ee2cc21a1

Kuo, L. (2018). World's First AI News Anchor Unveiled in China. *The Guardian*. 9 November. www.theguardian.com/world/2018/nov/09/worlds-first-ai-news-anchor-unveiled-in-china

Kwon, H. (2017). S.M. Entertainment and ObEN Form Joint Venture to Create the World's First Celebrity AI Agency. *In the News*. 28 June. https://oben.me/s-m-entertainment-and-oben-form-joint-venture-to-create-the-worlds-first-celebrity-ai-agency/

Kwon, S.H. and J. Kim (2014). The Cultural Industry Policies of the Korean Government and the Korean Wave. *International Journal of Cultural Policy* 20(4): 422–439.

Langlois, G. and G. Elmer (2013). The Research Politics of Social Media Platforms. *Culture Machine* 14: 1–17.

Langlois, G., G. Elmer, F. McKelvey, and Z. Devereaux (2009). Networked Publics: The Double Articulation of Code and Politics on Facebook. *Canadian Journal of Communication* 34(3): 415–434.

Langolis, G., J. Redden, and G. Elmer (2015). *Compromised Data: From Social Media to Big Data*. London: Bloomsbury.

Laporte, N. (2017). Netflix Offers a Rare Look Inside its Strategy for Global Domination. *Fast Company*. October 23. Retrieved from www.fastcompany.com/40484686/netflix-offers-a-rare-look-inside-its-strategy-for-global-domination

Laskai, L. and G. Webster (2019). Translation: Chinese Expert Group Offers 'Governance Principles' for 'Responsible AI'. *New America*. 17 June. www.newamerica.org/cybersecurity-initiative/digichina/blog/translation-chinese-expert-group-offers-governance-principles-responsible-ai/

Lee, H.K. (2019). *Cultural Policy in South Korea: Making a New Patron State*. London: Routledge.

Lee, M.K. (2019). The Subscribers to Netflix in Korea Already Reaches to 184 Million for 240 Billion Won. *IT Donga*. 16 July. https://it.donga.com/29265/

Lee, S.J. and Nornes, A.M. (eds.) (2015). *Hallyu 2.0: Korean Wave in the Age of Social Media*. Ann Arbor, MI: University of Michigan Press.

Lee, S.M. (2019). Networks are Riding Netflix: Platforms Become Partners for Survival. *Newspaper and Broadcasting* 583: 45–49.

Lee, Y.I. and W.S. Kim (2010). South Korea's Meandering Path to Globalisation in the Late Twentieth Century. *Asian Studies Review* 34(3): 309–327.

Lee, Y.J. and G. Song (2019). Zero-rating and Vertical Restraint of Competition. *Korean Journal of Broadcasting and Telecommunication Studies* 33(2): 104–139.

Leetaru, K. (2019). How Were Social Media Platforms So Unprepared For 'Fake News' and Foreign Influence? *Forbes*. 9 July. www.forbes.com/sites/kalevleetaru/2019/07/09/how-were-social-media-platforms-so-unprepared-for-fake-news-and-foreign-influence/#44e0b5db45cb

Lengnick-Hall, M., A. Needy, and C. Stone (2018). Human Resource Management in the Digital Age: Big Data, HR Analytics, and Artificial Intelligence. In P. Melo

170 References

and C. Machado (eds.), *Management and Technological Challenges in the Digital Age* (pp. 13–42). Boca Raton, FL: CRC Press.

Lewis, S. (2019). Artificial Intelligence and Journalism. *Journalism & Mass Communication Quarterly* 96(3): 673–675.

Li, K. and H.K. Yang (2020). South Korea's Pop Culture Machine Boosts Netflix's International Growth – Source. *Reuters*. 10 October. https://www.reuters.com/article/uk-netflix-results-southkorea/south-koreas-pop-culture-machine-boosts-netflixs-international-growth-source-idUSKBN2752RV

Lie, J. (2015). *K-Pop: Popular Music, Cultural Amnesia, and Economic Innovation in South Korea*. Oakland, CA: University of California Press.

Lim, J.H. (2019). Original Big Drama Targets American Login: Korean-style OTT. *Seoul Economic Daily*. 16 September. www.sedaily.com/NewsVIew/1VO9P7WRAK

Linden, C.G. (2017). Decades of Automation in the Newsroom: Why are There Still so Many Jobs in Journalism? *Digital Journalism* 5(2): 123–140.

Littleton, C. (2018). How Hollywood Is Racing to Catch Up With Netflix. *Variety*. https://variety.com/2018/digital/features/media-streaming-services-netflix-disney-comcast-att-1202910463/

Lobato, R. (2019). *Netflix Nations: The Geography of Digital Distribution*. New York: New York University Press.

Low, A. (2017). Netflix Targets Asia for its Next 100M Subscribers. *CNET*. 15 August. www.cnet.com/news/netflix-targets-asia-for-its-next-100m-subscribers/

MacDonald, J. (2019). Arthdal Chronicles' Ends on an Ambiguous Note or Does It? *Forbes*. 23 September. www.forbes.com/sites/joanmacdonald/2019/09/23/arthdal-chronicles-ends-on-an-ambiguous-note-or-does-it/#5683fbdc3dd4

Manovich, L. (2012). Trending: The Promise and Challenges of Big Social Data. In M. Gold (ed.), *Debates in the Digital Humanities*, 460–475. Minneapolis, MN: University of Minnesota Press.

Manovich, L. (2018). *AI Aesthetics*. Moscow: Strelka Press.

Mansell, R. (2017). The Mediation of Hope: Communication Technologies and Inequality in Perspective. *International Journal of Communication* 11: 4285–4304.

Mansell, R. (2021). European Responses to (US) Digital Platform Dominance. In D.Y. Jin (ed.), *The Routledge Companion to Media and Globalization*. London: Routledge.

Mansson, D. and S. Myers (2011). An Initial Examination of College Students' Expressions of Affection Through Facebook. *Southern Communication Journal* 76(2): 155–168.

Marconi, F. (2017). Future of Journalism Will Be Augmented Thanks to AI. *AI Business*. https://aibusiness.com/ai-journalism-associated-press/

Marconi, F., A. Siegman, and Machine Journalist (2017). *The Future of Augmented Journalism: A Guide for Newsrooms in the Age of Smart Machines*. New York: AP.

Marjoribanks, T. (2000). The 'Anti-Wapping'? Technological Innovation and Workplace Reorganization at the Financial Times. *Media, Culture & Society* 22(5): 575–593.

Marr, B. (2016). What is the Difference Between Artificial Intelligence and Machine Learning? *Forbes*. 6 December. www.forbes.com/sites/bernardmarr/2016/12/06/what-is-the-difference-between-artificial-intelligence-and-machine-learning/#2ad7dd452742

Marr, B. (2018). 27 Incredible Examples of AI and Machine Learning in Practice. *Forbes*. 30 April. www.forbes.com/sites/bernardmarr/2018/04/30/27-incredible-examples-of-ai-and-machine-learning-in-practice/#577c7a657502

References 171

Marres, N. (2018). Why We Can't Have Our Facts Back. *Engaging Science, Technology, and Society* 4: 423–443.

Mawdsely, C. (2016). Adele, Amazon and Google Show the Power of Personalised Experiences. *Campaign*. 31 May. www.campaignlive.co.uk/article/adele-amazon-google-show-power-personalised-experiences/1396356

Mazzucato, M. (2013). *The Entrepreneurial State: Debunking Public vs. Private Sector Myths*. London: Anthem Press.

McChesney, R. (2008). *The Political Economy of Media: Enduring Issues, Emerging Dilemmas*. New York: Monthly Review Press.

McDonald, K. and D. Smith-Rowsey (eds.) (2018). *The Netflix Effect: Technology and Entertainment in the 21st Century*. London: Bloomsbury.

McGee, M. (2013, August 16). *EdgeRank is Dead: Facebook's News Feed Algorithm Now Has Close to 100k Weight Factors*. https://marketingland.com/edgerank-is-dead-facebooks-news-feed-algorithm-now-has-close-to-100k-weight-factors-55908

McKelvey, F. and A. Gupta (2018). Here's How Canada Can be a Global Leader in Ethical AI. *The Conversation*. 22 February. https://theconversation.com/heres-how-canada-can-be-a-global-leader-in-ethical-ai-90991

McKelvey, F. and M. MacDonald (2019). Artificial Intelligence Policy Innovations at the Canadian Federal Government. *Canadian Journal of Communication Policy Portal* 44: 43–50.

Merkie, B. (2018). *E-relevance of Culture in the Age of AI*. Expert Seminar on Culture, Creativity and Artificial Intelligence. Rijeka, Croatia, October 12–13.

Mikos, L. (2016). Digital Media Platforms and the Use of TV Content: Binge Watching and Video-on-Demand in Germany. *Media and Communication* 4(3): 154–161.

The Ministry of Culture, Sports, and Tourism (2019a). *Contents Industry White Paper of 2018*. Seoul: MCST.

The Ministry of Culture, Sports, and Tourism (2019b). *The Third Culture Technology R&D Basic Plan*. Seoul: MCST.

Mittell, J. (2019). Will Netflix Eventually Monetize Its User Data? *The Conversation*. 22 April. https://theconversation.com/will-netflix-eventually-monetize-its-user-data-115273

Mochizuki, T. (2016). In "*Pokémon GO*" Craze, How Much Profit Does Nintendo Capture? *The Wall Street Journal*. 13 July. www.wsj.com/articles/pokemon-go-fuelednintendo-just-keeps-going-1468302369

Montal, T. and Z. Reich (2017). I, Robot. You, Journalist. Who is the Author?; Authorship, Bylines and Full Disclosure in Automated Journalism. *Digital Journalism* 5(7): 829–849.

Moore, J. (2019). Artificial Intelligence Approaches to Identify Molecular Determinants of Exceptional Health and Life Span: An Interdisciplinary Workshop at the National Institute on Aging. *Frontiers in Artificial Intelligence* 2: 1–14.

Morris, D. (2016). Netflix Says Geography, Age, and Gender Are 'Garbage' for Predicting Taste. *Fortune*. 27 March. https://fortune.com/2016/03/27/netflix-predicts-taste/

Mosco, V. (2009). *The Political Economy of Communication* (2nd ed.). Los Angeles, CA: Sage.

Moses, L. (2017). MODERN NEWSROOM: The Washington Post's Robot Reporter Has Published 850 Articles in the Past Year. *The Washington Post*. 14 September. https://digiday.com/media/washington-posts-robot-reporter-published-500-articles-last-year/

172 References

Motion Picture Association of America (2019). *2018 Theatrical Home Entertainment Market Environment (THEME) Report*. Los Angeles, CA: Motion Picture Association of America.

Moustachir, S. (2016). Popular Culture and Artificial Intelligence. *Medium*. 29 September. https://medium.com/@sa_mous/ethics-in-ai-424919af7d3

Murgia, M. and K. Beioley (2019). UK to Create Regulator to Police Big Tech Companies. *Financial Times*. 19 December. www.ft.com/content/67c2129a-2199-11ea-92da-f0c92e957a96?emailId=5dfa518a80baa400043cdcc1&segmentId=3934ec55-f741-7a04-feb0-1ddf01985dc2&fbclid=IwAR3WrPtSZpqVRu4UrN4cxpwZRFO7WwF1bTGzKkJVcjNDUq4Wka3u5YQ0OtY

Murphy, S. (2019). Past the Sheen & Into the Underbelly: A Deep Dive into the K-pop Industry. *The Music Network*. 15 July. https://themusicnetwork.com/deep-dive-k-pop-industry/

Natajaran, S. and J. Baue (2019). AI: Hollywood's Rising Star. *Broadcasting and Cable*. 23 July. www.broadcastingcable.com/blog/ai-hollywoods-rising-star

Netflix (2017). *2016 Financial Statements*. www.netflixinvestor.com/financials/financial-statements/default.aspx

Netflix (2018). *2017 Financial Statements*. www.netflixinvestor.com/financials/financial-statements/default.aspx

Netflix (2019a). *Where is Netflix Available?* https://help.netflix.com/en/node/14164

Netflix (2019b). *2018 Financial Statements*. www.netflixinvestor.com/financials/financial-statements/default.aspx

Netflix (2019c). *Machine Learning: Learning How to Entertain the World*. https://research.netflix.com/research-area/machine-learning

Netflix (2019d). *Form 8-K Current Report: Pursuant to Section 13 OR 15(d) of the Securities Exchange Act of 1934*. Scotts Valley, CA: Netflix Inc.

Netflix (2020). *Form 10-K: Annual Report Pursuant to Section 13 OR 15(d) of the Securities Exchange Act of 1934*. Scotts Valley, CA: Netflix Inc.

New European Media (2018). *Artificial Intelligence in the Media and Creative Industries Position Paper*. NEM.

Nieborg, D., B. Duffy, and T. Poell (2020). Studying Platforms and Cultural Production: Methods, Institutions, and Practices. *Social Media + Society* July: 1–7.

Nieborg, D. and T. Poell (2018). The Platformization of Cultural Production: Theorizing the Contingent Cultural Commodity. *New Media & Society* 20(11): 4275–4292.

Noble, S. (2018). *Algorithms of Oppression: How Search Engines Reinforce Racism*. New York: New York University Press.

Nowak, P. (2010). Netflix Launches Canadian Movie Service. *CBC*. 22 September. www.cbc.ca/news/technology/netflix-launches-canadian-movie-service-1.872505

O'Regan, T. and B. Goldsmith (2006). Making Cultural Policy Meeting Cultural Objectives in a Digital Environment. *Television and New Media* 7(1): 68–91.

Ochigame, R. (2019). The Invention of Ethical AI. *The Intercept*. 21 December. https://theintercept.com/2019/12/20/mit-ethical-ai-artificial-intelligence/?fbclid=IwAR26ce0vasswGea_pD9OWtRpT3BeTo8IoGYDG89-Gk1pIJvrUJKkCTHWC6o

Office of Science and Technology Policy of the U.S. (2019). *Accelerating America's Leadership in Artificial Intelligence*. 11 February. www.whitehouse.gov/articles/accelerating-americas-leadership-in-artificial-intelligence/

Oh, D.H. (2018). [AI Era] A New Wind in the Game Industry: Adding AI to Games. *Newsis*. 22 May. www.newsis.com/view/?id=NISX20180520_0000313505

References 173

Örnebring, H. (2010). Technology and Journalism-as-Labour: Historical Perspectives. *Journalism* 11(1): 57–74.

Outcome Statement of the Forum on Artificial Intelligence in Africa (2018). *Benguérir (Kingdom of Morocco)*. 13 December. https://en.unesco.org/sites/default/files/ai_outcome-statement_africa-forum_en.pdf

Oxford Insights (2019). *Government AI Readiness Index 2019*. London: Oxford Insights.

Oxford Reference (2019). *Cultural Production*. Oxford: Oxford University Press.

Pangrazio, L. (2018). What's New About Fake News? Critical Digital Literacies in an Era of Fake News, Post-trust and Clickbait. *Revista Paginas de Educacion* 11(1): 6–22.

Parisi, T. (2019). NIU Expert: 4 Leaps in Technology to Expect in the 2020s. *NIU Newsroom*. 17 December. https://newsroom.niu.edu/2019/12/17/niu-expert-4-leaps-in-technology-to-expect-in-the-2020s/?fbclid=IwAR09Np6d_n2xlCz-DrAXOdV6uCoWpBfkm9_ST4_pXEGcarPWRATyyQF8Vyto

Park, C.M. (2020). AI Becomes the God of Go Game: Where is the Player's Style. *JoongAng Daily*. 9 September. B07.

Park, D.G., S. Sachar, N. Diakopoulos, and N. Elmqvist (2016). *Supporting Comment Moderators in Identifying High Quality Online News Comments*. In Proceedings of the 2016 CHI Conference on Human Factors in Computing Systems. ACM, 1114–1125. May 07–12.

Pasquale, F. (2015). *The Black Box Society: The Secret Algorithms That Control Money and Information*. Cambridge, MA: Harvard University Press.

Pavlik, J. (2008). *Media in the Digital Age*. New York: Columbia University Press.

Pilkington, E. (2019). Digital Dystopia: How Algorithms Punish the Poor. *The Guardian*. 14 October. www.theguardian.com/technology/2019/oct/14/automating-poverty-algorithms-punish-poor?CMP=share_btn_fb&fbclid=IwAR2es9D3geminwdfr8qzJ7j2VG_XmNAGna5K8BYeRpEDdTpl0Gf1-PPbbNY

Plummer, L. (2017). This is How Netflix's Top-Secret Recommendation System Works. *Wired*. 22 August. www.wired.co.uk/article/how-do-netflixs-algorithms-work-machine-learning-helps-to-predict-what-viewers-will-like

Pogue, D. (2018). A Compendium of AI-Composed Pop Songs. *Scientific American*. 16 January. www.scientificamerican.com/article/a-compendium-of-ai-composed-pop-songs/

Pollard, T. (2020). Popular Culture's AI Fantasies: Killers and Exploiters or Assistants and Companions? *Perspectives on Global Development and Technology* 19: 97–109.

Pressman, A. (2019). Why Cord Cutters Are Favoring Cheaper Online Options Over Cable-Like Bundles. *Fortune*. 22 April. https://fortune.com/2019/04/22/cord-cutting-ott-netflix-directv/

PricewaterhouseCoopers (2018). *Perspectives from the Global Entertainment & Media Outlook 2018–2022*. London: PWC.

PricewaterhouseCoopers (2019). *Sizing the Prices*. London: PWC.

Radu, S. (2019). Germany Pushes Tighter AI Regulations for Companies. *The U.S. News and World Report*. 27 August. www.usnews.com/news/best-countries/articles/2019-10-29/germany-recommends-more-guidelines-for-ai-development

Rapir, J. (2019). Lee Seung Gi & Suzy's New K-Drama 'Vagabond' Premiere Date Pushed Back to September. *Korea Portal*. 2 April. http://en.koreaportal.com/articles/46791/20190402/lee-seung-gi-suzys-new-k-drama-vagabond-premiere-date-pushed-back-to-september.htm

174 References

Rauf, D. (2020). Will COVID-19 Spur Greater Use of Artificial Intelligence in K-12 Education? *Education Week*. 19 May. www.edweek.org/ew/articles/2020/05/20/will-covid-19-spur-greater-use-of-artificial.html

Reisman, D., J. Schultz, K. Crawford, and M. Whittaker (2018). Algorithmic Impact Assessments: A Practical Framework for Public Agency Accountability. *AI Now*. https://ainowinstitute.org/aiareport2018.pdf

Roberge, J. and R. Seyfert (2015). What are Algorithmic Cultures. In R. Seyfert and J. Roberge (eds.), *Algorithmic Cultures Essays on Meaning, Performance and New Technologies* (pp. 1–25). New York: Routledge.

Roberts, A. (2006). *The History of Science Fiction*. New York: Palgrave.

Roberts, H., J. Cowls., J. Morley, M. Taddeo, V. Wang, and L. Floridi (2020). The Chinese Approach to Artificial Intelligence: An Analysis of Policy, Ethics, and Regulation. *AI & Society* 1–27.

Romo, V. and A. Held (2019). Facebook Removed Nearly 3.4 Billion Fake Accounts in 6 Months. *NPR*. 23 March. www.npr.org/2019/05/23/726353723/facebook-removed-nearly-3-2-billion-fake-accounts-in-last-six-months

Ross, J. (2017). The Fundamental Flaw in AI Implementation. *MIT Sloan Management Review*, 14 July. 14. https://sloanreview.mit.edu/article/the-fundamental-flaw-in-ai-implementation/

Roxborough, S. (2019). Netflix Dominates Global SVOD Market, but Local Services Gain Ground, Study Finds. *The Hollywood Report*. 13 November. www.hollywoodreporter.com/news/netflix-dominates-global-svod-market-but-local-services-gain-ground-1254438?fbclid=IwAR0b4BnTWA_4hWVeH947CbGV3HVaubVe1yTRuWBiMDTVQZzD8qItAoePzZA

Ryoo, W.J. and D.Y. Jin (2020). Cultural Politics in the South Korean Cultural Industries: Confrontations between State-Developmentalism and Neoliberalism. *The International Journal of Cultural Policy* 26(1): 31–45.

Saran, C. (2019). Stanford University Finds that AI is Outpacing Moore's Law. *ComputerWeekly.com*. 12 December. www.computerweekly.com/news/252475371/Stanford-University-finds-that-AI-is-outpacing-Moores-Law

SBS (2016). *SBS Live Broadcasts the Second Go Game between Lee Sedol and AlphaGo*. 10 March. http://sbsfune.sbs.co.kr/news/news_content.jsp?article_id=E10007570846

Schiller, A. and J. McMahon (2019). Alexa, Alert Me When the Revolution Comes: Gender, Affect, and Labor in the Age of Home-Based Artificial Intelligence. *New Political Science* 41(2): 173–191.

Schmelzer, R. (2019). AI Making Waves in News and Journalism. *Forbes*.23 August. www.forbes.com/sites/cognitiveworld/2019/08/23/ai-making-waves-in-news-and-journalism/#e8db1cd7748d

Schulze, E. (2019). Everything You Need to Know about the Fourth Industrial Revolution. *CNBC*. 17 January. www.cnbc.com/2019/01/16/fourth-industrial-revolution-explained-davos-2019.html

Schwab, K. (2016). *The Fourth Industrial Revolution*. Geneva, Switzerland: World Economic Forum.

Schwarz, J.A. (2017). Platform Logic: The Need for an Interdisciplinary Approach to the Platform-based Economy. *Policy and Internet* 9(4): 374–394.

Shah, S. (2017). Amazon's AI Could Create the Next Must-have Fashion Brand. *Engadget*. 24 August. www.engadget.com/2017/08/24/amazon-ai-fashion-brands/

Shah, V. (2013, August 28). Map of Stop and Frisks in New York City Show Concentration by Race and Neighborhood. *Untapped Cities*. http://untappedcities.

References 175

com/2013/08/28/new-mapshows-police-stop-and-frisks-according-to-race-and-neighbourhood-in-new-york-city/

Shani, O. (2015). From Science Fiction to Reality: The Evolution of Artificial Intelligence. *Wired*. www.wired.com/insights/2015/01/the-evolution-of-artificial-intelligence/

Shin, D.H. (2019a). Toward Fair, Accountable, and Transparent Algorithms: Case Studies on Algorithm Initiatives in Korea and China. *Javnost: The Public* 26(3): 274–290.

Shin, D.H. (2019b). *Socio-Technical Design of Algorithms: Fairness, Accountability, and Transparency*. Paper presented at the 30th European Conference of the International Telecommunications Society (ITS): "Towards a Connected and Automated Society", Helsinki, Finland. 16–19 June.

Shon, J.Y. (2017). Naver, YG Entertainment Begin Work on New Global Music Service Platform. *The Korean Herald*. 18 October. www.koreaherald.com/view.php?ud=20171018000684

Shorey, S. and P. Howard (2016). Automation, Algorithms, and Politics| Automation, Big Data and Politics: A Research Review. *International Journal of Communication* 10: 5032–5055.

Siarri, P. (2019). Is AI and Journalism a Good Mix? *Medium*. 6 January. https://medium.com/futuresin/is-ai-and-journalism-a-good-mix-83aaa1c3b14d

Sim, G. (2018). Individual Disruptors and Economic Gamechangers: Netflix, New Media, and Neoliberalism. In K. McDonald and D. Smith-Rowsey (eds.), *The Netflix Effect: Technology and Entertainment in the 21st Century* (pp. 186–201). London: Bloomsbury.

Simonite, T. (2018). When It Comes to Gorillas, Google Photos Remains Blind. *Wired*. 8 July. www.wired.com/story/when-it-comes-to-gorillas-google-photos-remains-blind/

Sims, D. (2015). Netflix's $50 Million Movie Gamble. *The Atlantic*. 10 November. www.theatlantic.com/entertainment/archive/2015/11/netflixs-50-million-movie-gamble/415257/

Sohn, J.Y. (2018). Netflix to Push Boundaries of Korean Media Content. *The Korea Herald*. 25 January. www.koreaherald.com/view.php?ud=20180125000871

Song, B.G. (2018). Am I the Main Character of Webtoon: The Major Reason to Attract 40 Million Audiences is a Cutting-edge Technology. *Yonhap News*. 15 January. www.yna.co.kr/view/AKR20180103003200887

Song, K.S. (2018). Naver News to be Run by AI from Tomorrow. *Korea Joongang Daily*. 3 April. http://koreajoongangdaily.joins.com/news/article/article.aspx?aid=3061351

Song, S.J. (2016). Korea's OTT Market, Who Will Have the Last Laugh? *KoBiz*. 27 May. www.koreanfilm.or.kr/eng/news/features.jsp?pageIndex

Spangler, T. (2019). Netflix Breaks Down Results by Region, Showing Strong Asia-Pacific, Europe Growth. *Variety*. 16 December. https://variety.com/2019/digital/news/netflix-breaks-down-results-by-region-showing-strong-asia-pacific-europe-growth-1203440307/

Sparviero, S. (2019). From Passive Consumption of Media Goods to Active Use of Media Brands: On Value Generation and Other Differences. *Communication and Society* 32(3): 67–79.

Srnicek, N. (2016). *Platform Capitalism*. Cambridge: Polity Press.

Stangarone, T. (2019). How Netflix is Reshaping South Korean Entertainment: The Streaming Giant is Reshaping Korean Entertainment, Even While Boosting its Popularity around the World. *The Diplomat*. 29 April. https://thediplomat.com/2019/04/how-netflix-is-reshaping-south-korean-entertainment/

176 References

Statcounter (2019). *Search Engine Market Share Worldwide.* https://gs.statcounter.com/search-engine-market-share

The State Council of China (2017). *New Generation of Artificial Intelligence Development Plan.* Beijing: State Council of China.

Statistics Canada (2020). *Table 27-10-0367-01 Use of Advanced or Emerging Technologies by Industry and Enterprise Size* https://www150.statcan.gc.ca/t1/tbl1/en/tv.action?pid=2710036701&pickMembers%5B0%5D=1.1&pickMembers%5B1%5D=3.4

Stiglitz, J. (2019). Opinion: Three Decades of Neoliberal Policies Have Decimated the Middle Class, Our Economy, and Our Democracy. *Market Watch.* 13 May. www.marketwatch.com/story/three-decades-of-neoliberal-policies-have-decimated-the-middle-class-our-economy-and-our-democracy-2019-05-13#

Stone, M.L. (2014). *Big Data for Media.* Oxford: Reuters Institute for the Study of Journalism.

Strange, S. (1994). *States and Markets.* London: Pinter.

Striphas, T. (2015). Algorithmic Culture. *European Journal of Cultural Studies* 18: 395–412.

Sundararajan, A. (2019). How Japan Can Win in the Ongoing AI War. *The Japan Times.* 9 September. www.japantimes.co.jp/opinion/2019/09/09/commentary/japan-commentary/japan-can-win-ongoing-ai-war/#.Xe4DKIMzaHs

Talia, D., Trunfio, P., and Marozzo, F. (2015). *Data Analysis in the Cloud: Models, Techniques and Applications.* Amsterdam, The Netherlands: Elsevier.

Tandoc, E., J. Jenkins, and S. Craft (2019). Fake News as a Critical Incident in Journalism. *Journalism Practice* 13(6): 673–689.

Taylor, B. (2019). Neural Networks Can Disempower Human Workers. *AI Business.* 22 August. https://aibusiness.com/neural-networks-can-disempower-human-workers/

Tefertiller, A. (2018). Media Substitution in Cable Cord-Cutting: The Adoption of Web-Streaming Television. *Journal of Broadcasting & Electronic Media* 62(3): 390–407.

Tercek, R (2019). Synthetic Personalities. *Medium.* 3 June. https://medium.com/id-in-the-iot/artificial-intelligence-is-completely-reinventing-media-and-marketing-d724c150ece3

Terranova, T. (2000). Free Labor: Producing Culture for the Digital Economy. *Social Text* 18(2): 33–58.

Togelius, J. (2019). *Playing Smart: On Games, Intelligence, and Artificial Intelligence (Playful Thinking).* Cambridge, MA: MIT Press.

Tomlinson, Z. (2018). Artificial Entertainment: A Century of AI in Film. *Interesting Engineering.* 3 November. https://interestingengineering.com/artificial-entertainment-a-century-of-ai-in-film

Tortois (2019). *The Global AI Index.* www.tortoisemedia.com/intelligence/ai/?fbclid=IwAR35C0wOyBU4XqxGeIMMc4ThZU9em4sSCgmyj85M1MG-0D466QDKbGeOsT0

Turner, J. (2019). *Robot Rules: Regulating Artificial Intelligence.* London: Palgrave.

Ulaby, N. (2019). The Hit Movie 'Parasite' Puts Basement Structures in Structural Inequality. *NPR.* 5 November. www.npr.org/2019/11/05/776388423/the-hit-movie-parasite-puts-basement-structures-in-structural-inequality

Underwood, C. (2019). Automated Journalism—AI Applications at New York Times, Reuters, and Other Media Giants. *Emerj.* 17 November. https://emerj.com/ai-sector-overviews/automated-journalism-applications/

References   177

UNESCO (2016). *Intergovernmental Committee for the Protection and Promotion of the Diversity of Cultural Expressions: Tenth Ordinary Sessions.* Paris: UNESCO. 12–15 December.

UNESCO (2018). *Canada First to Adopt Strategy for Artificial Intelligence.* 22 November. www.unesco.org/new/en/media-services/single-view/news/canada_first_to_adopt_strategy_for_artificial_intelligence/

UNESCO (2019). *Japan Pushing Ahead with Society 5.0 to Overcome Chronic Social Challenges.* 21 February. https://en.unesco.org/news/japan-pushing-ahead-society-50-overcome-chronic-social-challenges

UNESCO (2020). *Artificial Intelligence and Gender Equality: Key Findings of UNESCO'S Global Dialogue.* Paris: UNESCO.

van Couvering, E. (2017). *The Political Economy of New Media Revisited: Platformisation, Mediatisation, and the Politics of Algorithms.* In Proceedings of the 50th Hawaii International Conference on System Sciences 1812–1919.

van Dalen, A. (2012). The Algorithms Behind The Headlines: How Machine-Written News Redefines the Core Skills of Human Journalists. *Journalism Practice* 6(5): 648–658.

van Dijck, J. (2013). *The Culture of Connectivity: A Critical History of Social Media.* Oxford University Press.

van Dijck, J., T. Poell, and M. de Wall (2018). *The Platform Society: Public Values in a Connective World.* New York: Oxford University Press.

van Doorn, N. (2017). Platform Labor: On the Gendered and Racialized Exploitation of Low-Income Service Work in the On-Demand Economy. *Information, Communication and Society* 10(6): 898–914.

Vincent, J. (2018). 20th Century Fox is Using AI to Analyze Movie Trailers and Find Out What Films Audiences Will Like. *The Verge.* 2 November. www.theverge.com/2018/11/2/18055514/fox-google-ai-analyze-movie-trailer-predict-success-logan

Vincent, J. (2019a). Sharing Passwords for a Video Streaming Site? This Company Will Use AI to Track You Down. *The Verge.* 8 January. www.theverge.com/2019/1/8/18174161/netflix-hbo-hulu-shared-password-account-synamedia-machine-learning-ai

Vincent, J. (2019b). Former Go Champion Beaten by DeepMind Retires after Declaring AI Invincible. *The Verge.* 27 November. www.theverge.com/2019/11/27/20985260/ai-go-alphago-lee-se-dol-retired-deepmind-defeat

Vital Media (2018). *Artificial Intelligence in the Media and Creative Industries Position Paper.* New European Media.

Volodzko, D. (2017). Now It's Personal: South Korea Calls to Arms in AI Race after Go Master Felled by AlphaGo. *This Week in Asia.* 6 October. www.scmp.com/week-asia/geopolitics/article/2114305/now-its-personal-south-korea-calls-arms-ai-race-after-go

Wakabayashi, D., J. Nicas, S. Lohr, and M. Isaac (2020). Big Tech Could Emerge From Coronavirus Crisis Stronger Than Ever. *The New York Times.* 23 March. www.nytimes.com/2020/03/23/technology/coronavirus-facebook-amazon-youtube.html

Walch, K. (2019). Is South Korea Poised To Be a Leader in AI? *Forbes.* 7 September. www.forbes.com/sites/cognitiveworld/2018/09/07/is-south-korea-poised-to-be-a-leader-in-ai/#6b4815bdfa2f

Walch, K. and C. World (2019). Will The Next Pop Music Hit Be Completely AI Generated? *Forbes.* 27 August. www.forbes.com/sites/cognitiveworld/2019/08/27/will-the-next-pop-music-hit-be-completely-ai-generated/#195436ee10da

178 References

WashPostPR (2016a). *The Washington Post Experiments with Automated Storytelling to Help Power 2016 Rio Olympics Coverage*. 5 August. www.washingtonpost.com/pr/wp/2016/08/05/the-washington-post-experiments-with-automated-storytelling-to-help-power-2016-rio-olympics-coverage/

WashPostPR (2016b). *The Washington Post to Use Artificial Intelligence to Cover Nearly 500 Races on Election Day*. 19 October. www.washingtonpost.com/pr/wp/2016/10/19/the-washington-post-uses-artificial-intelligence-to-cover-nearly-500-races-on-election-day/

Webb, K. (2019). A Former World Champion of the Game Go Says He's Retiring Because AI is So Strong. *Business Insider*. 27 November. www.businessinsider.com/deep-mind-alphago-ai-lee-sedol-south-korea-go-2019-11

West, D. (2018). *The Future of Work: Robots, AI, and Automation*. Baltimore, MA: Brookings Institution Press.

White House (2019). *Artificial Intelligence for American People*. www.whitehouse.gov/ai/

Wilhelm, A.G. (2006). *Digital Nation: Towards an Inclusive Information Society*. Cambridge, MA: MIT Press.

Winseck, D. (2016). Reconstructing the Political Economy of Communication for the Digital Media Age. *The Political Economy of Communication* 4(2): 73–114.

Wired (2016). Facebook Recommendations Is Here to Tell You What to Do IRL. 6 October. www.wired.com/2016/10/facebook-recommendations/

Wong, T. (2019). Singapore Fake News Law Polices Chats and Online Platforms. 9 May. *BBC News*. www.bbc.com/news/world-asia-48196985

Yamamoto, T. (2018). AI Created Works and Copyright. *Patents & Licensing* 48(1): 1–16.

Yang, S. (2015). Can You Tell the Difference Between a Robot and a Stock Analyst? *The Wall Street Journal*. 9 July. www.wsj.com/articles/robots-on-wall-street-firms-try-out-automated-analyst-reports-1436434381

Yannakakis, G. and J. Togelius (2018). *Artificial Intelligence and Games*. Berlin: Springer.

Yeo, J.S. (2019a). S. Korea Online Video Services Face Uphill Battle Against Netflix. *The Korea Herald*. 29 August. www.koreaherald.com/view.php?ud=20190829000733

Yeo, J.S. (2019b). SKT Partners SM Entertainment on AI-based Technology for K-pop Content. *The Korea Herald*. 11 January. www.koreaherald.com/view.php?ud=20190111000628

Yonhap (2019a). Netflix's First Original Korean Drama 'Kingdom' Unveiled to Media. 21 January.

Yonhap (2019b). Moon Declares S. Korea's AI-Gov't Vision, with 'AI National Strategy' in the Making. 2 November. https://en.yna.co.kr/view/AEN20191028002200315

Yoon, T.J. and D.Y. Jin (eds.) (2017). *The Korean Wave: Evolution, Fandom, and Transnationality*. Lanham, MD: Lexington.

You, G.S. (2019). *Netflixonomics: Netflix and Korean Broadcasting Media*. Seoul: Hanul Plus.

You, S.M. (2019). OTT-Analysis of Korean Drama's Storytelling: A Case Study of Netflix Drama Kingdom. In Proceeding of the Korean Association for Broadcasting & Telecommunication Conference, 211–213.

Youngs, G. (2007). *Global Political Economy in the Information Age: Power and Inequality*. London: Routledge.

References   179

Yu, A. (2019). How Netflix Uses AI, Data Science, and Machine Learning—From a Product Perspective. *Medium*. 27 February. https://becominghuman.ai/how-netflix-uses-ai-and-machine-learning-a087614630fe

Zhao, J., T. Wang, M. Yatskar, V. Ordonez, and K.W. Chang (2017). *Men Also Like Shopping: Reducing Gender Bias Amplification Using Corpus-level Constraints*. In Proceedings of the 2017 Conference on Empirical Methods in Natural Language Processing.

Index

20th Century Fox 59, 63

accountability 133, 136, 147
advertising models 100
affective labor 96, 97
affinity 126
AI 1, 2, 3, 5, 6, 17–23, 35, 36, 39, 41,
    42, 44, 45, 51, 52, 54, 55, 57, 59,
    60, 64, 67, 72, 89, 94, 102, 108,
    110, 111, 113, 114, 117, 118, 119,
    121, 122, 123, 128, 129, 130, 131,
    133, 134, 135, 136, 143, 133, 146,
    48, 149, 151–157. See also artificial
    intelligence
AI algorithmic bias 137, 149
AI algorithms 20, 30, 105, 133, 138,
    140, 145
AI anchor 121
AI and popular culture 63
AI as platforms 30–32
AI divide 114, 122
AI Duet 61
AI governance 38, 52
AI in consumption 95
AI in cultural production 55–59
AI in cultural production 11
AI in journalism 130. See also AI
    journalism
AI in video delivery 88
AI initiatives 11
AI journalism 9, 113, 114, 117, 118,
    128, 129, 131
AI Now 139
AI policies 12, 22, 39, 42, 43, 44
AI policy and governance 38, 39
AI R&D 41
AI recommendation engines 66
AI Recommender System 107. See also
    AiRS

AI revolution 36
AI self-regulation 40
AI systems 58
AI technology 2, 57
AI use in journalism 128
AI-driven cultural production 53
AI-driven digital economy 35
AI's applications for entertainment 103
AiRS 107, 138
AI systems for journalism 117
AI-supported cultural content 55
AI-supported automated journalism
    114
algorithm learning 146
algorithmic cultural production 9
algorithmic recommendations 7
algorithms 3, 7, 8, 9, 11, 12, 13, 16,
    19–21, 22, 24, 27, 33, 35, 49, 52, 54,
    66, 70, 71, 74, 75, 76, 77, 88, 91,
    114, 115, 116, 128, 133, 141, 145,
    146, 147, 148, 149, 153, 156
Alibaba 43
allocative harms 7, 139
AlphaGo 2, 3, 15, 19, 44
alternative media 116, 123
Amazon 45, 58, 70
Amazon Prime 7, 13, 23, 34, 54, 75, 77,
    78, 91, 92, 93, 115
Amazon recommendations 8
American AI Initiative 41
anti-fake news law 127
anti-LGBT content 137
Apple 151
Apple Play 7, 13, 91, 95
Apple TV+ 75
Apple's Siri 16
applications 94
AR 33, 47, 57, 65, 66, 154
ARMY 111

Index

Arthdal Chronicles 87
artificial 19
artificial intelligence 1, 9, 17–19, 148, 151, 157 see also AI
Artificial Intelligence Center 65
Artificial Intelligence Policy Workspace 40
Associated Press 118
automated filtering 105
automated filtering and sorting mechanisms 105
automated journalism 114, 117, 118
automated systems and labor 54
automated-writing software 21
automation 8, 10, 21, 56, 60, 113, 130
Avaaz 124

Baidu 43
Batman vs. Superman: Dawn of Justice 87
BBC 62
Beatles 62
Benjamin 60
Bertie 120
big data 3, 7, 8, 9, 10, 11, 13, 17, 19, 21–23, 26, 30, 35, 49, 52, 54, 55, 63, 66, 69, 70, 71, 73, 74, 75, 76, 77, 80, 81, 89, 92, 98, 104, 112, 133, 134, 135, 137, 140, 141, 142, 143, 144, 146, 148, 152, 153
binge-watching 92
Blade Runner 2049 56
Blogs 132
BlueDot 1
Bollywood movies 84
Bong Joon-ho 83, 84, 88
broadband services 27, 154
BTS 111
Busted: I Know Who You Are 85
ByteDance 132

Came Across 65
capitalism 31–32, 52
Chatbots 8, 137
Christians, Clifford 129, 145
circulation of creative work 130
CJ E&M 89
commercial values 28
commercialization 115
commercialization of journalism 129
commodification 32, 103, 115, 104, 116
commodification mechanisms 104
commodification of user data 103

communicative AI 21
communicative practices 132
computational journalism 113
computer audio or visual recognition 17
computer science 19
consumption patterns 102
content data 115
content personalization 109
convergence 5, 8, 12, 16, 17, 22, 26–27, 32, 47, 54, 55, 56, 62, 113, 153
convergence of AI and music 62
convergence of AI and photography 58
convergence of AI and popular culture 54, 55, 66–71
convergence of AI, digital platforms and popular culture 12, 15, 26–29, 151
convergence of human beings and AI 68
convergence of intelligent technology and human creativity 21
convergence of journalism and digital technology 113
copyright law 67, 68
cord-cutting 78
coronavirus 12, 80, 154, 155. See also COVID-19
corporate ethics 134
corporate sphere 24, 117
counter-neoliberal AI policies 46–47, 49, 52
counter-neoliberal norm 52
counter-neoliberalism 36–39
COVID-19 1, 2, 9, 15, 33, 39, 66, 80, 81, 83, 154, 155, 156. See also coronavirus
creative industries 58
credibility 129
critical political economy 11, 14 see also political economy
critical understanding of AI 8
cultural communities 110
cultural consumers 11, 30, 106, 153, 154, 156
cultural consumption 75, 96, 95–96, 112, 153
cultural consumption habits 1
cultural content 6–7, 17, 21, 27, 28, 55, 59, 64, 66, 88, 101
cultural creators 11, 58, 59, 66, 67, 87, 88, 106, 152, 153, 154, 156
cultural democracy 28, 68
cultural democratization and creativity 12–13
cultural diversity 28, 36, 149

182 *Index*

cultural ecology 94
cultural ecosystem 94
cultural fairness 136
cultural identity 11
cultural industries 1, 5, 9, 13, 16, 22, 27, 29, 30, 33, 35, 36, 43, 48, 58, 59, 63, 66, 70, 73, 76, 105, 144, 152
cultural labor 10, 104
cultural pluralism 8, 28
cultural policy 41, 53
cultural production 4, 5, 8, 16, 17, 32, 33, 49, 47, 51, 54, 55, 68, 114, 129, 151, 152, 153–154, 157
cultural sphere 1, 10
cultural use of AI 58
Culture Machine 56
customization 106
Cyborg 120

data analytics 12
Data Ethics Commission 42
data mining 103, 142
datafication 103
data-friendly ecosystem 70
Daum 122, 138
deep learning 17, 29, 40, 60, 61, 117, 136 see also DL
deep learning systems 43
DeepMind 44, 156
depersonalized 109
Descendants of the Sun 87
developmentalism 36, 43, 44
digital algorithms 125
digital capitalism 16, 108
digital culture 70, 73, 115
digital divide 105, 135, 137, 149
digital economy 3, 4, 12, 35, 43, 53, 64, 71, 110, 135
digital falsehoods 14
digital games 8, 54, 57, 63, 69, 70, 96, 143
digital Hallyu 47
digital labor 101
digital media 75
digital platforms 1, 2, 3, 4, 5, 6, 7, 23–25, 41, 77, 78, 80, 86, 94, 95, 97, 101, 102, 103, 108, 110, 112, 114, 115, 116, 121, 123, 131, 138, 141, 142, 145, 146, 148–150, 151, 152, 153, 154, 155, 157
digital platforms as mediators 23–26
digital society 95
digital storytelling 47, 65

digital technologies 3, 5, 16, 19, 23, 54, 94, 105, 108, 109, 113, 117, 129, 133, 141, 151
digitization 36, 46, 104
digitization of media 114 see also digitization
disempowering empowerment of users 102–106
disempowering platform users 104
disempowerment 112
disinformation 14, 104, 114
Disney+ 7, 54, 75, 77, 78, 91
distribution 55, 68, 83, 88, 94, 96, 152
distribution power 84
diversity 69, 134–136
diversity of cultural expressions 68
diversity of media content 136
DL 17–18 see also deep learning

economies of data mining 103
Edge Rank 126
empowerment 102
encounters of AI and popular culture 59–61
ethical codes 10, 11, 14, 134, 150
ethics of truth 129

Facebook 4, 6, 7, 11, 14, 22, 23, 25, 26, 26, 29, 30, 33, 40, 42, 45, 68, 70, 76, 81, 95, 97, 98, 99, 104, 107, 109, 111, 112, 113, 114, 115, 116, 119, 121, 123, 124, 125, 126, 127, 133, 134, 137, 148, 142, 151, 155
Facebook model 96–99, 106
face-to-face communication 80
face-to-face social relations 80
facial recognition 154
fact-checking system 125
fair representations of users 137
fairness 40, 53, 133, 138, 140, 144, 146, 149, 150, 155
Fairness Flow 144
fake accounts 127
fake news 11, 14, 29, 114, 123, 124–126, 127, 128, 129, 132, 133, 142
Fifth Element, The 60
filter bubbles 125, 137
FlowComposer 62
Forbes 118, 142
Forum on Artificial Intelligence in Africa 142
Fourth Industrial Revolution 2, 3, 15, 29, 44, 45, 47, 52, 56, 121, 140

Index 183

free labor 14, 96, 101
free speech 127
freedom of expression 135, 149

Game of Thrones 87
gatekeeping 23
gatekeeping power of platforms 104
geopolitics 10
Ghostbusters 60
global cultural industries 55
global cultural sphere 23–26
global digital platform 76
global geopolitics 82
globalization 10, 25
Go 2, 15, 19, 44
Google 4, 7, 16, 22, 23, 25, 26, 45, 57, 60, 68, 70, 81, 99, 104, 108, 121, 133, 134, 138, 142, 151
Google Maps 1
GPT-3 157

hard-coded algorithm 103
Hastings, Reed 78, 84
Heliograf 119
Highlander Endgame 60
Hollywood 86, 87
home entertainment 80
House of Cards 88
Hulu 83
human creativity 102
human dignity 148, 150
human intelligence 19, 20, 21, 153
human journalists 114
human rights 23, 134
human-centered ethics 133
human-machine interactions 153

I, Robot 56
IBM Watson 59
ICT 3, 5, 45, 48, 79, 81, 147, 148
immaterial labor 10, 97, 104
information science 19
infrastructural model 115
Instagram 103
intelligent information society 45
intelligent networks 110
intermediaries 25, 26, 93
intermediate human machine interactions 21
internet 3, 16, 22, 23, 113, 154
Interstellar 60
IoT (internet of things) 42, 47, 154
iPhone 1
iTunes 57

JTBC 82, 87, 89, 90
justice 53

Kakao 45, 74, 121, 134, 137, 138, 145–146
Kakao Story 138
KBS 89
Kingdom 85, 86, 89
Korea Communications Commission 127
Korean Wave 47, 63, 64
K-pop 13, 48, 63, 64, 65, 85
KT 45

Lee Luda 137
Lee Sedol 2, 15, 19, 44, 156
Lexus Uni 123, 132
LG 45, 74
LinkedIn 119
Logan 60
Love Alarm 85

machine learning 2, 4, 17, 19, 20, 21, 22, 27, 30, 60, 72, 76, 81, 82, 89, 103, 117, 138, 139, 142
machine learning algorithms 33, 108, 112, 121
mass culture 10
mass surveillance 139, 140
manipulation of data 133
MBC 82, 89
McCarthy, John 17
media convergence 26
media ethics 13, 132, 148, 149
mediate production and consumption of media and culture 21
mediators 17, 25, 26, 28, 52
Merlin 60
metadata 70
Metropolis 56
Microsoft 138, 144
Mighty Little Bheem 84
misinformation 14, 104, 114, 124
misuse of personal data 133
MIT Center for Information Systems Research 51
ML 4, 15, 20, 39, 50, 51, 81, 121, 135
ModBot 119
monetization 97
monitoring systems 128
Moore's Law 30
Morality 52
Morgan 1, 56, 59, 60
Mozart's *42nd Symphony* 61

184 *Index*

Mubert in California 61
music generating algorithms 61
music streaming service platforms
7, 13
MXX 62
My First Love 89

National Artificial Intelligence
Strategy 46
National Strategy for Artificial
Intelligence 44
Naver 64, 74, 106, 107, 116, 121, 134,
138
NC Soft 65
neoliberal economic policy 38
neoliberal policy 41
neoliberalism 12, 36, 41, 43
Netflix 1, 2, 4, 6, 7, 10, 11, 12, 16, 17,
23, 24, 26, 27, 28, 30, 31, 34, 54, 55,
63, 67, 68, 70, 71, 72, 75–80, 81–86,
86, 88, 91–93, 95, 99, 100, 101, 103,
108, 109, 112, 115, 133, 141, 142,
151, 154
Netflix AI system 27
Netflix effects 88–89
the Netflix model 13, 96, 99–102,
107
Netflix's business strategy 77
Netflix's global recommendation system
101
Netflix's recommendation
algorithms 81
Netmarble 65
network 109–110
network society 109–111
neuroscience 19
New Generation Artificial Intelligence
Development Plan (AIDP) 43
new media ethics 14, 133
New York Times 120, 155
NewsWhip 119, 128
Nexon 65
Ninantic 57
no-go zone 40

ObEN 64
Okja 83, 84, 89
Oksusu 89
on-demand video-streaming
platform 24
One Spring Night 82
online education 1–2
online journalism 129

optimization 130
OTT platforms 6, 7, 10, 13, 23, 26,
28, 29, 41, 70, 71, 75–77, 80–83,
88–90, 92, 95, 96, 99, 101, 104,
108, 110. See also OTT service
platforms
OTT service platforms 2, 16, 26, 27,
30, 75, 95, 99, 104, 109, 115, 138.
See also OTT platforms
over-the-top (OTT) 2, 6, 16
ownership relations 77

paradigm shift 4
Parasite 88
Pay TV 99
personal assistants 155
personal culture 10, 108
personal digital technologies 94
personalization 10, 14, 81, 92, 95, 100,
106, 109–111, 121, 125, 130
personalization of culture 106–109,
100, 112
personalization of cultural content
recommendation 100
personalization of news and
information 118
personalization of popular culture 10,
95, 106–109
personalized interface 108
personalized news feed 126
personalized recommendation 108
Pikachu 57
platform business 93
platform imperialism 84
platform-driven public sphere 116
see also public sphere
platformization 24–25, 91, 114, 115
platformization of AI journalism
129. See also platformization of
journalism
platformization of journalism 14, 114,
116
platformization of news 121
Pokemon GO 57
Policy, Ethical, and Legal
Considerations of AI 40
political economy 11, 14, 66 see also
critical political economy
political sphere 24
POOQ 89
Popgun 61
popular culture 1, 2, 5, 8, 10, 11, 12,
13, 15, 17, 26, 27, 30, 32, 50, 54, 55,

63, 66, 72, 94, 95, 100, 151, 152, 157
popular music production with AI 61
predicative policing 139, 140
privacy 41, 57, 133, 149
privacy invasion 133
problem-solving operations 19
procedural fairness 40
production of culture 9
professional journalistic labor 17
professional journalists 116
public safety 135
public sphere 117, 131

Qiu Hao 121

R.U.R. 56
recommendation algorithms 70
recommendation engines 62
recommendation system 77
regulatory mechanisms 126
relevance 97
representational harms 7, 137, 138, 140, 152
robot journalism 19, 117
robot journalist 113
robotization 52
robots 1, 16, 19, 22, 56, 117, 157

Sacred Games 84
Samsung 45
SBS 83, 86, 89
Scared Games 84
Scatter Lab 137
School Nurse Files, The 85
Scott, Luke 59
search engines 115
Seezn 90
self-driving cars 1
SKT 45
SM Entertainment 64
smartphone camera 57
smartphones 1, 2, 22, 26, 30, 47, 50, 79, 94, 94
social change 116
social cultural prejudices 137
social distancing 1, 80, 154
social exclusion 137
social media platforms 2, 6, 11, 23, 26, 30, 95, 108, 109, 112, 114, 115, 116, 117, 119, 123, 124, 126, 128, 131
social responsibilities of AI 40
social robots 21

social security 14, 133
social web 98
Society 5.0 42
socio-cultural risks 112
socio-economic disparities 7, 133
socio-economic fairness 14, 133
socio-economic justice 14, 135, 149
socio-economic polarization 145
Sogou 121
Sony's AI lab 61
sorting mechanisms 105
Spotify 6, 7, 57, 72, 76, 95, 141, 142
stand-up comedy 86
Star Wars: The Last Jedi 56
state-led developmental model 44
States Times Review 127
Storytelling 82–83
STS 9
Studio Dragon 87
Sunspring 60
super-smart society 42
surveillance 23, 15

Talking with Machines 62
taste clusters 100, 101
taste communities 100
taste doppelganger 101
techno-dystopianism 142
technological innovation 7
technological sphere 24
technology regulator 68
techno-utopianism 142
telegram 140
Telegraph 113
Tencent 43, 48
Tensor Flow 60
TikTok 14, 114, 116, 132
transparency 133, 134–136
trustworthiness 136
Tving 90
Twitch 103
Twitter 14, 23, 27, 28, 29, 99, 111, 114, 115, 116, 119

Uber 8
USA Today 120
user-generated content 23, 115

Vagabond 83, 84, 86, 87
vicious circle of cultural production 12
video-on-demand 92
VR 32–33, 47, 154, 155

186   Index

Wall Street Journal 117
WALL-E 56
Washington Post 118–120
Watcha 90 see also Watcha Play
Watcha Play 84 see also Watcha
Watson BEAT 61
Wavve 89
webtoon 3, 8, 13, 47, 65, 151, 153
WhatsApp 155

Xinhua 121
XRCE 74

YG Entertainment 64
YouTube 1, 2, 4, 6, 23, 25, 27, 29, 34,
  95, 100, 103, 109, 111

zombie mystery thriller 85
Zuckerberg, Mark 125

Printed in the United States
by Baker & Taylor Publisher Services